THE HOUSE OF NASI

The Duke of Naxos

THE HOUSE OF NASI

THE DUKE OF NAXOS

by

CECIL ROTH

PHILADELPHIA

THE JEWISH PUBLICATION SOCIETY OF AMERICA

5708–1948

TO

CHAIM WEIZMANN

PRINTED IN THE UNITED STATES OF AMERICA
THE JEWISH PUBLICATION SOCIETY
PHILADELPHIA, PENNA.

Paperback edition, ISBN 0–8276–0412–2, 1992

TABLE OF CONTENTS

Preface

IN 1947, I completed a biography of Doña Gracia Nasi, one of the most remarkable figures of sixteenth-century history and one of the outstanding Jewish women of all time. I intimated at the time that this volume would in due course be rounded off by a sequel dealing with the astonishing career of her nephew and son-in-law, Joseph Nasi, Duke of Naxos. This is now presented to the reader. It is complete in itself, but should be read in conjunction with the other work, the two forming in fact successive parts of the same romantic history.

As in *Doña Gracia*, I have given references to my sources only when they are difficult to find or have been overlooked by previous writers on the subject. They are most numerous in the last chapter, which I thought it desirable to round off with an account — to a large extent entirely new — of the Jewish statesmen at the Turkish court at the close of the sixteenth century, after Joseph Nasi's fall.

It is a pleasure for me to express my thanks to Mr. Meir Benayahu of Jerusalem for providing me with some information that was inaccessible to me in England; and to Professor A. Galante of Istanbul for reading the proofs and thus removing my diffidence at publishing a work which deals with an aspect of Jewish history formerly unfamiliar to me.

CECIL ROTH

OXFORD
January, 1948

Foreword

The companion volume to the present work (The House of Nasi — Doña Gracia) *deals with the remarkable history of the Marrano heroine, Beatrice de Luna, descended from a family which had fled from Spain to Portugal at the time of the expulsion of 1492 and there had been victims of the forced conversion five years later. She had married Francisco, head of the great firm of Mendes, who had built up out of a business in precious stones a banking establishment of international fame, with a branch at Antwerp (directed by his brother Diogo) which outdid the main establishment in importance. On her husband's death in 1536, the widow went with her family, including her nephew, João Miguez, to the Low Countries, where she joined her brother-in-law. Here, the Queen Regent of the Netherlands solicited the hand of her beautiful daughter, Reyna, for one of the court favorites. The mother replied without mincing words that she would rather see the maiden dead.*

Unable to continue a life of perpetual subterfuge, she fled from Flanders, in 1545, leaving her nephew behind for a while to settle up her affairs, and settled in Venice. When she was denounced to the authorities here by her own sister as a Judaizer, João Miguez secured Turkish diplomatic intervention on her behalf. She and her family then settled in Ferrara, where she threw off the disguise of Christianity and became known by her Jewish name of Gracia Nasi. Here, she earned undying gratitude and fame among her coreligionists by her great work in organizing the flight of

*Marranos from the ferocious persecutions of the Inquisition
in Portugal. In 1553, she settled in Constantinople, where
she continued this and similar activities. Everywhere in
the Ottoman Empire, she was known as* La Señora, *or Ha-
Gevereth—"the Lady." She patronized scholarship, founded
synagogues, supported academies, and unremittingly continued her work to assist the escape of persecuted Jews
from lands of oppression. The most remarkable episode in
her career was in 1556–7, when she attempted to organize
a punitive boycott of the port of Ancona, in Italy, in retalia-
tion for the burning there of twenty-five Marranos as renegades from the Christian faith; but unfortunately there was
not sufficient discipline among the Jews of Turkey to make
this effective.*

*Long before her death, which took place in 1569, her
nephew, the former João Miguez, now her son-in-law, had
been closely associated with everything that she did. The
present volume deals with his career.*

THE HOUSE OF NASI

The Duke of Naxos

GENEALOGICAL TREE

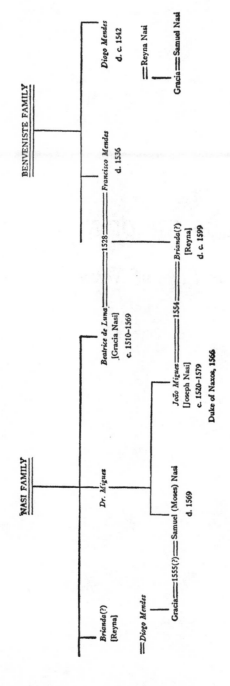

Marrano names are in italics; Jewish names in brackets.
Marriages are indicated by a double line.
Year of death is preceded by the letter d.

CHAPTER I

João Miguez

DOÑA Gracia Nasi, *alias* Beatrice de Luna, the pride
of Jewish womanhood in the middle of the sixteenth century, who played so great a role in her day in Antwerp,
Venice, Ferrara, Constantinople, had it seems a single
brother, a Spaniard or Portuguese like herself. He was
privily known among his fellow-Marranos as Samuel
Nasi,[1] but he had been baptized under the name of
Miguez, had studied medicine (a calling much favored
by the New Christians, both because of the traditional
Jewish proclivity and because of the opportunities it
gave for the observance of the Jewish ceremonial laws,
especially as regards the Sabbath) and became one of the
royal physicians. "Doctor Miguez," as he was usually
called, might have made a greater name in his profession
but for an early death. He had two sons — the one baptized as João Miguez but secretly known as Joseph, the
other, perhaps posthumous, domestically named Samuel
like himself. The exact date of their birth is unknown,
but we may fix it tentatively in either case about the year
1520 — perhaps a little before, and certainly not much
after.

João Miguez had the upbringing of any other Marrano
boy of good family. It would have been suicidal not to

give him an ostensibly Catholic background. He was therefore christened as a baby, called publicly by his baptismal name, brought up to perform the formalities of the Christian religion, carried to hear Mass on occasion, accustomed to be shriven and to take the sacraments from time to time. But he did it all without conviction, perhaps muttering some secret formula of self-excuse, as so many other Marranos did, whenever he entered a church, and performing private austerities to atone for his outward Christian observances. For at home he was called by his Jewish name of Joseph or Joseph Nasi, taught perhaps the meaning of that surname — derived from former "princes" of their people in the Diaspora — accustomed little by little to Jewish ways, and in the end (in all probability, this was when he had reached the traditional Jewish age of confirmation and the performance of full religious rites, at thirteen) was informed that he was of the seed of Israel and inducted into the cardinal tenets of Jewish belief and practice.

On his father's death, he was brought up, it seems, by his aunt (the latter's sister), Beatrice or Gracia, wife of the wealthy spice-broker and banker Francisco Mendes. For the rest, his education was that of the young Portuguese of the upper bourgeoisie. He was master of many languages, at home in society, and a skilled swordsman and jouster who distinguished himself in games and martial exercises, to which he always remained addicted. When Doña Gracia removed to Antwerp in 1536, on Francisco Mendes' death, she took her nephew with her. On the way, they visited England, so that the youth had first-hand experience, however brief, of yet another country, widening the knowledge of international affairs which was subsequently to prove so valuable to him.

In the Low Countries, he grew to maturity. He made the acquaintance in Antwerp of merchants from many lands who came to traffic in that great port, as well as of the artists and scholars whom they patronized. He learned at first hand of the movement for religious reform, which had begun to manifest itself in Christian Europe, and was on familiar terms with some of its local leaders. His smooth manners, his accomplishments and his wealth made him welcome at the court of the Queen Regent Mary, in Brussels. He was known to the redoubtable, fanatical, ever-needy Charles V, by whom he was knighted[2] — a dignity not so cheap as it was afterwards to become. He became a jousting-partner of their nephew, the future Emperor Maximilian. At this period, moreover, he was inducted into the work of the great Mendes banking house, his journeys through Europe on behalf of the firm now beginning; and it seems that the development of the branch at Lyons, and the important loans contracted with the Crown of France, were largely due to his enterprise. Diogo Mendes, his uncle by marriage, learned to value his judgment, and in his will recommended Doña Beatrice to rely for advice on him and another kinsman, Agostino Henriques, who were designated to succeed to the administration of the estate should she die before his daughter came of age.[3]

In the following years, Doña Beatrice depended on him more and more. While she managed the firm's transactions in Flanders, he looked after those in other lands; and, when finally she made her secret, hurried departure, it was in his hands that she left her affairs.

It was now that he first came into real prominence —
bargaining, imploring, intriguing; going to see the queen
regent at Brussels and the emperor himself at Ratisbon;
always ready with a fresh offer and a fresh expedient if
it were needed; but inexorably pressed from all sides,
until in the end he had to abandon the struggle and follow the family into flight, leaving a great part of the
disputed property behind.[4] It was rumored that he had
eloped in the first instance to Venice with one of his
beautiful cousins, Doña Beatrice posting at his heels;
but (as has been suggested) this may have been only a
canard, which they themselves put into circulation in
order to explain their hurried movements. When proceedings were started against the members of the family
in Venice, owing to the unhappy dispute between his
two aunts, it was Joseph who appealed to his correspondents in Turkey (notably Moses Hamon, the sultan's
physician) and obtained the diplomatic intervention on
their behalf which resulted in their release. He must
have been a familiar figure at this period in Venice and
afterwards at Ferrara. In 1547 he was apparently living
in Milan, if he was identical with the "Juan Mickas" of
that city who was now denounced to the Inquisition.[5]

But he spent the greatest part of his time elsewhere,
looking after the interests of the firm — especially, it
seems, at Lyons, where, as well as in Paris, his transactions were on the largest possible scale. His loans to the
French treasury ran into six figures. As a result, he obtained the good opinion of many persons who stood high
in the state, including King Francis I, to whom he was

personally known. He was also a familiar figure at this time in Rome and in Naples,[6] then under Spanish rule. In consequence of all this, he was as yet unable to re-embrace Judaism formally, as the other members of the family now did. But he was meanwhile settling the firm's affairs in Europe, with the intention of leaving as soon as possible.

At last everything was arranged, though apparently at great financial loss. Most of the family, with Doña Beatrice (now known as Gracia Nasi) at their head, had reached Constantinople in 1553. Early in the following year, he came to join them, followed (it was said) by a caravan of five hundred Marranos who had found a temporary resting-place in Italy. He traveled across the Balkans in great state. He was fashionably dressed. He had a train of twenty liveried servants and was preceded by two mounted janissaries, in the Turkish style, as his bodyguard. No less attention was attracted by his arrival than by that of his redoubtable aunt in the previous year. In April, 1554, the period of subterfuge ended. He now formally entered the Covenant of Abraham, the attendants who had come with him following his example.

The reversion to Judaism was not unopposed. Andrés Laguna, the Spanish litterateur — who had been brought to Constantinople not long before as a captive and, ingeniously posing as a physician, was now engaged in a spluttering guerilla warfare against the Jewish medical practitioners who were his only serious rivals — gives an obviously biased account in his autobiographical *Viaje de Turquía* (Turkish Voyage), which has already been quoted more than once in connection with the family history at this stage:[7]

The first days that Juan Micas was living in Constantinople as a Christian, I went to him every day and begged him not to do such a thing as to become converted to Judaism for the sake of four *reals* of money, for one day the Devil would take them from him. I found him so firm [in his faith] that naturally I went away consoled; for he assured me that he would not go to visit his aunt again, and that he wished to return [westwards] at once. You can judge my suprise when I learned that he had already become one of the Devil's own. When I asked him why he had done this, he said that it was so that he should not remain subject to the Spanish Inquisition. I replied: "You may as well know that you will come under it here much more so if you live; but I do not think that it will be for long, and ill and repentant at that."

The author goes on to say that his prophecy came true, and that before two months had passed he saw the neo-convert weeping for the sin he had committed, though the Devil consoled him with money. It was an almost obligatory conclusion for an orthodox Spaniard; the historian can only add that, whatever faults of character Don Joseph may ultimately have shown, insincerity and lack of Jewish conviction were certainly not to be found among them.

At the risk of a certain amount of repetition of details already given, let us hear too what the German merchant, Hans Dernschwam, has to say about the episode:

He has been at the court of the Emperor of the Holy Roman Empire. Christian prisoners know him by sight ... The Jews who are around him daily do not agree as to his name, in order that people should not learn to know such rogues. He is said to have been named Zuan Mykas, or Six; his father is said to have been a physician by the name of Samuel. This rogue whom I just mentioned came to Constantinople in 1554 with over twenty well-dressed Spanish servants. They attend him as if he were a prince. He himself wore silk clothes lined with sable. Before him went two janissaries with staves, as mounted lackeys, as is the Turkish custom, in order that nothing should happen to him. He had himself circumcised in the month of April 1554 . . . He is a large person with a trimmed black beard . . . The servants who came with him and with the women have also all been circumcised and have become Jews. . .[8]

Some little while since, his brother, Samuel Nasi (still living in Ferrara), had espoused their cousin, Gracia *la Chica*. For himself, Doña Gracia's own daughter, Reyna (formerly Brianda), the greater match of the two, had been held in reserve, notwithstanding the gossip which linked her name with that of the son of Moses Hamon, the sultan's physician, who is said to have solicited his master's intervention with the Venetian republic on this understanding. As we have seen, it had been reported long before that the two, João and Reyna, had eloped together from Antwerp. This was untrue; but their union seems to have been far more than a mere *mariage de convenance*, arranged by the family in the fashion normal at this time, especially when great fortunes were involved. According to Stephen Gerlach, domestic chaplain and preacher to the imperial ambassador in Constantinople, Reyna's friends had been opposed to the match, but she was unable to resist her cousin's handsome appearance, of which more than one contemporary speaks admiringly. Nevertheless, like Dinah of old, she would not presumably consent to marry unless her husband openly professed Judaism. Now, there was no further obstacle. As soon as possible after

his conversion, the wedding took place at last, the bride's
dowry being no less than 90,000 ducats[9] (rumor exaggerated the amount to 300,000 — more than the fortune
of the Medici!) in addition to a quantity of pearls and
precious stones. For months before and after the event,
there was banqueting and lavish entertainment of the
poor, without which no Jewish festivity could be complete.[10] The climax of the celebrations was reached when,
on August 24 (it was St. Bartholomew's Day — not yet
a shameful anniversary in the Gallican calendar), the
French ambassador, M. d'Aramon (to whom Don Joseph
had brought letters of recommendation from his colleague
at Rome, the Seigneur de Lansac),[11] crossed specially
over from Constantinople to Galata to congratulate the
young couple. ("They were very ceremonious to one
another," sneered Hans Dernschwam, almost as much
anti-French as he was anti-Jewish. "So the Jews tell
me, who were with them daily. Even as birds of a feather
flock together, so do other scoundrels and betrayers of
Christendom.")

The period of the Portuguese business magnate, João
Miguez, is now over, though non-Jews continued to call
him generally by that name or some approximation to
it. It was as the Jew, Joseph Nasi, that he was to continue his remarkable career and that it was to reach its
most dramatic heights.

CHAPTER II

Joseph Nasi

DON Joseph took up his abode together with his redoubtable mother-in-law in her splendid mansion at
Galata, with its swarms of servants, its unending pro-
cessions of mendicants, its interminable benevolences.
Later on, he removed to Ortakewy, in the outskirts of
this same suburb (where a small Jewish community had
existed from Byzantine days), to a residence of his own,
enjoying an extensive view over the Bosphorus and the
Asiatic mainland beyond. This was called, in the Italian
fashion, by the name *Belvedere*[1], or "Fair View." We may
picture him as he rode through the streets of Constantinople with his escort of janissaries and chokidars — a
slightly incongruous figure in that setting, in his stylish
European costume, notwithstanding the well-trimmed
black beard which he allowed to grow in the fashion of
the day. He made a gallant attempt to perpetuate in
his new home something of the courtly occidental atmosphere to which he had been accustomed. He had with
him when he came to Constantinople a goodly supply of
weapons and armor, not intended perhaps only for exercise. In the garden of his mansion a jousting-ground
was fitted up, where he and his attendants would enter
the lists one against the other, for all the world as though

it were the pleasances of Italy or the Court of Brussels.
To quote the supercilious Hans Dernschwam once again:

The above-mentioned Portuguese, like other Spaniards at
the Imperial Court, must have practiced jousting and tilting.
He brought with him all sorts of equipment, such as armor,
helmets, fire-arms, long and short lances, as well as battle-axes
and muskets, both large and small. And even at Galata in his
garden he retained this mummery of having his servants tilt
and joust.

He lived, as is obvious, in great style. He had a numerous retinue. Three "gentlemen" in personal attendance on him had accompanied him to Constantinople,
one of them calling himself now Don Abraham, one Don
Samuel, and one Solomon.[2] Solomon Senior (Coronel),
an ex-Marrano (formerly, it was said, governor of Segovia), his "vicar" or principal agent, was constantly
consulted by him and was generally spoken of as being
his "right eye"; of his son, Francisco, "João Miguez's
heart and soul," who later ruled the duchy of Naxos as
his lieutenant governor, it will be necessary to speak at
length later on.[3] A certain physician named David, or
Daoud, was his representative for official business at
Court where he served as his interpreter, and thus knew
all his secrets.[4] Joseph Cohen, or Cohen Pomar (Ibn
Ardut) was his secretary and amanuensis, and sometimes
acted as his deputy for official transactions.[5] The scholarly Isaac Onkeneira, a member of a famous Salonican
family of Spanish descent, was in his employment as
dragoman or interpreter.[6] There were numerous other
dependents of various degrees. It was more than a household, in the modern sense, that Don Joseph had about
him: it was almost a court.

He was now some thirty-five years of age, in the prime
of his life. He must have been a singularly fascinating
person at this period. Contemporaries with no reason
to flatter testify to his powerful build, his handsome
appearance and his personal charm. To all this he added
great wealth, polished manners, and extensive experience. His knowledge of the world was memorable. He
had been a familiar figure at the Court of Brussels.
He had known intimately the queen regent of the Netherlands, King Francis I of France, even the Holy Roman
Emperor himself, the dour, fanatical Charles V, by whom
he had been knighted, and the latter's son, the priest-
ridden Philip II of Spain. He had been the companion
of Maximilian of Habsburg, Charles' nephew, in the lists
and at play. He knew all the courts of Italy at first hand.
"There are few persons of account in Spain, Italy or Flanders who are not personally acquainted with him," wrote
a Christian contemporary, not without a touch of envy.

He was excellent as well as profitable company, with
his supple manners, his extensive travels, his recollections
of courts and cabinets all over Europe, his many adventures and escapes. A contemporary Jewish scholar, Moses
Almosnino, who knew him well, spoke of him as "a great
gentleman, of subtle intellect, most generous, a lover of
justice and merciful, all in a high degree of perfection,
as is demanded of such a person, elevated to so high a
rank." Anton Verancsics (Verantius), later Archbishop
of Gran, who was in Constantinople in 1567 as Hungarian peace-plenipotentiary,[7] described him at some
length in one of his despatches as being a man who "both
in his appearance and in his open address and in the
entire bearing of his body and in his conversation was

more fitting to be a Christian than a Jew" and who "comported himself in humane and dignified fashion in all things." Similarly, the Spanish captive, Andrés Laguna, who detested his religious principles, could not withhold his admiration for his personality and his social graces. Referring to his intimacy at the Courts of the Holy Roman Emperor and the King of France, this cynical observer adds: "He deserved it all, for he was a gentleman, expert in arms, well read, and a friend of his friends."

That does not imply that he lacked the defects of his qualities. These he had in full measure, and some more perhaps as well. Ingratiating enough when he pleased, it seems that he was overbearing and irascible with persons of a lower social status, flying into a passion and threatening summary vengeance if he were thwarted. But his anger seldom lasted, and if his threats were implemented it was not for long. On the other hand, he never forgot or forgave what he and his family had suffered in the past, the grievances rankling for many years until he found the opportunity for vengeance. For himself, he was highly ambitious, but lacked fixity of purpose. He elaborated brilliant plans, but when prospects seemed brightest was beguiled by others still more brilliant and abandoned the first. Ideas were picked up, toyed with, partially carried into effect and then discarded. (One of the Venetian ambassadors spoke of him with keen insight as being better able to impede than to forward any particular line of policy.) So long as his aunt, Doña Gracia, lived, he was stiffened by her stamina and determination. After her death, his ambitions soared, but they henceforth lacked sustaining power; and he died, still resplendent, but thwarted.

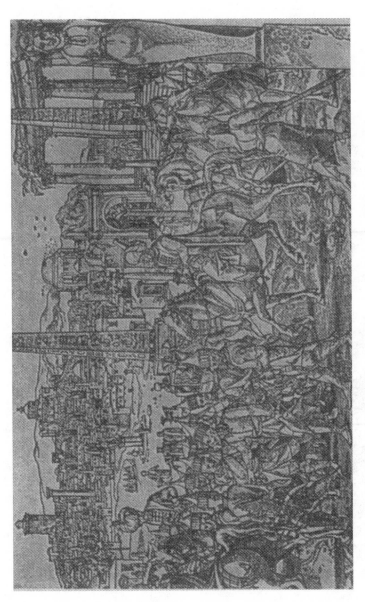

The Sultan and his Train Passing through the Roman Circus in Constantinople

(16th-century woodcut)

A Palace on the Bosphorus
(from an engraving)

It was natural that, almost as soon as he arrived in Constantinople, in 1554, Don Joseph was brought into touch with Court circles. The age of Turkish expansion was then at its height. There was an almost perpetual state of hostility between Turkey and the Christian powers, and open warfare was never far remote. Every scrap of information regarding the latter — their strength and weakness, their policy and intentions, their finances and economy, above all their military organization — was therefore of supreme interest and supreme importance at the Sublime Porte. Owing to the profound differences of language, faith, costume, social habits and everything else, there was indeed an almost impenetrable veil between the Moslem and the Christian worlds. The foreign merchant-colonies in Constantinople, whose services might have been utilized to overcome this, were for obvious reasons unreliable. Hence the arrival of a man like Joseph Nasi, with his knowledge of many countries, his powers of observation, his experience of courts and capitals, and his personal acquaintance with rulers and statesmen, all combined with an unquestionable (because inevitable) loyalty to his new home, created tremendous interest. He had already been in relations with the Sublime Porte long before his coming; these were automatically renewed. One may imagine him taking an early opportunity to wait upon the grand vizier to express his gratitude, and being plied with questions. But the information that he had was too important to be transmitted at second hand. Before long, he was summoned to the presence of the sultan, Suleiman the Magnificent, himself; and it became customary for the latter to ask his opinion and advice when any matter touching on European politics was concerned. In return, he and his relatives received important commercial concessions and could count on special measures of protection when any sort of difficulty arose in connection with them.

The family's arrival in Turkey coincided with a sordid, sanguinary dynastic dispute which in the end turned greatly to Don Joseph's advantage. The heir-apparent to the throne was the Prince Mustapha, child of Suleiman's first wife, "the Rose of Spring" — the darling of the army and of the people, and said in sentimental retrospect to be the heir to all his father's good qualities but none of the bad. Suleiman was pre-eminently uxorious, and it was in his reign that the harem came to be a power in the state, as it was to remain henceforth for centuries. At present, his principal wife, who had acquired immense power over him, was the Russian-born Churrem, who has gone down in history, owing to the genius of the French poets, Marmontel and Favart, as Roxalana. Desiring, in the classical fashion, to secure the throne for her own offspring, she began to intrigue against Mustapha and persuaded the elderly sultan that he was conspiring with the janissaries to seize the throne. Rustam Pasha, grand vizier since 1544, who had married her daughter and was likely to lose his appointment if Mustapha succeeded to power, added his efforts to her blandishments and the sultan was won over. During the course of the campaign against Persia in 1553, the warlike prince was summoned to the imperial camp at Eregli. On entering his father's tent he was strangled. A revolt of the janissaries was averted, if with difficulty, though it was found desirable to depose the scheming grand vizier temporarily, the ineffectual Ahmed Pasha being appointed in his place.

When Joseph Nasi reached Constantinople in 1554, the succession lay between Roxalana's two sons, Selim and Bajazet. The former was the elder of the two and thus had (for what it counted) the better hereditary right: he had the support, too, of Rustam Pasha, who shortly afterwards returnèd to office as grand vizier. (It is said that Roxalana secured Ahmed Pasha's murder, shortly before her own death in 1555, with this object in view.) Bajazet on the other hand inherited the temperament as well as the name of one of the most warlike and successful of all Turkish rulers and was thus extremely popular with the generals and the troops. Nasi came to be on good terms with both of the princes, his influence with them being a matter of common knowledge.[8] Selim however, who was at this time governor of Anatolia, treated him with special favor, appointing him his purveyor and jeweller (*djevahirdji*).

In 1559, the struggle for the succession to the throne suddenly flared up afresh. In accordance with Turkish precedent, Bajazet's success in the tussle seemed highly probable. Don Joseph realized no doubt that if the military party gained the upper hand, his lot, like that of other aliens in the Turkish empire, would be precarious. He, moreover, perhaps saw in Selim reserves of ability and tenacity which were lacking in his brother. He decided therefore to throw in his lot decisively with the former. While most of the great officers of state and other notables were prudently holding aloof, or else showed their lack of sympathy in a more positive fashion, he obtained the sultan's permission to visit Selim at Kutahia, in Asia Minor, where he had his official residence, taking with him a magnificent gift of treasure, clothing, arms and horses — enough almost to finance the approaching campaign.[9] (Contemporaries valued what he brought at 50,000 ducats in specie and 30,000 in kind, but this was without doubt an exaggeration.) It was an act of friendship which Selim never forgot.

Not long thereafter, in the summer of 1559, open hostilities broke out between the two brothers, Bajazet opening his attack with characteristic dash. Selim was now better prepared to resist, and after he gained the upper hand his father, who had hitherto shown himself impartial as between the two, gave him his support in a fashion which some historians find wholly inexplicable. Bajazet was decisively defeated at Konia and fled to Persia, but was handed over for execution, together with his four sons, in return for an enormous bribe. (A fifth met the same fate in Asia Minor.) Selim's accession to the throne was now as certain as assassination and intrigue could make it; indeed, even in his father's lifetime he was henceforth often referred to as "Sultan." He showed himself profoundly grateful for the support he had received at the crucial moment, and Joseph Nasi, the Portuguese Jew, became one of his prime favorites.

A curious story was told of how the latter consolidated his influence. Islamic law, highly lenient as regards some other fleshly indulgences, stringently forbade the faithful to drink wine. This was an unpopular restriction, especially in a grape-growing region, but it was impossible to flout it openly. For Prince Selim, accustomed to soft living and self-indulgence, this was an almost unbearable deprivation. Don Joseph, a connoisseur in wines and with very considerable interests in the trade (in which, as we shall see, he ultimately acquired a monopoly in the

Turkish Empire), is said to have assisted him to evade the restrictions. In the boxes of trinkets, which he sent from time to time to the Castle at Magnesia, bottles of choice vintages were packed, and the young man was enabled to indulge in his favorite petty vice while continuing to pose to the outside world as a model of orthodox observance.

Whether or no there is any truth in these details, it is certain that Selim became deeply attached to Don Joseph, whom he found amusing, useful and informative. (One is reminded in a way of the intimacy three hundred years later between the future King Edward VII of England, when he was Prince of Wales, and the Jewish *bon-vivants*, who similarly assisted him to escape from the oppressive atmosphere of the Court.) So close did their friendship become that absurd stories began to circulate regarding the prince's parentage. It was told that he was in fact a changeling, without a drop of Ottoman blood, passed off by Roxalana as her own, but in reality child of a sister of Nasi's (otherwise unrecorded);[10] and henceforth he was constantly referred to by his enemies as "the Jew's son."

There was in any case no possibility of mistaking Don Joseph's position of favor. As a non-Moslem or *raya*, he could not be admitted to any official government appointment — that would have been contrary to Islamic law. Selim, however, had him raised to the rank of *muteferik*, or "Gentleman of the Imperial Retinue," granting him, moreover, fifty-five aspri (5½ ducats) daily;[11] and he was consistently spoken of in official documents as *Frenk Bey Oglu*, or Frankish (that is to say, European) Prince, or else "Model of the Notables of the Mosaic Nation."

Henceforth, Joseph Nasi was one of the great personages in the Turkish state. It was no question of secret, backstairs influence; his position was openly recognized, and he himself was universally courted. In Constantinople, he was generally known as "The Great Jew" or else "The Rich Jew." Foreign ambassadors waited on him as a matter of course, listened deferentially to his opinions, and tried hard to see whether they might derive from them some inkling as to the future policy of the Sublime Porte, or influence him to their own advantage. The conversations with him were faithfully reported in their despatches home, sometimes at great length. References to him are constantly found in diplomatic correspondence from now on, under the names of Giovanni (or Jean, perhaps Jehan or Zan) Miches, or Michel, or Miques, or Micas; or else *il Marzano* (i. e., Marrano?). No single individual, other than the sultan and the grand vizier, figures perhaps so prominently in the despatches of the representatives of the sultan's ally, the Most Christian King of France. He was included among those high officers of state whom it was considered desirable to conciliate with gifts and pensions, in accordance with the immemorial tradition of the Golden Horn. Less exalted observers, like Stephen Gerlach, preacher to the German colony, or Hans Dernschwam, the inquisitive Fugger factor, or Andrés Laguna, the Spanish litterateur who was lightening the burden of captivity by posing as a medical expert, all noted his activities in their reminiscences and writings, as the passages quoted from time to time in the foregoing pages have illustrated. His influence was all the more remarkable in view of the fact that he did not entirely master the Turkish language, making use of the services of an interpreter when he was admitted to audience.[12]

His position owed not a little to his close intimacy with some of the more prominent Turkish politicians and public officers — for example, the gifted but inordinately avaricious ex-swineherd, Rustam Pasha, so long grand vizier, whose name recurs time after time in connection with Don Joseph's career, though he does not seem to have been above speaking against him when he was not present; or this dignitary's brother-in-law, the Captain Pasha Piale, one of the most brilliant of Turkish admirals.

The great position that Nasi occupied in Constantinople henceforth was not only dependent on his wealth, his personality and his ingratiating ways, to which he owed his advancement in the first instance. In the sequel, his influence was probably due quite as much to his remarkably extensive knowledge of European affairs and conditions, to which reference has already been made. Others in Constantinople relied on hearsay, on prejudice, on the favor of Allah or the invincibility of the Turkish arms. He, on the other hand, knew at first hand of the strength and weakness of every part of Europe — of Portugal where he had been born, of Spain under whose rule he had so long lived, of England which he had visited, of the Low Countries with which the family had been so closely associated, of the Holy Roman Empire where he had great interests, of France where he had carried on business for many years, of the various states of Italy, through all of which he had passed at one time or the other. Even in these days, personal knowledge so extensive would be found useful in similar circumstances. In the sixteenth century, when the East and the West, the Moslem world and the Christian, were cut off from one another by so profound a cleavage, it was almost unique.

Apart from his range of experience and knowledge, there was one other factor which made Joseph Nasi's advice invaluable. All over Europe, he had devoted agents, correspondents and acquaintances who constantly primed him with information of what was going on. Thus his intelligence service was far in advance of that maintained by the government. From every capital he was regularly supplied with the court gossip — what was the state of the king's health, whether any change of minister was likely, and so on. If a military expedition was in contemplation, his factors knew of it and hastened to inform him. The foreign diplomatic representatives in Constantinople were at one in calling the attention of their governments to this fact. (Thus, for example, even in 1573, when his star was definitely in the decline, the Venetian envoy reported how the intelligence garnered from all countries by Nasi, "being the head of all his Nation," was harmful not only to Venice but to all Christendom.) It was a system not unlike that organized for the English government a hundred years later by the Marrano Carvajal, at the time of Oliver Cromwell, or in the early nineteenth century by the House of Rothschild. There was one occasion when thanks to him the Turkish government was informed of the approaching arrival of a French special envoy, and the object of his mission, even before he had left Paris!

It seems as though he acted almost as an associate minister for foreign affairs, even under the Sultan Suleiman, where European relations were concerned. In any case, when in 1563 the Turkish government conceived the idea of embarrassing Venice by inciting the Duke of Savoy to put forward a remote dynastic claim on the island of Cyprus, the envoy who was sent to the Court of Turin with this object had his credentials countersigned by Don Joseph. In the subsequent correspondence on this matter, the latter took the principal part; and it is recorded how one of the Turkish agents, Niccolò Giustiniani, brought the Duke a personal letter from him, dated November 9, 1565, indicating that all the pashas favored the enterprise so greatly that it was certain of success, and urging the despatch of an ambassador to Constantinople to make the final arrangements. The cautious Italian decided in the end that discretion was the better part of Christian solidarity, and informed the Pope and other potentates about the proposals; so that Cyprus remained for a few years longer in Venetian hands and was later on to enter into the orbit of Don Joseph's own overweening ambition.[12a]

When João Miguez (as he was then) came to Turkey, he brought with him cordial letters of recommendation from the French ambassador in Rome, the Seigneur de Lansac, with whom he must have been intimately acquainted, to M. d'Aramon, his colleague in Constantinople, who was requested to favor the new arrival in certain affairs (the nature of which it is not difficult to guess, in the light of what afterwards happened) which he had in hand. As we have seen, d'Aramon went over in state to Galata to visit him and his bride shortly after their wedding, and the intimacy between the two scandalized at least one jealous observer.[13] Nasi had, as a matter of fact, resided for a long time in France and still had business interests there, and it was to be anticipated that his relations with the French diplomatic representatives would be close and cordial. Since 1555, there existed a somewhat incongruous Franco-Turkish alliance directed against their common enemy, the House of Habsburg, which controlled Spain, much of Italy, the Low Countries, the Holy Roman Empire and what was left of Hungary. This understanding horrified contemporary opinion, which considered that Christendom should stand united against the Crescent. Nevertheless, it survived criticism, intrigues and difficulties, and was one of the determining factors in European politics in the sixteenth century. The friendly relations betweeen Don Joseph and d'Aramon were therefore natural and, from the point of view of the Turkish government, welcome. They continued under the latter's successor, M. de Codignac. The French Court was now desperately in need of funds (at one time, an attempt was made to raise 2,000,000 crowns from the sultan, who intimated that to lend money to a Christian was against his religion, and to an ally beneath his dignity!) and had difficulty even in remitting the ambassador's expenses. Nasi came to his help with some substantial advances. By this means, he presumably hoped to prepare the way for friendly consideration of his personal claims on the French government, which the ambassador in Rome had so warmly recommended to his colleague's good offices. (It is hardly to be doubted that this had been the object of his communication.)

Codignac was, however, succeeded in 1557 by M. de la Vigne (notorious for his rudeness, and a personal enemy of Rustam Pasha), who regarded the haughty Portuguese as though he were an importunate usurer and treated him accordingly. He showed this clearly in one of his first despatches home, not long after his appointment. It is the old story. Personal dislike made everything that the Jew did appear suspicious. The fact that the man was rich, that he had agents in Italy, that he had been on good terms with the former French ambassador, was taken as proof of his treasonable practices and intrigues against France; while his attempt to obtain payment for his business debts was bitterly resented. The only tangible piece of evidence concerning him was that he was in correspondence with the French Court — testimony, if anything, to his devotion. But what matter? That too could be twisted into a weapon against him; there was no need to be discriminating in the choice of spittle to bespatter a Jewish gaberdine. The ambassador's words are more graphic than any paraphrase:

There is here a certain Jehan Micques who, from being a Christian, became a Jew in order to marry a rich Jewish heiress who at one time left Flanders and passed through France on her way here.[14] This fellow, pretending to be devoted to your service, and lending a certain sum of money to Codignac, inserted and intruded himself, and still does, to hear the secret of your affairs at the Porte in order to profit as and where he pleases. Having the convenience to hear all the news from France by means of his agents in Italy, he communicates them daily to the Pasha and thereby makes us dependent on him and frequently frustrates our designs. It is therefore necessary for your interest to make him lose the credit that he has gained by this means and by the presents which he is constantly making. Therefore may it please you to write a letter to the Grand Seigneur to the effect that the said Migues makes a practice of warning your enemies of everything that happens here, even of your private affairs, since he is a Spaniard[15] born, and to ask that he should be punished. At the same time write also to the

Pasha, informing him of the other insolences that he ventures upon daily with your poor subjects, merchants and servants, because of his great wealth; and demand and ask that he should be punished, so that a rascal of this sort should not dare to attempt anything further against you and your servants. Since my return, I have heard that he has written you certain letters, copies of which I should very much like to have in order to show them to the said Pasha; for the fact that, being a subject of the sultan, he has dared to write to so great a Prince as you, is enough to abate his pride and have him severely punished . . .

The French king, Henri II, could not fail to be influenced by his ambassador's opinion and advice. Writing to de la Vigne immediately after, on June 24, 1557, he told him to instruct Nasi to submit for scrutiny to the Council the accounts or receipts of what he had advanced to Codignac, on the verification of which he would be paid. Events were to show that this was not the language to use with regard to one of the other's temperament and position.

The correspondence that followed is long and prolix. One thing only emerges from it clearly. De la Vigne was now on the worst possible terms with Nasi and did everything possible to discredit him; and Petremol, who was left in charge of French interests on his recall in 1559, followed his example. The French king showed by his actions that he was in complete agreement with his representatives. As a result, Don Joseph's relations with the French Court, formerly so cordial, came to be worse and worse, until further deterioration was impossible. As we have seen, he followed closely throughout his life the principle of Jewish conduct laid down by his fictitious contemporary in Shakespeare's play, "If you wrong us, shall we not revenge?" Furious at the manner in which he had been treated, he determined to make his enemies regret it.

He had certain business claims against the French Crown, which he now determined to press to the full. It was not only a question of the relatively unimportant advances he had made to Codignac, but also of debts of far greater magnitude and far longer standing which he had formerly been content to leave dormant.[16] We do not know the exact details of his early activities and travels, but a good part of his time had apparently been spent at Lyons. This city, from being a center of the silk and textile industry, which attracted a considerable foreign colony — including large numbers of Spaniards and Italians, especially Florentines — had developed into one of the most important money-markets of Europe. Thus the Mendes banking house had found exceptional opportunities there. Among its clients was the French treasury, to which it made very considerable advances. When, in 1549, proceedings were opened at Venice against Gracia Nasi at the instigation of her irresponsible sister, on the score of being a secret Judaizer, the king of France was encouraged to follow suit, an embargo being laid on the same pretext on the property of the firm in France. It is not on record that this was ever lifted, though we know that later on certain French assets of Doña Gracia's were registered in the name of the Albizzi firm of Florence. In any case, what with all this and what with subsequent advances, Don Joseph had a claim against the French Crown to a total of 150,000 ducats — a truly vast fortune for those days. On his first arrival in Turkey, he had not pressed it very seriously, either because he imagined that more could be

obtained by persuasion than by persistence, or because
he considered that the maintenance of good relations mattered more in the long run than any sum of money,
however large. Now that the good relations were at an
end, and he was treated as an actual enemy, he saw no
further reason for forebearance, and began to press his
claim.

The reply of the French government to his demand
for payment was ingenious, but far from ingenuous.
Joseph Nasi was a Jew, they said. While resident in
France, he had therefore been a secret Jew. But Jews
were forbidden to live and traffic in France. Hence,
whatever business he had transacted there was illegal,
and engagements made in connection with it were not
binding. The debt was therefore repudiated entirely.

It was a peculiarly ignoble piece of casuistry. The
other was now driven to have recourse to the old device
of the family in such circumstances, and solicited the
support of the Turkish court. After all, the Sublime
Porte had more than once thought fit to intervene on
behalf of the House of Mendes and its property even
when they were living in Italy, while they were Turkish
subjects only potentially. It had far better justification
for doing so now, when they were settled in Constantinople and their economic interests were those of the
country at large. Accordingly, within the broad setting
of the Franco-Turkish alliance there was now enacted a
minor but long-protracted diplomatic tussle on behalf of
Don Joseph Nasi, in which international amity was
tested and almost endangered by the unusual touchstone
of common honesty. Don Joseph's bosom friend, Selim,
the heir-apparent to the throne, pressed his case upon

SELIM II, SULTAN OF TURKEY, 1524–1574

THE SEA OF MARMORA
(from an engraving)

his father and the grand vizier, Ali the Fat, who had succeeded Rustam Pasha on the latter's death in 1561. Their
warmth in the matter was not, as a matter of fact, dis-
interested, for by now Nasi in turn owed great sums to
the Imperial treasury on account of various state mono-
polies and customs dues which he farmed, and which he
professed to be unable to pay unless his claims on the
French Crown were satisfied — an argument which he
was now always able to employ.

Accordingly, the Turkish government took up his ap-
lication in the most serious and formal fashion. In the
summer of 1562, the inevitable *chaus*, or court messenger, was sent to France to request the government officially to satisfy Nasi's claim. He reached Venice without
incident. Here, however, difficulties began to arise, as
the French representative refused to give him a safe-
conduct to go further, using as a pretext the disturbed
state of France. The grand vizier was, as a matter of fact,
relieved rather than otherwise; for he did not attach
much importance to the *chaus'* mission, which (as he
confided to the French ambassador) had been due mainly
to Nasi's importunity. But, in spite of this half-hearted
support, the messenger ultimately obtained a safe-conduct
from Paris, and another from the governor of Milan,
and was able to continue his voyage.

Meanwhile, the French government had been stirred
to action on its side. A special envoy of Italian origin,
Vincenzo Giustiniani, had gone to Constantinople on
behalf of Charles IX, the boy king of France, to explain
why the payment of a debt to an infidel could be considered superfluous. He waited on Selim to expound this
point of view; but Nasi, most unreasonably, was there

first. (M. de Petremol called this "his Jewish tricks".)
Hence the remonstration failed. The French government,
pressed by its enemies, was in no position to risk estrang-
ing its only friend and now admitted the debt, though
asking for time to discharge it. Here the matter rested
for a short while.

On the conclusion of the Peace of Amboise, in 1563,
which temporarily restored domestic tranquillity in
France, the question was reopened. Nasi now insisted
once more that he was unable to pay the Turkish treasury
the vast sums he owed it in connection with various
transactions unless this claim were settled. Hence the
payment again became one of the foremost matters under
discussion between the two governments. In April, 1564,
the grand vizier, in a conversation with M. de Petremol,
told him that the sultan and his son were so insistent, not
only because of the special relations between the latter
and Nasi, but also because of their personal interests. He
coldly hinted that, if the French king had no ready
money available for the purpose, he could settle it by
transference of raw materials — metal and textiles —
which were needed in Turkey. The sultan and Selim sent
personal letters to Paris pressing the claim, avoiding the
dangers of transmission through Italy by utilizing the
good offices of the king of Algiers. Selim, moreover, requested the French ambassador at Constantinople, as a
personal favor, to see that Nasi's debts should be given
preferential treatment, when the financial settlement
began, and not allowed to drag on. The ambassador
replied in a conciliatory fashion, stating that it had been
only through the domestic troubles and the difficulties of
verification that the matter had not been concluded long

before. Meanwhile he wrote home, reporting on the state of affairs in a burst of exceptional candor. If the French government wished to continue to maintain good relations with the Sublime Porte, he said, the debt could be satisfied without an excessive strain — either in specie or, if this were undesirable, in kind; otherwise, the old excuses might still serve — that France did not tolerate Jews such as Nasi to live and traffic there, and that the property they held in the country was legally forfeit to the Crown. However, a spirit of conciliation seemed to be in the air; and Nasi instructed his personal agent at Venice, Duarte Gomes (the Portuguese poet and patron of letters who had stood in such close relationship with the House of Mendes for so long)[17] to go to Paris with all the necessary documents in order to substantiate his claims.

For the Most Christian King to make a payment of such magnitude when there was a colorable pretext to refrain from doing so, in the name of true religion, was almost to fly in the face of Providence. Notwithstanding all the promises, remonstrations and proof, the debt was even now not discharged. The Turkish government at length lost its patience. On March 23, 1565, the sultan sent a peremptory personal letter to the king of France — the third on this subject — not asking but demanding the immediate payment of the amount "as a sign of justice and loyalty, and a token of friendship towards Us." It was, moreover, despatched, not by the normal diplomatic channel, but by the medium of the Admiral Mustapha Pasha, who was instructed to send a special messenger to Paris bearing his master's communication, while he was making a naval demonstration in the western Mediterranean with the Turkish fleet — auspices which were almost ominous. At the same time, the French representative was instructed to forward urgent despatches to the same effect to his government. The terms of the reply are unknown. It was obviously a temporizing one, or else promises were once again made for payment, as so often before, which were not fulfilled. Meanwhile, M. de Petremol was succeeded as French agent by M. de Grantrie de Grandchamp who, however, continued his predecessor's disdainful treatment of Nasi and his claims. It was he who was to suffer for it; for, as will be seen later, the Jew had by no means attained as yet the height of his influence.

Even after the attitude of the French representatives in Constantinople towards him had altered so drastically, Don Joseph, on one occasion at least, went out of his way to do the French government a service. In July, 1560, after the destruction of the Spanish fleet off Gerba by Piale Pasha and the famous corsair Torgut, the Spanish garrison on the island was overwhelmed and numerous prisoners of war taken back to Constantinople. Catherine de Médicis, queen mother of France, was anxious to secure the release of certain of them, in particular the commander of the force, Don Alvaro de Saude, and for that purpose sent to Constantinople a special envoy, named Salviati, to see what he could do in the matter. Thanks to his highly-organized intelligence service, Don Joseph knew about the mission before the Turkish government did and tried to secure the same object independently — presumably for the sake of the prestige which would accrue to him. As the French ambassador waspishly reported in February 1562:

The last time I presented him [the grand vizier] with the
King's letters, he informed me that he knew of the coming of
the said Salviati and its reason even before he left France. The
person who informed him was the Jew, Jean Micques, who
makes a practice of giving information about our Court and
other places by the means of spies, whom he maintains under
the name of factors. He even wished to use his influence with
the Pasha for the liberty of Don Alvaro. This he did, as I believe, so that if there were a successful outcome he would be
able to boast publicly everywhere that he was responsible!

As a matter of fact, Nasi was disappointed in the
event. There was in Constantinople at that time, acting
as imperial envoy, the famous Flemish diplomat and man
of letters Ogier Ghislain de Busbecq, who was also using
his influence with the same object; and it was his efforts
(so at least he claimed) that were ultimately crowned
with success.

There was one area, later to be associated with Jewish
life in an exceptionally intense degree, with the fate of
which Don Joseph was intimately concerned. Since the
beginning of the sixteenth century, Moldavia, the heter-
ogeneous province on what was then the Polish border,
had been tributary to the Turk, whose hold there gradu-
ally strengthened. In the intrigues in favor of the various
aspirants to authority, which went on in Constantinople
throughout the century, Jews played an active part.
Notwithstanding this, they were able to do nothing for
their Moldavian brethren (as yet, fortunately, few in
number). Thus in 1541, Peter Rares, the last ruler who
enjoyed a show of independence, was assisted in the
recovery of his throne by a Jewess, the confidante of the
sultan's mother (perhaps Esther Kyra),[18] who also gave

him pecuniary assistance. Nevertheless, his first action
when he resumed rule was to despoil the Jewish merchants
of the country in a most dastardly manner. His example
was followed by the voivode Alexander Lapuseanu. The
latter, however, was displaced in 1561 by a picturesque
Greek adventurer named John (Jacob) Basilikós Era-
clides, who claimed to be descended from the former
despots of Serbia and had adopted their name. He
managed to obtain confirmation of his title from the
sultan and gallantly attempted to introduce what he
considered an enlightened administration. His career
was in some respects curiously similar to that of Joseph
Nasi, and he, like the other, had political interests in the
islands of the archipelago, where he had somehow obtained recognition as Marquis Palatine of Samos and
Paros, where Nasi was afterwards to rule.[19] We know
nothing, however, of the relations between the two men.
In any case, his relatively efficient government in Moldavia needed heavy taxation to support it, and in consequence of the discontent which was thus aroused he was
assassinated after only two years. Busy intrigues for the
succession now began in Constantinople. Notwithstanding his former record, Lapuseanu managed to enlist
the support of Joseph Nasi, and partly as a result of this
he recovered his throne. It may have been in consequence
of Don Joseph's influence that in the few years that
remained of his reign the lot of the Moldavian Jews was
more tranquil. Later on, as we shall see, the influential
Jews of the capital were again closely concerned in
political developments in this area; while Nasi (who was
reported to have received from Lapuseanu a payment of
10,000 galbeni) actually had his name associated for a

while with the supreme office of voivode of the adjoining Province of Muntenia or Wallachia.

A strong interest in this border province was naturally maintained also by the Polish Court. Here, too, Nasi's name carried great weight. Striking testimony of this was forthcoming in 1562, when a treaty of peace with Turkey was under discussion. In connection with this, Selim addressed King Sigismund Augustus a personal letter (dated "Caramania", March 2, 1562). In this, he mentioned the *Frenk Bey Oglu* Joseph Nasi, who was well known in European countries and greatly honored at the Turkish Court, and told of the prominent part he was taking in the negotiations and how anxious he was for the sultan to conclude peace. It may be that this was because he wished to extend his commercial operations further north, into Poland itself, as indeed happened in due course.[20]

While playing so prominent a role in political life, Joseph Nasi did not relinquish his business interests. His influence was indeed mainly due to his wealth, but had he been content to live on his capital he would have counted for very little. As we have seen, Doña Gracia, after her arrival in Turkey, had continued to direct the affairs of the former House of Mendes, her interests apparently centering upon the importation and distribution of textiles and manufactured materials throughout the Turkish Empire. Her nephew had, of course, become associated with her; and in Ragusa, for example, the names figured side by side on official documents and agreements. Naturally, he soon began to venture out in new directions on his own account, adapting his former banking experience to the special circumstances of the

Turkish Empire. He thus became interested in the farming of the taxes — advancing, that is, a considerable sum
in anticipation and receiving in return the right to collect
the entire revenue from the impost on one or another
commodity.

In addition to this, he imported choice wines from all
over Europe, his cellar being famous. Court circles, at least
in moments of religious laxity, learned to appreciate his
palate, and his remarkable supply and excellent taste
were, according to common gossip, among the reasons
for the influence he enjoyed over Selim. He is said to
have owned the most famous vineyards in Chios, as well
as in Sicily and Cyprus. When, in 1563, Alexander
Lapuseanu regained his fief as voivode of Moldavia and
had to give a feast in Constantinople to celebrate the
occasion, it was anticipated that Nasi would net no less
than 10,000 ducats for supplying the wine, though so vast
a sum must surely have included incidental perquisites
as well.

His travels were now confined to the Turkish Empire,
generally in Selim's train, as he moved with his cumbrous
retinue from Constantinople to Magnesia or Kutahia, or
took the field on his rare military campaigns. This relative inactivity was not entirely of his own free will. On
one occasion, at least, he had desired to go back to Italy
on a visit, with his brother Samuel. The Turkish government now approached the Signoria of Venice for a safe-
conduct for "the Model of Persons of quality, the Frankish Bey, Joseph Nasi (may his obedience increase!)."[21]
But he was too notorious and too unpopular a figure to
be welcome — especially in this city, where he was considered a traitor. The doge not only refused point blank,

but went so far as to state that, in view of Don Joseph's many misdemeanors, he could never be admitted to any Venetian possession or territory. It was an injury that he could never overlook, though he professed to forgive it. He obtained from the sultan the doge's letter of refusal, which he thenceforth retained, a somewhat truculent souvenir. The Secretary to the Venetian embassy, when he returned home in 1565, told the full story in the report he presented to the doge, which illustrates incidentally Nasi's prominence in the eyes of the diplomatic corps in Constantinople:

I am unwilling, most Serene Prince, to refrain from telling you of another matter which I think of some moment; Your Serenity may take it into such consideration as seems fitting to your most pertinent and sapient judgment, for I do not think that I should keep silent about it. During this mission, I had occasion to converse frequently with Giovanni Michel (sic), who calls himself now Don Josef Nasi. At length, finding myself in his company two days before I left, after other conversation, he came to speak of the banishment he had from this most excellent State.[22] He showed me the actual letter in parchment that Your Serenity wrote to the Most Serene Sultan Selim in reply to the request by His Highness for a safe-conduct for the persons of this Giovanni and his brother. He then said to me, and indeed swore affectionately, that although this letter made many charges against him, he nevertheless mitigated the matter with the Sultan Selim as adroitly as he could, saying that it was caused by reason of certain private affairs, and not because Your Serenity is not determined to satisfy and gratify His Highness in major matters. He did this, he says, to prevent His Highness from remaining discontented because he had not been listened to, and also in the hope that the benignity of Your Serenity would in return confer some kindness upon him. He begged me, moreover, to assure everyone here warmly that he and his brother are and will always remain most devoted servants of this State; and outwardly he showed that he could not desire anything more dearly in this world than to be restored to Your Serenity's favor.

It would have been well for Venice had the doge and Signoria responded to this friendly gesture in the same spirit. For Joseph Nasi never forgot an injury, and the time was approaching when he would be in a position to avenge himself.

CHAPTER III

Imperial Favorite

ON MAY 1, 1566, Sultan Suleiman the Magnificent, now in his seventy-third year, rode out of Constantinople at the head of his army, to take the field against his enemies for the thirteenth and last time. In August, he began the siege of Szigétvár in Hungary, which was stoutly defended. On the morning of September 5, a great part of the wall of the city was destroyed by mines, in preparation for the final assault. During the following night, the sultan died in his tent, worn out by the hardships of war.

The grand vizier, Mehemet Sokolli, succeeded in keeping the sad event secret so as to secure peaceful succession for the heir, as was not infrequently done at the Turkish Court. (It is said that for greater certainty he had the monarch's physician strangled!) Three days later, the beleaguered city fell, but with hardly credible cunning the minister still concealed the fact of his master's demise until the arrival of Prince Selim, for whom he had sent posthaste, in the midst of the army at Belgrade. Only then were the tidings publicly announced, the accession of the new sovereign proclaimed and the customary largesse (though not indeed in what was considered sufficient quantity) made to the troops. Thus, after a reign of forty-six years in life, Suleiman's body received homage in the midst of his forces for a further forty-six days after his death.

At the time of his accession, Selim II, son of the late sultan and his exotic Russian favorite, Roxalana, was forty-two years of age — a little Don Joseph's junior. From his youth, he had a reputation for indolence and luxurious living, which left a visible trace on his bloated, rubicund features and gave him among historians the nickname of Selim the Sot. Nearly ten years before he came to the throne, one of the Venetian envoys, Antonio Erizzo, had described him as being "unpopular with his subjects, because they say that he is not a man of honor; much addicted to drink, cruel and very haughty." Daniel Barbarigo, in 1558, though giving a more pleasant account of his personality ("He is jovial and cheerful, and much loved by his servants"), similarly accentuated the fact that he was "luxurious, and very fond of wine." Dandolo spoke of him as being "altogether devoted to his pleasures, and slave to his senses." But there was another side to his character. Another contemporary depicted him as being "haughty and warlike, because of his long exercise in arms," and suggested that he knew when to call a halt to his self-indulgence and take vigorous action. He had the truly imperial faculty of taking good advice; and even though he did not have the vigor and driving force of his magnificent father, his life was not, on the other hand, disgraced by any similar succession of harem intrigues. His rule was on the whole successful and his campaigns fortunate in the long run. He did not take much ostensible share in the work of government, but, from the languid recesses of the seraglio, he watched, observed and, when necessary, acted. He reminds one in a way of Charles II of England, both in his apparent indolence and his real though seldom-asserted ability.

One of the fashions in which this was shown was, as has been indicated, in his choice of able ministers and advisers; and among these Joseph Nasi was pre-eminent. It was he more than anyone else who, in the opinion of one of the Venetian envoys, was responsible for stirring the sultan's naturally sluggish nature and spurring him on to a more vigorous and ambitious policy.

He was one of the trusted handful who had accompanied his master from Constantinople when he went to be hailed as sovereign by the army, after he had received the news of his father's death at Kutahia. This was itself a sufficient token of the prestige which he enjoyed. It was already obvious to the world how close was the association between the somewhat incongruous pair, and how he could count on his master's support in all things, sometimes even against the advice of the ministers of state. More and more signs of favor were henceforth showered upon him. On the road to Belgrade, even before Selim's formal assumption of power, he was enfeoffed with the island of Naxos and the adjacent Archipelago — once considered the premier duchy of Christendom — in succession to the deposed Giacomo Crispi.[1] (It will be necessary to devote a separate chapter to this extraordinary episode.) He hastened away immediately to visit his feud. Thus, he was not present at the resplendent ceremony in the camp on the banks of the Danube, when the officers of state paid homage to their new master, nor at his resplendent entry into Constantinople, when the Jews of all nations spread the roadway about the Adrianople Gate with cloths of gold and scarlet, which were

promptly looted by the greedy janissaries. But Don
Joseph was back again before long at his master's side
and in a position to reap the fullest advantages of the
favor he enjoyed. He received valuable commercial privileges. He was given lucrative financial grants. He
could count not only on diplomatic support, but sometimes even on the sultan's direct intervention, to further
his personal and economic interests. The French Court
was taught at last that his claims had to be taken seriously. His brother shared something of his refulgence,
in the few years of life left to him, becoming an imperial
muteferik like himself, with a daily allowance of twenty-
five aspri. His influence in the imperial Divan, at least
when foreign affairs were being discussed, was almost
comparable to that of the grand vizier himself, and sometimes outweighed it. To state that he controlled Turkish
policy at this period would be a great exaggeration; yet
it indubitably reflected his influence, not to say his personal predilections, at every turn. He attained a truly
dizzy height of dignity, authority and power.

He still could not occupy any official position in the
hierarchy of the Turkish Empire, this being impossible
for an unbeliever. Nevertheless, his power was at least
as great as though this had been the case. The phenomenon did not arouse such attention as it might
have done in other circumstances, for many of the most
powerful persons in the state were not Turks in origin.
Mehemet Sokolli, long grand vizier, was by birth a Bosnian; Ali the Fat, his predecessor, a Dalmatian; Rustam,
Nasi's close associate, a Bulgarian; Ahmed, who had
filled the office between his two periods of administration, a Styrian. The same was the case with the military

commanders: Piale, the captain pasha, was Hungarian; and Ochiali, the most famous corsair of the age, a renegade Calabrian. All of these, indeed, had formally embraced Islam. Joseph Nasi, alone, out of the entire group, had the manliness to withstand all temptation to abjure his faith. But for this, it is not inconceivable that he might have aspired to the position of grand vizier in Sokolli's place.

It was through the palate — or perhaps it is more correct to say the gullet — that he had first commended himself to his gourmandizing master, long before he came to the throne. Naturally, he did not forget this now. Every Friday, a gift of choice wines and delicacies was borne by his servants to the imperial seraglio. They were welcomed not only for gastronomical but also for political reasons. There was at this time in Constantinople, as in all the capitals and cabinets of Europe, a constant danger of poison. (Had not the Signoria of Venice more than once entered into negotiations for the removal of the Grand Signior by this means?) This could most easily be conveyed, not in the staple articles of diet, but in illicit delights, which had to be obtained clandestinely. What was supplied by the Jewish favorite was, however, beyond suspicion, and could be indulged in without fear of ulterior consequences, at least in this world. Stephen Gerlach was informed by his master, the imperial ambassador, that Selim would eat only what "the Great Jew" sent him each week. This is amply borne out in the report of one of the Venetian diplomatic representatives of the time:

His Highness drinks much wine, and the said Don Joseph sends him many bottles of it from time to time, together with

all manner of other delicacies. When His Serene Highness sees
these flasks and delicacies, marked with his seal, he drinks the
wine and eats the delicacies without any further thought, and
shows thus that he trusts him, as being his most loving servant.

We may obtain a picture of the background before
which Don Joseph's activity was now deployed from the
graphic descriptions of the magnificence of the Turkish
Court, combining all the uncouth pomp of the East with
the last survivals of Byzantine splendor. There his master
spent his time among a vast servile retinue of janissaries,
heralds, courtiers, physicians, minstrels, eunuchs, valets,
freaks and concubines. The following vivid impression,
of a slightly later date, is from the pen of a most remarkable English traveller, the organ-builder Thomas Dallam:

The Grand Sinyor . . . sat in great state . . . . . His people
that stood behind him . . . was four hundred persons in number.
Two hundred of them were his principal pages, the youngest of
them sixteen years of age, some twenty and some thirty. They
were apparelled in rich cloth of gold made in gowns to the
middle leg; upon their heads little caps of cloth of gold, and
some cloth of tissue; great pieces of silk around their waists
instead of girdles; upon their legs Cordovan buskins, red.
Their heads were all shaven, saving that behind their ears did
hang a lock of hair like a squirrel's tail; their beards shaven,
all saving their upper lips. Those two hundred men were all
proper men, and Christians born.
  The third hundred were dumb men, that could neither hear
nor speak, and they were likewise in gowns of rich cloth of gold
and Cordovan buskins; but their caps were of violet velvet,
the crown of them made like a leather bottle, the brims divided
into five peaked corners. Some of them had hawks in their
fists.
  The fourth hundred were all dwarfs, bigbodied men, but
very low of stature. Every dwarf did wear a scimitar by his

side, and they were also apparelled in gown of cloth of gold . . . .
The Grand Sinyor . . . sat in a very rich chair of estate, upon
his thumb a ring with a diamond in it half an inch square, a
fair scimitar by his side, a bow and a quiver of arrows.

It is legitimate to place our picture of the handsome
Jewish favorite, in his incongruous occidental clothing,
in this bizarre setting as he wended his way amid the
kiosks and courts, half-concealed in lovely gardens slop-
ing down to the sea, famous throughout Europe under
the name of the imperial palace or seraglio.

How great Don Joseph's influence now was may be
deduced from the fact that non-Jews in the highest position — even supercilious functionaries of the Orthodox
church — had recourse on occasion to his good offices.
On the accession of the new sultan, it is recounted, the
Greek Patriarch himself approached Don Joseph in person and, presenting him with 1,000 sultani to expend on
the necessary baksheesh, begged him to secure the confirmation of the privileges which the Patriarchate had
enjoyed under previous rulers. Not so much through
his personal interest as from a sense of gratification at
the thought that a Jew could help the ecclesiastical dignitary in such an important matter, the other did what
was asked, and with conspicuous success. Rabbi Moses
Almosnino of Salonica records how he was himself present when the Patriarch came to receive the imperial firman that had been obtained for him, superbly illuminated
in gold. Overjoyed, he bent low to kiss his benefactor's
hand. This the courteous Jew would not permit, though
he did not return the magnificent gift that was sent to
him subsequently as a token of gratitude.[2]

Fortified by the close support of the sultan, who doubt-

less did not fail to profit thereby, Don Joseph extended
his commercial operations to a far more ambitious scale
than before. Above all, the wine-trade in which he
engaged assumed vast proportions. Alcohol had of course
been forbidden by Mohammed to true believers. It was
a highly unpopular restriction, as is clear; and in the
Turkish Empire, with perhaps more infidel inhabitants
than Moslems, its enforcement was none too easy.
(Andrés Laguna, in the *Viaje de Turquía*, gives a most
appreciative account of the exquisite variety of wines that
had formerly been available in the wineshops of Galata,
the foreign quarter — sweet malmsey and muscatel from
Crete, white wines from Gallipoli, red or *topico* from Asia
Minor and the Greek islands.) Nevertheless, in 1562,
Suleiman the Magnificent had forbidden wine to be
brought into Constantinople even for Jewish and Christian consumption. There was, on the other hand, no
reason in logic or in law why this pious (though short-
lived) ordinance should impede the transit trade. The
recent Turkish conquests included some of the most
famous grape-growing areas of the Mediterranean. Turkey's neighbors to the north, and the border territories
between them, consumed large quantities of wine — a
primary necessity before tea and coffee were known in
Europe. It would have been absurd to cut off the infidels
from the supply which was legally permitted to them, or
to deprive the imperial treasury and the sultan's loyal
servants of the resultant profit. Nasi had accordingly
obtained an imperial firman permitting him to export to
Moldavia, by way of the Bosphorus, a thousand barrels
of wine every year from Crete. At the beginning of
Selim's reign, this was converted into a monopoly; for in

1568 the captain pasha and other officials were instructed to permit no wines other than his to pass through the Straits, and to treat all other concessions as null. Later on, Nasi contracted for the entire customs on all wines (as well as certain other merchandise) whether from the "Black" or the "White" (i. e. Ionian) sea, at the rate of one-tenth of the total value. For this privilege, he paid 2,000 ducats each year; gossip said that the amount he derived from it came to as much as 15,000!

Henceforth, all ships that entered the Bosphorus were boarded by his agents, accompanied by the imperial janissaries, who inspected the cargoes and exacted his dues. This concession, which gave him almost sovereign power on one of the highways of international commerce, was said to have attracted even more notice than his enfeoffment with the duchy of Naxos, the crowning triumph of his career. When, in 1574, the sultan, in hypocritical deference to Moslem religious law, renewed the ban on the importation of wine and alcohol into his dominions, he (unlike his father) expressly permitted Jews and Christians to sell it privately among themselves. This in effect nullified the pious regulation, and the wine trade continued to flourish, providing a good part of Nasi's income. It is reported that, in addition to these financial operations, he advanced money to the Crown in a more commonplace fashion.

His commercial operations in Poland were on an exceptionally large scale. Thanks to the sultan's cordial recommendation, in 1567–8 he obtained from Sigismund Augustus, king of that country, important privileges for his personal agents, Hayim Cohen and Abraham Mosso — the same who had formerly represented Doña Gracia

at Ancona and had escaped the holocaust through the
Grand Signior's intervention. For a five-year period, they
were empowered to import into the country muscatel and
malmsey wines, and other incidental commodities, on the
same terms as the highly-favored merchants of Lemberg;
while what had already been imported by another agent
of his, Abraham Hasef,² was retroactively exempted from
duties. The imports made by this means through Lemberg
in the second year of the concession (May, 1569–May,
1570) were to the value of 5,800 florins, in addition to
374 barrels of malmsey wine and 70 of muscatel, the
normal import-dues on which amounted in all to 1,000
florins. The Lemberg merchants were, of course, intensely
jealous and tried to put an end to this foreign competition.
The King's communication ordering them to desist
eloquently expressed the reason for his policy; it was
necessary, he said, in order to ensure maintenance of good
relations between himself and the Turkish emperor. Notwithstanding the scale of their transactions, the agents
were short of money for brief periods and were compelled
to have recourse to non-Jews for loans, at truly usurious
rates of interest, varying between 60 and 150 per cent.
When the war of Cyprus broke out in 1570, Mosso made
a declaration testifying to the good character of a number
of Turkish Jewish merchants arrested as enemy aliens in
Venice, whose release he tried to secure. On his leaving
Poland at the expiration of his concession, he was empowered to export with him 500 bales of cloth.

Another agent or associate of Nasi's in Poland, the Jew
Gianomore (?), enjoyed the monopoly of the import of
Turkish wax. The infringement of this elicited a sharp

letter of protest from the sultan to the Polish king, calling attention to the fact that he· always made a point of covering with benefits those, like Nasi, who had distinguished themselves for their fidelity and devotion to the imperial throne.[4]

As with Selim's accession Don Joseph's influence at Court grew, he came into headlong collision with Mehemet Sokolli, grand vizier since 1565 in succession to Ali Pasha "the Fat." A renegade Bosnian by origin (his real name was Sokolic, "the Eagle's Nest"), he still retained something of the Christian's contempt for the Jew; intensely ambitious, though intensely capable (he was without doubt the greatest Turkish statesman of his age), he strongly resented Nasi's political influence; eager for the fruits as well as the status of office, he was envious of the other's privileges; on the other hand, as the sultan's son-in-law, he had made his position wellnigh impregnable. The two men's tendencies in foreign politics were diverse. Their personalities were poles apart. Nor were the reasons for their opposition merely personal and political. At Constantinople, perhaps even more than elsewhere at this period (which is to say a great deal), considerations of the most sordid nature always entered into play in public affairs: and, as a counterpoise to Nasi, Sokolli extended his favor and patronage to the enormously rich Christian financier Michael Cantacuzenos, called by the Turks *Shaitan Oglu* or "son of the Devil," whose name was remembered in folk songs for centuries after as a type of wealth. The latter belonged to the Greek element which, from about 1560 onwards, had begun to challenge the short-lived

Jewish supremacy in this field. His name (unlike that
of Nasi, against which no similar charges were brought
up even by his bitterest enemies) was associated with
one financial scandal after the other; but he shared the
spoils of office with the grand vizier, who therefore supported him in all things. The enmity between Nasi and
Sokolli was thus notorious as it was inevitable. It was
typical of Selim that he retained them both in his service — turning for advice to the one, entrusting the
administration to the other. That Nasi should have
maintained his position for so long in spite of this precarious state of affairs says much for his adroitness; for
Sokolli was a past master in the art of ruining his enemies,
and that this did not happen in the present case was
certainly not due to any forbearance on his side. It was
in part the result of the consistent support of Nasi by a
few powerful sympathizers — not only the great officers
of state, such as Piale, the captain pasha, but also the
latter's wife, Selim's sister, who (perhaps through the influence of Esther Kyra and the other Jewish women who
enjoyed a position of privilege in the imperial harem)[5]
aided him through thick and thin. This sympathy was
kept alive through other means of Lucullan type that
have already been indicated. As the Venetian envoy,
Marcantonio Barbaro, reported to the Doge:

> In this connection I should mention that, although the Jew
> Michel (*sic*) is so hated by the pasha that he has often tried
> to reduce him to ruin in various ways, the other has always
> managed to save himself, the Grand Signior himself excusing
> him and defending him on several occasions. Many persons
> think that the reason for this is that he very frequently pleases
> the Grand Signior and various of the principal Agas of his

court with trivial presents of comestibles. As a result of these gifts, the latter take every occasion to be of service to him with the Grand Signior. It is thus that he is able to maintain himself in spite of Mehemet Pasha, who is his mortal enemy!

However that may be, Don Joseph's influence, even when it was at its greatest, was qualified and restricted by that of his supremely capable rival. There was a painful indication of this in 1568, when he found himself powerless to prevent the promulgation of two sumptuary laws in the sultan's name, regulating the nature and color of the clothing worn by Jews, both men and women, as well as (plainly a redeeming feature) by Christians.[6] Doubtless, the imperial favorite and his family were able to secure exemption from these regulations for themselves; but it was in any case a bitter reminder of the limitation of his power, as well as of his rival's influence.

For many years, nevertheless, Nasi was the leading spirit of the party of opposition in the imperial Divan in matters bearing upon the relations with the Christian states of Europe. Sokolli, as will be seen, inherited the anti-Habsburg tendency of the former sultan, regarding Spain as Turkey's ultimate enemy and subordinating everything else to the inevitable conflict between the two powers for the mastery of the Mediterranean. With this object in view, he steadfastly supported the alliance with France, which was the keystone of his foreign policy, with the corollary of an understanding with Venice. Nasi, on the other hand, knowing Europe, aware of French internal weaknesses, confident (perhaps excessively) in the might of Turkey, and incidentally with various personal grievances to remember, favored what was in the short view a more nationalistic, but in fact perhaps a more far-sighted policy. He inclined, it seems (so far as it is possible to generalize from the slender data at our disposal), to a more self-reliant line of action. He advocated, in fact, uncompromising opposition to both of the great Catholic powers as well as to their Italian clients, coupled with an entente with the Inquisition-hating Protestants who were now beginning to become a force in northern Europe and with whom, as he felt, the future lay. It was not a unique phenomenon, but remarkable nevertheless, to find the recently settled immigrant taking so broad a view, with such intense confidence in the power of his adopted coutry. Modern Turkish historians suggest that, had he arrived in Constantinople a little earlier, he might have been able to prevent the growth of the fatal system of capitulations, conferring extraordinary rights on the subjects of the Western European powers, which subsequently had so baneful an effect in the country's history.

Before long, the importance of the position that he occupied became generally recognized, both at home and abroad. The Hungarian war continued inconclusively for a full year after Sultan Suleiman's death. The Holy Roman Emperor, Maximilian, could not hope for any noteworthy success; the new sultan was not very much interested in the enterprise begun by his father, being bent on enlarging his dominions in another direction. When, therefore, the Habsburg wrote to congratulate his infidel fellow ruler on his accession to the throne, at the same time suggesting that peace negotiations should be opened, a safe-conduct for his representatives was readily forthcoming. In the summer of 1567, peace commissioners appeared in Constantinople, headed by Anton Verancsics

(Verantius), later Archbishop of Gran. As was inevitable when negotiations were carried on at the Turkish Court, the plenipotentiaries brought with them gifts for those it was deemed necessary to placate; so much for the sultan himself, so much annually for the grand vizier, and 2,000 thalers to be distributed amongst other persons of authority in the state. Among these was specifically mentioned the Jewish favorite, whose voice could carry such weight in the negotiations.[7] At the same time, Maximilian (who had known Don Joseph well in his old Marrano days as João Miguez, when he was in the Low Countries at the Court of his aunt, Mary of Hungary), sent a personal letter asking him for his assistance. "What! a great emperor demean himself to approach a Jewish jobber?" cried the grand vizier, Mehemet Sokolli, when he heard of it; but it was from jealousy rather than sincere indignation.

In obedience to their instructions, the ambassadors waited on Don Joseph when they first came to Constantinople, and reported on the interview at some length in their next despatches home: how he had been converted to Judaism (this was their tale!) in order to marry a wealthy Jewish maiden, how he had become friendly with the sultan at Magnesia before his accession to the throne, and how favorable his personality had impressed them.[8] He on his side informed them how attached he was to Maximilian and his family and offered his services to procure the conclusion of a lasting peace, on which subject he had already spoken to the pasha (Mehemet Sokolli). But he had no hesitation in pointing out what, in his opinion, the relations between the two powers should be. "You see how strong the sultan is in arms and in men," he informed them roundly. "You and the Christians are all unwarlike and powerless to resist him." The ambassadors continued in close relations with him. In the course of the mission, they had frequent conversations together, during which Don Joseph indicated that he had been on terms of intimacy in former days with Philip II, the emperor's cousin, now king of Spain; and Verancsics decided that he was a less assertive personality than he had thought at the outset. On one occasion, when he was newly returned from attendance on the sultan, two secretaries were sent to him from the embassy for confidential discussions, at his special request, and he advised the ambassadors to follow the Court to Adrianople if they desired to secure their object speedily. Their diary shows, moreover, that on September 11, 1567, Don Joseph paid them a formal visit. They were by now short of funds and borrowed 2,000 Turkish ducats from him to defray their immediate expenses — apparently without interest, for this was the precise amount ultimately repaid. Finally, in the following February, after long discussions, a peace intended to last for eight years was signed.

Nasi remained thereafter on the pension list of the Imperial Court. In the Vienna archives there is preserved a list of gifts to be presented in the emperor's name by the envoys sent to Constantinople in the following year, 1569. His name figures immediately after that of the three viziers:

To the said Don Joseph the Jew there is to be given as a present two flasks value 22 marks and 5 lots, which at 16 florins and 30 kreuzers the mark amounts to . . . .
. . . . 368 florins, 9 kreuzers.

A further double drink-vessel from the Imperial Treasury worth 5 marks, 14 lots, 3 groschen, at 20 gulden the mark amounts to.............. 118 florins, 26 kreuzers, 1 pfennig.
In all, the honorific present to Joseph the Jew costs ....
.... 486 florins, 35 kreuzers, 1 pfennig.[9]

As a result of his great trade with Poland, Nasi was able, in due course, to negotiate with that country almost as though he were a territorial potentate. The culmination of the commercial transactions which have been described above (unless it was the original condition, as may well be the case) was reached when he advanced Sigismund Augustus a loan which ultimately amounted, with accumulated interest, to 150,000 ducats. This gave him a status in his negotiations with the king which he was not reluctant to utilize. An anonymous Hebrew letter, preserved by chance in a model letter collection, informs us cryptically that the writer had heard "from behind the veil" how "Joseph Nasi (may his might increase!) sent a special envoy to the king of Poland, with various princes and servants accompanying him. Great honor was done to him and to all his attendants, and the king showed him his treasure-house and his gold and silver and precious vessels and everything else he had in his deposits, witholding nothing .... But the purpose of the envoy's coming is not known."[10] The story is carried on, however, in a letter in Latin from the king himself to Don Joseph, dated Warsaw, February 25, 1570. The phraseology is perhaps more informative than the text, which is somewhat obscure:

Excellent Sir and well-beloved Friend!

Johannes Vancimulius (*Vincentinus*) will treat with Your Excellency in order to despatch the business whereof he has spoken to Us. We are confident, that there will be a happy issue, in accordance with our mutual desires. Meanwhile, we will endeavor to bring together promptly all that sum of money [owing to you], which in a certain time will come to 150,000 florins. May God Almighty give us His aid by means of His servant, so that all that which we have promised may be fulfilled.

From the same person Your Excellency may learn, how ready is our desire and inclination towards you, both as regards the confirmation of the privileges in due course and as regards any other service, as you will hear more fully from Vancimulius himself, whom we heartily commend to you for his security.

The nature of the "privileges" referred to in this document, concerning which historians have long speculated, is obvious. There is no question here, as has been fancifully thought, of any attempt on the part of Don Joseph to secure special rights for the Jews of Poland. The reference is clearly something far more personal: to the renewal of his commercial concessions in connection with imports to Poland, granted for five years in 1567–8, and now about to lapse.

It appears that the results of this communication proved satisfactory, the envoy reporting to his master on his return how well he had been received, how useful Don Joseph had been and what influence he enjoyed. This is apparent from the next letter in the series, which is even more significant than the first. The intermittent dispute about the government of the border province of Moldavia had again come to a head, after the death of the voivode Alexander Lapuseanu, whose claims Joseph Nasi had supported.[11] The Turkish nominee was now one Imonia, but the Poles favored the candidacy of Bogdan

IV, who temporarily secured control. In connection with this, Sigismund Augustus sent a certain Andrew Taranowsky to Constantinople in 1570, as his envoy. Among his credentials there was a letter of recommendation to Joseph Nasi, couched in the most flattering terms:

Illustrious prince and beloved friend!

Most welcome to Us is the demonstration of Your Excellency's great good will towards Us, which We know in part from your letters and in part from the information of those messengers who have returned thence to Us. This being so, Your Excellency must be assured, that We in our turn are and will be prepared to render similar good will to Your Excellency, whensoever the opportunity may offer. Since now We are sending to the Sublime Porte for our own affairs Andrew Taranowsky as our ambassador, We do not wish him to leave without letters from Us to Your Excellency; desiring from Your Excellency, that if he may need Your Excellency's assistance, service or protection in Our business, he will know that by virtue of these letters he may count upon your support in all things.

May 8th, 1570.

Never before perhaps in history had a Jew been addressed by a European monarch in such flattering terms. But how the royal chancellery envisaged the matter is to be seen from the contemptuous caption to the correspondence in the official transcript: "Sigismund Augustus, King of Poland, etc., to the Jew Nasi"![12]

All this diplomatic tangle was subordinate to the major political issue of the time — the great struggle between Spain and Turkey for dominance in the Mediterranean. It was never very difficult to enlist verbal agreement at least among Catholic powers against the Grand Turk; but where could the latter look for allies? Mehemet

Sokolli pinned his faith upon the downtrodden Moriscos of Granada, always ready to rise in revolt — as happened in 1568, in consequence of a brutal attempt to break their traditions and individuality. Don Joseph — rightly, as events turned out — did not overestimate their value as allies, for he knew Spain and Spanish conditions. At the same time, he realized that the menace to the Spanish power lay in a totally different area, with which he himself was exceptionally familiar. It will be recalled that he had spent many years of his life in the Low Countries, and as it happens he was still in touch with some leading figures among the burghers of Antwerp. Here the Reformation had taken root early — in part through the work of the highly intelligent group of Spaniards and Portuguese of Jewish descent settled there, who, ignorant of Judaism and alienated from Catholicism, greeted the new doctrines with avidity. Among the leaders of the local Calvinist Consistory was Marco Perez, one of the most remarkable figures in the history of the Reformation in the Low Countries; he was energetically assisted by his brother-in-law, Martin Lopéz (de Villanueva), Montaigne's close kinsman and an active lay preacher, and the Spaniard Ferdinando Bernuy, similarly said to be of Marrano origin, whose family had been settled in the city since the close of the previous century.[13]

It is more than probable that the members of this group, whom Don Joseph had known intimately in his Marrano days, were among those who remained in correspondence with him. Thus he was fully primed with all the details of what was going on and knew every stage by which the loyalty of the Netherlanders was being undermined, almost deliberately, by the religious fanaticism, economic exploitation and political misgovernment of Spain.

Others in Constantinople listened with incomprehension and contempt to the reports that trickled through of the bickerings of the infidels over unintelligible points of doctrine. When, in 1568, the Netherlands broke out into open revolt, he, perhaps alone, realized the opportunity. Spain was too strong to be attached frontally, but the Low Countries constituted an exposed flank. Without the wealth derived from its busy trading and manufacturing cities, King Philip II would be powerless. On the banks of the Scheldt perhaps lay the key to the Mediterranean.

Moreover, there was the specific question of Marrano and Jewish interests. During the past decade, the persecution of the Spanish and Portuguese New Christians in the Netherlands had been intensified. If the dominance of the Catholic Church there were destroyed, if a Protestant regime were established, a greater tolerance might be expected and the Flemish cities might harbor entire colonies of Jews from Spain and Portugal instead of a trickle of furtive refugees — as indeed was to happen in the United Provinces a generation later, when the great Amsterdam community was founded. Once again, Jewish and Turkish interests coincided — and coincided too with the opportunity of personal revenge for past indignities and wrongs.

Hence, through the medium of his correspondents and secret agents in the Netherlands, Nasi did whatever lay in his power to encourage the revolt, confidently promising the Turkish military succour which was looked forward to so eagerly at this time by all the malcontents in Europe. In 1569, after the bloody Duke of Alva had begun his ruthless work of repression, the Prince of Orange sent a personal agent to Nasi asking him to use his influence with the sultan to commence hostilities against Spain, so as to draw away forces from the Low Countries. The French envoy, who faithfully reported this as a matter of major importance in his despatch of March 14, 1569, could not discover that there had been any positive outcome. But his information service failed him on this occasion, for it seems that, in personal communications to his old associates in Antwerp, Nasi had made certain definite promises, which were jubilantly received. We do not know many details, but Strada, the contemporary historian of the revolt of the Netherlands, gives a lively account:

The people of Flanders were receiving encouragement from all parts, including the most distant places, to rise in rebellion, by reason of the hatred that existed for the Catholic religion or for the House of Austria. About this time, in fact, there were read out in the Consistory of Antwerp letters written by Jean Miches, a powerful person in Turkey and favorite of the Grand Signior, in which he encouraged the Calvinists of Antwerp to hasten to carry into effect the conspiracy that they had made with such courage and tenacity against the Catholics. He gave them to understand that the Turkish emperor would carry out great enterprises against the Christians, and that within a short while the Ottoman arms would give such preoccupation to King Philip that he would not even have time to think about Flanders. It is certain that Miches did not send them false intelligence . . . . As regards the Flemings, Miches' letters and persuasions had no little influence on them. By this news, courage was generally heightened; and it was resolved in the

Consistory of Antwerp, that since there was such a promising opportunity to strengthen the enterprise, they should raise as much money as possible to use in emergency. . . .[14]

The ultimate outcome was of supreme importance. For it was this encouragement, it is said, which resulted in the presentation to Margaret of Parma of the famous petition which was the first step in the great Revolt.

The promised diversion did not in fact take place, or at least not as immediately and decisively as had been hoped. As a preliminary to engaging the force of Spain, it was found desirable to eliminate the naval might of Venice — a project which for personal reasons (as will be seen) was by no means unwelcome to Nasi.[15] Moreover, when Spain was drawn into the conflict, the naval engagement at Lepanto resulted in a Turkish disaster, from which she recovered only precariously. But as happened on other occasions as well, Mehemet Sokolli did not object to profiting from his rival's policy, and the political relations which the latter had so painstakingly fostered continued to influence the course of history. When, not long afterwards, the Prince of Orange, who had assumed the leadership in the revolt of the Netherlands, entered into peace negotiations with the Spanish governor-general, the grand vizier urged him by special messenger to make no concessions, as he could be certain that military pressure would soon be brought to bear on Spain from the Ottoman side as well. On the other hand, when the Spaniards asked the Porte for an armistice, the grand vizier obstinately insisted that the Netherlands should be included in it — a condition which he knew very well would be found unacceptable. In this respect, therefore, Joseph Nasi's influence on Turkish policy was enduring, and he takes a place, even though it be a modest one, among the creators of Dutch independence.

Meanwhile, his long-standing financial dispute with the French Crown had reached a climax. His claims dated back by now some fifteen years or more, but there seemed to be no prospect that they would ever be honorably admitted or spontaneously discharged. King had succeeded king at St. Germain since he had first presented his demands, and agent had succeeded agent in Constantinople. There had been continuity of policy on relatively few points, but one of them was to withhold his payment; the only detail on which uncertainty ruled was the precise pretext, for everything had been tried in turn, from indignant repudiation to a plea of poverty. Diplomatic intervention had elicted fair words, but it had proved as little effective as personal remonstrance. It was time to attempt something drastic; and, now that Sultan Selim sat upon the throne of Turkey, this was well within the bounds of possibility. Moreover, by this time Don Joseph owed the imperial treasury very considerable sums on account of the customs dues which he farmed, and whether justifiably or not professed himself unable to pay unless the amounts due to him from France were forthcoming. Thus, the Turkish government had all the pretext for action that it needed.

On this occasion, everything was carefully planned and organized, down to the last detail. All of a sudden, the French agent at Constantinople, Grantrie de Grandchamp, found himself out of favor. Even the grand vizier, as he thought, changed his attitude, encouraging his debtors to take proceedings against him and going out of the way to embarrass him in every possible fashion. "Never before has any of your servants received such treatment," he complained bitterly to the king. Ultimately, he was compelled to acknowledge the French government's indebtedness to Nasi before the Turkish courts, over his own seal and signature — an action for which he was strongly censured afterwards. He was then induced to agree that the debt should be settled by seizing, up to the amount in question, the goods of the merchants who sailed to the Levant under the French flag (he envisaged apparently the Sicilians, Anconitans and Genoese, rather than the French themselves!) on the understanding that his king would in due course reimburse them for their losses.

Thus the sultan had all the legal justification he needed for the unprecedented action which he now took in the interests of his Jewish favorite, implementing the agreement entered into by the ambassador. An imperial firman (issued apparently in the second half of 1568) ordered that one-third of the merchandise on board all ships flying the French flag — provided that the total value exceeded 1,000 ducats — should be sequestered until the amount due to the Duke of Naxos was satisfied in full. Thus, in effect, the commercial treaty of 1535 between France and Turkey, guaranteeing the subjects of the former power free navigation and commerce in eastern waters — one of the most important measures of the sort in sixteenth-century economic history — was abrogated on account of the claims of a private individual. The Duke did not dally; and before long his ships were at sea and his representatives were on their way to Alexandria, the greatest entrepôt of European commerce in the Levant, to intercept French vessels and ensure that the firman was carried into effect.

It was like a bombshell in the life of the foreign colony in Egypt. The complications that ensued can be imagined. The local tax-farmers, unable to distinguish easily between one species of Frank and another, took measures against the vessels belonging to Venetian, Ragusan and other traders, to the manifest disturbance of international relations and loss to the imperial customs; and a further communication from the sultan was needed in order to regularize matters (December 25, 1568). It was now a particular indignity for the French merchants, formerly so favored, to witness the release of the vessels of all those nationalities who had hitherto sailed under the French flag, in order to share in their special privileges, while they themselves still remained under the embargo. They protested vigorously to the pasha of Egypt, but in vain; for he (or was it the grand vizier?) received for his own pocket one-quarter of the proceeds, which before long came to some 42,000 ducats — about one-quarter of the total amount of Don Joseph's claim. Meanwhile, steps were taken by Nasi to extend the embargo to Algiers (to which he despatched two ships for the purpose) and to Tripoli, the most important Syrian seaport, though here the French consul got wind of the plan in time, with the result that the French trading colony was able to withdraw to Cyprus.[16]

By now the French government had taken vigorous action. On March 13, 1569, the sieur Claude du Bourg, Seigneur de Guerines (formerly treasurer of France, and personally much interested in the Levant trade) was despatched to Constantinople to take matters in hand as ambassador — an office that had been vacant for the past ten years. He was not a little impatient of Grandchamp's bungling, amateurish way of conducting affairs, through he admitted that Nasi's great indebtedness to the imperial treasury complicated his task, as it made his interests and the sultan's coincide. On the other hand, he found that he could count on the support of the grand vizier, the unswerving advocate of the French alliance, whose star was now again in the ascendant. Nasi needed all his coolness, all his wits and all his concentration to face the combination. As ill-fortune would have it, he found himself, instead, overwhelmed by personal disaster.

In the spring of 1569, Doña Gracia Nasi passed away. She had lived long enough to see her daughter elevated to the dignity of Duchess, and her son-in-law become a force in European politics. She had been his counsellor and his inspiration, and the removal of her influence seems to have left its mark upon him. There is perhaps henceforth more dash and ambition, but something of the former nobility and restraint is lacking.

Yet another intimate breach with the past took place at this time. Throughout his life Samuel Nasi had played a relatively insignificant role, overshadowed by his magnificent aunt and his ambitious brother. Since the latter's rise to fame, indeed, he had enjoyed some reflection of his glory. (It is clear that the dispute over the family property had not embittered their relationship, as might have been expected.) He also had been taken into Selim's favor and likewise appointed an imperial *muteferik*. Visitors who came to Constantinople on official business found the younger brother at Joseph's side assisting him, though clearly in a subordinate capacity.[17] At the time of Doña Gracia's death, he too was suffering from a serious illness, in the course of which the Cabalists of the capital had resorted to the device of symbolically changing his name, as it were in order to mislead the Angel of Death. But Don Moses Nasi died as Don Samuel would have done, in the summer of 1569, immediately after Doña Gracia. When the news reached Salonica, Rabbi Moses Almosnino (who had made his acquaintance on the occasion of his recent missions to the capital) gave a memorial address in the Castilian synagogue, devoted to the not wholly connected topics of the immortality of the soul and the eminence of the Duke of Naxos, "in benefitting whom the Lord benefits us too and all Israel."[18]

It was just at the time of his brother's death, and while he was still grappling with the complications occasioned by that of Doña Gracia, that Du Bourg began his grand assault on Don Joseph at Constantinople. The latter, overwhelmed by his difficulties, and perhaps kept away from Court during the period of the crucial debates, was powerless. The grand vizier had long awaited his opportunity; he pressed home his advantage remorselessly, vigorously and (above all) effectively. In August, 1569 — within a few days of the second bereavement — the sultan was persuaded to revoke the firman by which the embargo had been placed on French shipping and merchandise and to repudiate the attempt made to extend its operation beyond Alexandria. (He had, he said, not without a touch of sarcasm, been misled by the admissions made before the Turkish courts by Grandchamp, whom he had been told to trust as he trusted the Most Christian

King himself!) The resumption of normal intercourse between the two countries was now possible, and a fresh commercial treaty was signed in October. How intimately the Jews were associated with Turkish public life at this time may be gauged from the fact that the original document was drawn up not in Turkish nor in French, but in Hebrew — presumably for the convenience of the Jewish agents and dragomen employed by either side. Over two centuries later, when a translation was needed in Paris, a scholar versed in that language had to be found to interpret it![19]

After a lengthy preamble setting forth the title and status of the high contracting parties, the treaty rehearsed the cause of the interruption of normal intercourse between the two countries and the recent embargo, arising out of the claims of the lord of the island of Naxos, named Joseph (otherwise known as Micques), on account of a debt "neither unencumbered nor admitted, which he pretended to be due to him from the said Emperor of France." The sultan expressed his regret at what had happened, stating roundly that he had been "circumvented and abused." (It is easy to see Sokolli's influence in this phraseology.) In the circumstances, he had given orders for the embargo on French shipping to be withdrawn; moreover, although it was impossible to restore at this stage what had already been confiscated (since it had been used by Don Joseph to pay his own debts), ultimate reparation was promised. This settled, the way was clear for a renewal of the capitulations guaranteeing French trade in the Levant, much as they had been concluded in 1535 and were to be renewed again in 1589 — the model of the Capitulation System which governed the trade of

all western nations with Turkey until the twentieth
century.[20]

The check was indeed more apparent than real. It was
in fact a typical piece of diplomatic chicanery. Though
what Don Joseph had done was formally repudiated, no
effective provision was made for undoing it. What he had
exacted was divided between him, the viziers, and the
exchequer, and, as we shall see, the clause regarding
restitution provided valueless. The sultan had managed
to secure the best of both worlds.

The original draft of the treaty (drawn up apparently
by Grandchamp) was a good deal more favorable to Don
Joseph than the final recension, for it mentioned the fact
that the French representative had formally acknowledged his sovereign's debt in the Turkish law-courts,
and made no provision for reimbursement for the sequestered property.[21] The reason for the revision of the document in a sense so sharply antagonistic to his interests
seems to be bound up with an egregious piece of intrigue.
Just at this stage, he had one of the narrowest escapes of
his adventurous life.

Having failed to ruin him by direct attack, or by
plotting with his opponents at the Sublime Porte, Grandchamp had latterly embarked upon a fresh strategy. The
Duke had long had in his employment a physician named
David, or Daoud, who had become his confidential agent,
attained position and riches in his service, acted as his
interpreter at Court, and thus knew all of his secrets as
few others did.[22] Indeed, Nasi used him as his intermediary for important communications with the Grand
Signior, and he prided himself that he had a greater share
than anyone else in securing the imperial edict for the

recent embargo on French property. He was of humble origin, according to Nasi's friends; but he himself asserted the contrary, even claiming that he had been mainly responsible for his employer's brilliant success in Turkey by introducing him to the sultan before his accession.

The two had now quarreled. The truth of the matter is by no means easy to disentangle. Don Joseph alleged that the other had shown himself not only unreliable, but dishonest as well; Daoud, on the other hand, considered that his services were not only insufficiently appreciated, but also insufficiently rewarded. On hearing what had happened, Grandchamp set to work on him through the medium of a French acquaintance, Master Jacques de Mercer, and tried to enlist him into his own service, in the same capacity of interpreter in which he had formerly served Nasi on occasion. His salary was to be no less than 12,000 crowns a year (the same amount that he had formerly received at the palace of Belvedere) with a further 10,000 by way of *douceur*. In return for this, Daoud was prepared to demonstrate that his former master had never had any honest claim on the French Crown, his demands being based on falsified documents which he had somehow obtained from the Spanish merchants at Lyons; and, moreover, that the official Turkish communications on this subject had been altered in translation by the imperial dragoman, in return for a heavy bribe.

On the basis of this elaborate but over-ingenious piece of mendacity, Grandchamp hatched a puerile plot. He suggested to the king that he should send some aged dotard to Turkey under the guise of special ambassador, taking care to select a person with a long grey beard who would impress the Turks, always susceptible to facial hirsuteness. He was to allege that the Most Christian King had ordered the examination of all the royal archives for hundreds of years, and discovered that no one named Miguez had ever performed any service to the Crown of France or had any claim on it. Meanwhile, all official communications received from the Turkish government should be sent back to Constantinople for diligent comparison with the originals, in the hope of finding some discrepancy. If this advice were carried out, the agent was prepared to wager that Don Joseph would be unable to substantiate his claims and would even be compelled to restore what had been seized at Alexandria; for Daoud undertook to reveal a fund of 200,000 ducats which he had secreted. In addition, so as to complete his former master's ruin, he promised to demonstrate that he was engaged in treasonable correspondence with the sultan's enemies — the Pope, the king of Spain, the duke of Florence, and so on — to whom he wrote regularly. He even undertook to abstract from the Duke's cabinet various private papers, letters and documents bearing on this, which he was convinced would suffice to cost anyone his head .... But it was of the utmost importance that closest secrecy should be observed in connection with the whole matter, for if the Turkish ambassador in Paris heard what was intended, he might warn Don Joseph and the scheme would fail.

Grandchamp was not ashamed to communicate the details of this precious and somewhat ridiculous proposal in cipher to his master, the Most Christian King of France, Charles IX, as well as to the Queen Mother, Catherine de Médicis, in a separate letter (October 3,

1569). It was a barefaced attempt to evade an obligation by sheer fraudulence, backed up by perjury and a little undignified play-acting. One can imagine how it would have been qualified had the roles been reversed, and the Jew been the guilty party; but M. de Grandchamp saw in it nothing disgraceful or remarkable.

In point of fact the news leaked out, and the idea was not pursued to the end. But there is good reason to believe that this was a contributory reason at least for the Sultan's brusque change of front, the raising of the embargo on French shipping, the repudiation of Don Joseph claims and the neglect of his interests in the treaty as it was finally concluded a few days after this amazing letter was penned.

Nasi's fury with his former dependent and physician, who had been responsible for the whole ignoble conspiracy, knew no bounds. It says a good deal for his humanity, that he contented himself with having him banished to the delectable island of Rhodes — then the criminal colony of the Turkish empire — where life could have been not unpleasant, even though as part of the sentence he was not allowed to stir beyond the city gates. The rabbinate of Constantinople, moreover, were persuaded to take action, on the grounds that Daoud's intrigues had prejudiced not only Don Joseph's position but, indirectly, that of Turkish Jewry as a whole. They were nothing loath to oblige their protector, and a sentence of excommunication against the errant physician and two of his associates was fulminated in crowded synagogues in the capital in the Judaeo-Spanish dialect. (The actual wording is preserved.)[23] Later on, the rabbinates of Safed (headed by Joseph Caro and Moses di Trani), of Salonica,

of Alexandria, of Cairo and of other cities associated
themselves with the ban.[21] Though for some time the
culprit attempted to continue his intrigues, in the end
he made his peace with his former master. The latter,
easygoing and tolerant, was prepared to forgive if not
forget, and persuaded the sultan to rescind the edict of
banishment. But talmudic sanctions were less malleable;
and even though, for mutual convenience, the sages
of Rhodes were particularly anxious to withdraw the ban
that had been pronounced, it continued in force. The
difficulties involved are obvious enough. It was from the
point of view of strict rabbinic law questionable whether
in such a case as this rescindment was feasible without
the previous assent of the same authorities who had been
responsible for the proceedings in the first instance; while
certain scholars held, moreover, that the same degree of
unanimity and the same degree of publicity were needed
now as on the former occasion — a highly difficult condition, as some of the original signatories had died in the
meantime. Underlying the dispute there seems to have
been the feeling, natural enough in the circumstances,
that in a matter of this sort it was wrong for the rabbinate
to be a weather-cock, merely registering the desires of
the all-powerful Duke. The latter, it seems, now tried to
secure his object by his habitual method, of threatening
to cut off the allowance of persons who continued to be
recalcitrant. He did not succeed this time. Only two of
the Constantinople scholars, Elijah ben Hayim[25] and
Judah Algazi, did what he asked; the remainder refused,
following the lead of Joseph ibn Leb, who was still pre-
siding over the Academy established by Doña Gracia
when she came to Turkey and was perhaps anxious to

demonstrate, now that his patroness was dead, his complete independence of her nephew. As a matter of fact, the recalcitrant rabbis did not apparently suffer in consequence of their hardihood, Don Joseph's passion proving, as it always did, for all his blustering, as shortlived as his determination. Nevertheless, this interesting point of law continued to be discussed, long afterwards, by some of the scholars concerned.

As for the settlement of the problems arising out of the embargo at Alexandria, all was not yet smooth sailing. Grandchamp and Du Bourg, so self-righteous in their criticisms of others, had been quick to realize the possibilities of personal profit at this stage and were accused of swindling the Marseilles merchants of 50,000 crowns in the process of "safeguarding" their interests. In consequence, their mission ended under a cloud. The Turkish government, on the other hand, did nothing to compel Don Joseph to repay the amounts he had received, as was stipulated by the treaty. When, in 1572, the new French ambassador, François de Noailles, Bishop of Acqs, arrived in Constantinople, the second of the four points contained in the memorial he submitted to the sultan at his first audience, on March 23, was that all property taken from the Marseilles merchants and other French subjects at the instance of "the Jew Miches" should be immediately restored, and the culprit punished for his insolence. The sultan replied that he assumed all responsibility for what had been done, and perforce the matter had to be dropped.[26] Nevertheless, even after Nasi's death, attempts were repeatedly made by the French to secure reimbursement from his estate, and for years thereafter this continued to be a sore point in

Franco-Turkish relations. As far as he himself was concerned, this episode, which might have proved fatal to a less pliable and resilient personality, left his position unweakened. The days of his greatest influence were still to come.

CHAPTER IV

Duke of Naxos

AMONG the band of trusted followers who rode out from Constantinople with Selim in September 1566, when he went to be hailed as sultan by the army in the field, was Don Joseph Nasi, the new ruler's favorite, now at the height of his expectations. But he was not with the cavalcade when they reached their destination. While they were in mid-journey, during a halt at the city of Philippopolis in Eastern Roumelia, a signal mark of favor had been conferred upon him. Joseph Nasi came from the imperial presence, that memorable day, as Duke of Naxos and the Archipelago, and left the camp, posthaste, to visit his resplendent fief.[1]

It was a singular, an astonishing, guerdon. It was, according to classical mythology, on the shores of Naxos, famous for its vineyards and its wines, that Bacchus had found Ariadne sleeping after she had been deserted by Theseus. At the time of the so-called Fourth Crusade at the beginning of the thirteenth century, the bold, predatory Venetian adventurer Marco Sanudo seized this and other islands of the Cyclades from the Byzantine emperor and fixed his residence there. His accomplice, the "Latin" Emperor Henry, erected this realm into a duchy, known as that of the Aegean Sea (*Egeo Pelago* or Archipelago). Like the other adventurers (and they were many) who installed themselves in the Greek seas at this time, he

Italianized his domain. He built a magnificent castle for his residence and a cathedral, in which his arms may still be seen, for the Roman Catholic bishop whom he introduced. For nearly two centuries his descendants ruled there after him, not without glory, and certainly not without enjoyment; and when they died out in 1383 they were succeeded by the Crispi, a family hailing from Verona. This dynasty lasted until the middle of the sixteenth century, under Venetian protection and with a couple of interludes of immediate Venetian rule, Naxos and the adjacent islands still being liberally sprinkled with their relics and their monuments. The ruler was considered to be the premier duke of Christendom and was treated on that account with the highest possible deference. When he visited Venice, four nobles clad in scarlet and many more in black were sent to escort him to the palace, the procession thither being headed by six trumpeters and the crew of the ducal galley; and, when he entered the Hall of Audience, clad in crimson velvet and with a golden chain of honor round his neck, the doge rose to embrace him and seated him at his side.

Such ceremonial glories were no protection against the rising tide of Ottoman might. When war broke out between Venice and Turkey in 1536, the notorious corsair, Barbarossa, sailed with a powerful fleet into the Cyclades, where one petty dynasty after the other fell before him. Naxos did not even put up a resistance. The reigning duke, Giovanni IV, was therefore allowed to retain his duchy as a Turkish fief on the payment of an annual tribute of 5,000 ducats. He continued to rule ingloriously for another twenty-odd years, his sole thought, according to the Venetian envoy, being how to scrape together

enough money to bribe the Turkish captains and ministers
of state. He thus managed to end his days in peace.
His son, Giacomo IV, the last Christian duke, who
succeeded him in 1564, maintained himself in the face of
increasing difficulties for two years more. The Turks,
however, were becoming more and more exigent in their
demands. His personal debauchery, imitated by the
nobility of his petty court, grossly outdone by his son
and affecting even the clergy, caused general scandal.
(The baron of Santorin is said to have confessed that he
could not recall having performed a single virtuous action
throughout his life.) His Greek subjects, who formed the
overwhelming majority of the population, saw no reason
why they should be kept under Latin rule when the Latin
ascendancy was obviously at an end. At length they could
bear it no longer and sent a deputation to Constantinople
imploring the sultan to appoint some person more fit to
govern them. The duke hastily gathered 12,000 ducats
as a bribe and sailed after them. But he arrived too late
and, as soon as he landed, was stripped of his dignity and
thrown into prison. Meanwhile, a little revolution took
place also in Andros, whence the population expelled the
duke's brother-in-law, Gianfrancesco Sommaripa. The
people of the islands waited anxiously to receive the
sultan's nominee.[2]

This was one of the problems that awaited Selim II on
his accession, in the early autumn of 1566. Obviously the
proper ruler for the island, accustomed for centuries past
to an occidental dynasty, was a man with some political
experience, acquainted with the occidental environment,
but at the same time possessing a knowledge of the eastern
world. There was perhaps only one person of note in

Constantinople who fulfilled these conditions — Joseph
Nasi, the former Marrano. True, he was a Jew. But to
the sultan a Jew was no more and no less obnoxious than
a Christian. One of the islanders' complaints had been
that, although they followed the Greek Orthodox form
of Christianity, they had been under the sway of a Roman
Catholic. If they were not to be ruled over by one of
their own (and they had not been for four centuries), it
seemed to a Moslem superfluous to pay excessive attention
to trivialities of religious eccentricity as between one
raya and another; and the sultan may perhaps have
thought it a pleasing sarcasm to appoint a Jew where the
islanders were indulging in intolerant distinctions in the
matter of Christianity. But all such considerations obviously entered into play only to a minor extent. The duchy
was vacant, and Joseph Nasi was an imperial favorite;
moreover, while the last duke had paid a yearly tribute
of only 5,000 ducats, Nasi was prepared to increase the
amount to 6,000. This assuredly was decisive. Even in
his father's lifetime, according to one contemporary,
Selim had been pressing for this appointment to be made.
Now, the decision lay in his own hands.

One of his first official actions after his accession to the
imperial throne was then (as we have already seen) to
create his Jewish favorite Duke of Naxos and the Archipelago. Thirty years before, he had been a despised New
Christian in Portugal, unable to aspire to any public
appointment or honor. Twenty years before, he had been
in peril of his life as a secret Judaizer in the Low Countries.
It was only a dozen years since he had arrived in Constantinople, a stranger. Other Jews, in the Golden Age in
Spain, had wielded an influence in politics comparable to

NAXOS

25°30′   C Stavrós

Apóllona

Koróni

Énga es
Akapsi   Mitriá   Skadhíón
Náxos   Vóthroi   Korónou
                  Kinídharos

                        Moní
Ayersani   Moutsoúna
                    Khal: Grani los
                        Filoti

37°   37°

A   Angídhia
G   Glinádhos
Ga   Galanádhos
T   Trípodhes

        5 Miles
                    C Katoméri   Koufó Islands
                    25°30′

THE ISLAND OF NAXOS

CONSTANTINOPLE AND ITS ENVIRONS
(from an old map)

his, though it is improbable that he was aware of the fact. Never before, however, in history, since the fall of the Jewish Commonwealth — except perhaps in the fabulously remote kingdoms of the Khazars or the Himyarites — had one enjoyed sovereign state, as Don Joseph now did. Mention has been made above of the curious coincidence that the name "Nasi," derived perhaps in the first instance from some long-distant autocratic ancestor, means "Prince." *Nomen fuit omen.*

The realm over which the ex-Marrano now ruled consisted of a group of islands — famous in ancient history, and still strewn with impressive classical monuments — lying to the north of Crete, between the mainland of the Peloponnese and the Dodecanese group, west of the coast of Asia Minor. Naxos (Naxia, as it was then generally called), the principal one of them and the seat of government, was nearly 400 square miles in extent. Her immediate dependencies included Santorin (Thera: this medieval name is a corruption of St. Irene), Milo (Melos), Syra (Syros) and Paros (Minoa). Antiparos, with Nio (Ios) and Namfio (Anapher), latterly ruled by the Pisani family, had been conquered by the Turks as early as 1536, and now became part of the duchy again. The same was the case with Seriphos — the island associated in classical mythology with Perseus and the Gorgon's Head — which the Michieli had governed for over a century as an independent barony, and with Amorgos and Stamphalia (Astypalaea), at one time subject to the Querini, whose name and style are still so familiar in Venice. Another dependent feud was Sifanto (the former Siphnos), with a number of smaller islands formerly ruled by the old Italian family of Gozzadini. Later on, in circumstances

of which we know nothing, Don Joseph's domain was
increased by the fertile island of Andros to the north, near
Euboea, a place of streams and orange-groves and ferns,
whose lord had formerly considered himself independent
and even gone so far as to style himself "Duke."³ (There
had presumably been an interlude of direct Turkish
administration since the recent petty insurrection which
had driven him out.) Mykoni (Mykonos), north of Naxos,
which the Venetians had been forced to abandon to the
Turks after its complete devastation, was presumably
considered part of this feud, as it had been bestowed by
Duke Giovanni IV on his daughter at the time of her
marriage to Gianfrancesco Sommaripa, the last Latin
lord of Andros, together with half of the fertile island of
Zea (Ceos), just off the coast of Attica, formerly ruled by
the Premarini family (the other half had been left in the
hands of the Gozzadini).⁴ Near Mykoni lay Rhenaia and
Delos, once world-famous but now deserted. The duchy
(which sprawled over about 120 miles at its greatest from
north to south, and 100 from east to west) thus consisted
of rather more than a dozen islands, in addition to a few
others of some size which were now uninhabited, or
nearly so. Nasi's official title illustrated the diversity of
his domain: "Duke of Naxos, Count of Andros and
Paros, Lord of Milo and the Islands."⁵

Some of these appanages were, to be sure, of very small
significance, for they had long passed their prime. Syra,
for example, had only some four hundred inhabitants at
present, and Santorin (sadly fallen from its former opu-
lence) perhaps twice that number. Nio, which was of
approximately the same size, was blessed with a fine and
much-used anchorage, and a traveller who visited it just

about the time of Joseph Nasi's enfeoffment found the
food and the women exceptionally attractive; but the
mountain-castle which the Crispi had built there reminded
him of nothing so much as a pigsty, the inhabitants
crowding in it at nights pell-mell for fear of the pirates.
Melos, on the other hand, which also had a good harbor
much frequented by shipping, was famous for its salt-
petre, its pumice, its millstones and, especially, its hot
baths; Ceos and Ios furnished vallonia from their oak-
trees for use in dyeing and tanning, both traditional
industries of the Jews in the Mediterranean areas; while
Seriphos was rich in minerals, and Paros still produced
the finest marble, exported even to Italy. But the most
flourishing island of the duchy, as might be expected,
was Naxos itself, "the largest, most fertile and most
agreeable of the Cyclades."

"The principal things that render this island celebrated," wrote a French visitor about this period, "are
the height of the mountains, the quantity of white marble
quarried from them, the number of springs and streams
that water the meadows, the vast number of gardens
filled with fruit trees of every sort, the groves of olive,
orange, lemon and pomegranate of exceptional height.
All these advantages which distinguish it have acquired
it the name of Queen of the Cyclades." The absence of
a good port was made up by several useful anchorages
suitable for small craft. The products included, besides
its famous wines, its emery, used especially for polishing,
of which it was the great source since classical times.
(Down to the close of the nineteenth century — at which
time, as it happens, a Jew administered the Turkish
government monopoly — the island produced three-quar-

ers of the total world supply.) The inhabitants were indolent and easygoing; according to a traveller's tale current at the time, whenever a ship put into port, the women and girls went down to the shore and placed their charms at the disposal of the mariners. But the duchy had other attractions for the visitor as well. Naxos and Paros were considered "places of much diversion," and we have a picturesque account of how, not long before this time, the Venetian ambassador was honored here by festivities and dances "at which there was no lack of polished and gracious ladies." Nor of course was there any lack of ecclesiastics; for Naxos, Paros and Melos were all episcopal sees. In some of the islands there were often no more than two working days in each week. Some religious festival was observed almost every day, the people spending the best part of their time in the performance of their picturesque traditional dances, just as their ancestors had done in Homeric times, or gazing at some wonder-working image, which the Turks too thought fit to propitiate.

Jews had been settled all over these islands in antiquity, and there was a small Jewish community in Naxos even now, perhaps reinforced by the commercial representatives of the firm of Nasi, which had done business there for some time past. Apparently, the majority came from Rhodes and dealt in wine, which they prepared in their own homes in accordance with the religious prescriptions laid down by that community.[6] How this little group reacted to the new conditions, and whether it expanded under the rule of a coreligionist, there is no evidence whatsoever.

The seat of administration of the duchy was the ducal

palace or "Castro" built by Marin Sanudo, the first duke, on the site of the ancient Acropolis overhanging the town of Naxos, on the west side of the island. It was a square building with massive walls; a balcony supported on marble struts, with a balustrade of wrought iron, ran all round it, commanding a marvellous view over a great part of the countryside and wide stretches of turquoise-blue sea. It was considered exceptionally strong, making up for the defensive weakness of the island itself, though hitherto it had been inadequately equipped. Besides this, there were two other castles in the island. Santorin, on the other hand, boasted five, Paros four (one of them built of fragments of classical temples!), Melos two, and the lesser islands at least one apiece; a necessary defence against the pirates of all races and creeds who were the scourge of the Eastern Mediterranean.

The dignity to which Don Joseph was raised was no empty one, the duke of Naxos being the absolute seigneur and overlord of the island, and not merely its titular patron. The feudal system, introduced with the Latin conquest, remained in force until the Turkish government abolished seigniorial rights a century and a half after the events with which we are now dealing. The principal tenants held their lands for the most part only on condition that they discharged military service when called upon, while those lower down in the social scale were required to provide for their maintenance; the mountainous part of the island was let out to herdsmen, who paid quantities of cheese by way of rent. The common people were little better than serfs and had to attend their lords on demand — for example, when they went to their country houses, on which occasions they were followed by long trains of dependents bearing their food, their furniture, their clothing, their children, and anything else that could make the cortège seem more important. The castle of Naxos was under the control of a captain; other important officials were the *apanochinigari* —.originally the chief huntsmen of the ducal household, but now endowed with executive functions. In the other islands — e. g., Santorin — the duke was represented by a ducal factor.

Immediately on his appointment at Philippopolis in September 1566, Duke Joseph left the imperial camp and went to visit his newly-acquired state, the sultan benignly excusing him (through the intermediary of his tutor, Hasan Pasha) from the duty of accompanying him any further;¹ thus the new vassal was not present at the resplendent ceremony which took place shortly afterwards in the camp before Belgrade, when the military commanders and officers of state kissed their new ruler's feet. He must have arrived in Naxos towards the beginning of the boisterous Aegean winter. He took up his residence in the four-square ducal palace at Naxos, the former duke afterwards complaining that he had lost his home and all his possessions. One can imagine the commotion among the islanders, the ceremonial performance of homage by the tenants-in-chief, the attempt to renew the magnificence of the ducal entourage, the imitation by the waters of the Mediterranean of the fashions and procedure dimly recollected from the courts of Brussels or Ratisbon, Reyna's stiff-lipped essay to maintain the dignity of Duchess before the supercilious eyes of the island aristocracy. But a profound disappointment awaited the ducal couple. General conditions in their island realm were far from satisfactory, and not even tranquil. There were frequent onslaughts by pirates, Turkish as well as Christian, which the inhabitants were unable to check. (The most notorious at this time was a certain Chaaban Reis, whose successes were so considerable as to encourage others to follow his example.) Although the sultan had forbidden Moslems to take up their residence in places in his dominions where there was no mosque or established Moslem community, the island was now in military occupation, and there was constant friction between the predatory Turkish soldiers and the long-suffering Christian inhabitants. The partisans of the dispossessed duke were hovering in the neighborhood and causing perpetual unrest. It was found necessary to despatch a special messenger to the Sublime Porte to solicit help.

By a sultanic missive, dated March 23, 1568, Piale Pasha, who commanded the Turkish fleet in Greek waters, was instructed to put things in order. Military rule was ended, the Turkish soldiery being withdrawn and those Moslems who had no business in the island (who were indeed a liability and no asset, as true believers were exempt from paying taxes!) sent home. Vigorous action was ordered against the pirates and malcontents.[8] But more than this was needed in order to adjust matters. The general atmosphere on the island was without doubt unfriendly. It is not difficult to picture the anti-climax of a court which no courtier willingly attended, the receptions at which there were no guests, the averted faces and sullen glances when the Duke and his Duchess went outside their palace walls. We are given no details. But before long Don Joseph was back in Constantinople; and although he visited his little realm again from time to time — he was probably there in 1568, certainly in 1570 and perhaps in 1571 and 1572 — he gave up the attempt to make it his home.[9]

It was dangerous indeed for him to be away from the sultan's side, leaving the field free for the intrigues of his detractors and rivals — perhaps he had personal experience of this during his absence. In any case, he had little interest in the external trappings of power; he had learned by long and bitter experience that it was only the reality of power that mattered. He had ambitious long-term plans, and the grant of Naxos may possibly have been linked up with his wider political schemes. Whatever the reason, so far as the published records go, it appears that the Duke's connection with his duchy after 1568 was mainly formal. Henceforth he ruled it, not from the impressive *castro* of Marin Sanudo overhanging the town of Naxos, but from his "Palace" of Belvedere outside Constantinople.

He chose his deputy ingeniously: a professing Christian (so that the islanders could not object) but by descent and perhaps sympathy a New Christian like himself. At the time of the expulsion of the Jews from Spain, seventy years before, one of the outstanding Jews of the country had been Don Abraham Senior of Segovia. Financier, tax-farmer and a shrewd man of affairs (it was he who had suggested the match between Ferdinand and Isabella, which brought about the political unity of Spain), he enjoyed too the status of Court Rabbi (*Rab de la Corte*) of Castile. It was not so much a religious as a civil office, the incumbent (who was arbitrarily appointed by the Crown) being regarded as the official representa-

tive of the Jews of the country. This does not excuse the
fact that, when the edict of expulsion was signed in 1492,
Abraham Senior became converted to Christianity and
was thus allowed to remain. Though some persons remembered that his orthodoxy had long been considered
questionable, his apologists said that he did this in order
to avoid the retribution threatened against his coreligionists if he continued obdurate. However that may be, he
was baptized with all his family, at Valladolid, on June 15,
1492, at the age of eighty, the king, the queen and the
primate of Spain acting as his sponsors at the font. For
the few remaining years of his life, he was known as
Fernando Perez Coronel. As Christians, his descendants
attained distinction, secretly retaining nevertheless their
Jewish allegiances to some extent. In the sixteenth century, a member of the family, who is said to have been
formerly governor of Segovia, escaped from the rigors of
the Inquisition and settled in Constantinople. Here he
became known as Solomon and entered the service of
Joseph Nasi, who did nothing without him and relied so
much on his judgment that people spoke of him as the
Jew's "right eye." With him came his son, Francisco,
Doctor of Civil and Canon Law, who, however, remained
nominally a Christian.[19] It was believed in the Cyclades
that these two were mainly responsible for the deposition
of Giacomo IV and Don Joseph's appointment as Duke of
Naxos in his place. Dr. Francisco Coronel, or Coronello
(in the Italian form), Jewish by descent but ostensibly a
Catholic, was now nominated by the new duke as his lieutenant governor in his distant and seldom-visited duchy.

No alien government — Italian, Turkish, least of all
Jewish — was likely to be popular with the islanders.

Any taxation was sure to be considered excessive — and in view of the heavy tribute that he had to pay, that exacted by Coronello for Don Joseph, ultimately scaled up to 14,000 ducats, could hardly be light. Nevertheless, his rule seems to have been just and efficient, being referred to in complimentary fashion in the Capitulations granted to his former subjects after his death[11] and spoken of laudatorily even by a Jesuit historian of a somewhat later generation, who stated that "no Duke had ever been more loved nor more respected" than was Coronel throughout his administration.[12] He maintained the ancient laws and customs of the Latins; his officials were all Christians; and he did his best to conciliate the older families, such as the D'Argenta or Argyroi, barons of the castle of St. Nicholas in the island of Santorin, by giving them places in the administration and confirming them in their former fiefs. Everything possible was done to maintain the prevailing position in the duchy from the religious and racial points of view. As has been seen, military rule was ended speedily. Full religious toleration, besides being a Jewish virtue, was in this case a political necessity. There is no indication that the diminutive Jewish community enjoyed any special privileges, whatever elation it may have felt; the Moslems were not allowed to abuse their position; the Christians obviously had no positive grounds of complaint, for they would not have failed to be vocal upon this point; and it was apparently at this time that the Archbishop Domenico delle Craspere carried out his embellishments in the Roman Catholic cathedral.

The duchy enjoyed, however, only a qualified independence. At every turn — for protection, for the resto-

MURAD III, SULTAN OF TURKEY,
1574–1595

ORIENTAL AMBASSADOR IN VENICE

ration of order, and so on — Don Joseph had to solicit
the sultan's help. When he found that his revenues suffered by reason of the emigration of so many of his subjects to Constantinople, he had to appeal for an order to
send them home. In matters concerned, however re-
motely, with the Mohammedan faith, his realm was
subject to the jurisdiction of the cadi, or religious judge,
of the island of Chios. In 1567, for instance, this dignitary
was instructed to proceed to the isles of the duchy and
levy the special tax, or *kharadj*, which was supposed to be
paid by all non-Muslims, the tax lists having to be sent
subsequently to Constantinople for purposes of record.
(It is interesting to speculate whether the Duke himself
was among those assessed under this head.)

One of the endemic problems with which the rulers of
the Archipelago were confronted was that of piracy, a
lucrative and at that time by no means disreputable
occupation.[13] Naxos was still most unfortunately situated in this respect, for it was spared by neither Christian
nor Moslem. (The former sovereign, Duke Giovanni IV,
had been captured at the outset of his reign while on
a hunting expedition, and carried off as a prize; and it
was not long since a celebrated Turkish corsair, driven
ashore at Naxos, was roasted for three hours by the in-
furiated populace.) It was their inability to cope with
this menace that had helped to discredit the former
dynasty. Don Joseph was fortunate in having the might
of the Turkish fleet to help him and in being on friendly
terms with the high admiral; but he, too, was not completely successful. In 1577, his most important feuda-
tories, the Barons D'Argenta, were attacked by ten
pirate galleys in their island of Santorin and carried off

into captivity. From some points of view, however, this turned out to be not entirely disadvantageous; for though they subsequently recovered their liberty, they never regained their barony.

Don Joseph's period of rule was not by any means uneventful. When the news of his enfeoffment reached Naxos, the inhabitants felt themselves deeply affronted and petitioned the sultan to release the former duke, Giacomo IV, and restore him to the faithful subjects who had so vigorously protested against his rule. It says much for Nasi's kindliness that Selim, who must obviously have consulted him in a matter which concerned him so closely, granted half the petition and set the prisoner free, though of course refusing to reinstate him. Accompanied by his sister, the former Lady of Andros, he now fled — first to the Venetian possessions in the south of Greece and then, by way of Ragusa, to Rome. Here Pope Pius V, that arch-enemy of the Jews, received him graciously, granted him a pension of 1,400 ducats, on which to maintain his ducal state, and encouraged him to prosecute his claims. Thence he went on to Venice, where he had an equally resplendent reception. In the summer of 1568, he rallied a body of supporters and made a raid on his former duchy, establishing himself in one of the adjacent islands and intriguing industriously with his late subjects. Don Joseph had to appeal to the sultan for assistance, and the pretender was dislodged, orders being issued to the cadis of Roumelia and Anatolia to keep on the watch for him and arrest him if they could.[14]

The main center of intrigue against the Duke's authority was the island of Tenos which, although it lay in the middle of the Archipelago, between Naxos and Andros, and commanded the entrance to the Dardanelles, was under Venetian rule. Coronello became convinced that there was no possibility of tranquillity in the duchy so long as this state of affairs continued. He was determined not to allow it to remain a source of embarrassment any longer than was absolutely necessary. He constantly egged on the Turkish authorities to take military action so as to remove this focus of trouble. On one occasion, it is said, he sent the sultan a painting of a lovely garden, in the midst of which there was a particularly fruitful tree. "The garden," the monarch was informed, "is the Cyclades and the Archipelago. It all belongs to Your Majesty, except for this one tree, which is the island of Tenos." The corollary was obvious.

Matters were in this state when the war of Cyprus between Turkey and Venice became imminent — largely, it was believed, through the instrumentality and intrigues of the sultan's Jewish favorite.[15] This seemed to give Coronello his opportunity. Hoping to starve Tenos out, he allowed neither news nor food to be sent thither or to other Venetian possessions from the islands under his control. A lucky chance put him into a position to seize a Cretan brig, laden with gunpowder and supplies for the garrison at Tenos, which had been forced into Naxos by the weather. He immediately despatched a frigate to Constantinople bearing the news and a specimen of the bread which the Teniotes were now obliged to eat, so as to show to what extremities they had already been reduced. It was captured on the way. Nevertheless, he transferred himself to Andros, ready for action. Thence he appealed to the Turkish admiral, Piale Pasha, to complete his conquest of the islands of the Archipelago by subduing this last Venetian stronghold — the key to the Cyclades, the refuge of all fugitive Christian slaves and all rebellious vassals — whose capture and addition to his master's domain was necessary to ensure the peace and tranquility of the Aegean. Rumor, of course, added that the appeal was reinforced by a magnificent bribe.

The result was a determined onslaught by a Turkish amphibious force of 8,000 men, led by Piale Pasha and Coronello himself, who fought presumably under the ducal banner. The rounding-off of Don Joseph's duchy seemed imminent. But the Venetian resistance, directed by the governor, Girolamo Paruta, proved to be unexpectedly staunch. The invaders found fortifications prepared and buildings in strategic positions levelled to the ground. Nevertheless, a landing was effected in force, and a sudden attempt made on the castle. The alarm was, however, given in time, and the assailants were repulsed. No preparations had been made for a formal siege; and after laying the island waste, the landing parties had to withdraw.

Coronello, with his reputation as a mortal enemy of Venice, was now a marked man. One night, during an official visit to the island of Syra, he was kidnapped and placed in the custody of the commander of a Venetian squadron from Crete (still at that time under the rule of the Most Serene Republic) which happened to be lying in harbor. When the Teniotes heard this good news, they were overjoyed and forthwith offered a large bribe if their arch-enemy, "the heart and soul of Zan Micas (João Miguez), traitor to this blessed State," were handed over to their tender mercies. But they were outbidden by Coronello, who astutely suggested a larger sum which he would give if he were taken instead to Crete, as was indeed the captain's obvious duty.[16] His life was thus saved. But Don Joseph was deprived of his services when they were most needed.

The War of Cyprus was now in full progress, and the Aegean was within the sphere of hostilities. Taking advantage of the absence of the Turkish fleet from home waters, the Venetians sent an expedition to the Cyclades, under the *provveditore* Antonio Canal. It seems that, in view of the imminent danger, Nasi now hastened to his dominions to direct the defence; clearly, the martial exercises to which he had been so addicted from his youth could now be useful. As early as September, 1570, it was rumored in Constantinople that Naxos had been mastered after a desperate struggle, and Don Joseph himself captured.[17] This news was premature; but not long afterwards the Venetian forces effected a landing on the island, which was speedily overrun. (Whether Don Joseph took any part in the operations is not recorded.) The rest of the Cyclades did not resist much longer, though the force under one Querini, which seized Andros, behaved so badly to the inhabitants that it had to be withdrawn before long. The island dynasties were automatically restored. Niccolò Gozzadini recovered Siphnos for good; Angelo Giudizzi was appointed by the Republic as military governor of Naxos; and Duke Giacomo IV gratefully led a force of 500 men to assist the allied Christian powers at the great naval battle of Lepanto.

But the change of rule was only temporary. Naxos was recovered by the Turks under Mehemet Pasha almost as quickly as it had been lost; Coronello somehow regained his liberty, notwithstanding the venomous accusations of the Teniotes and the receipt by his captor of instructions from Venice to put him to death, while announcing that he had died of sickness.[18] It was nevertheless some time before Don Joseph's hold on his domains was fully restored, and in the following period he more than once had to apply to the sultan for help. For the past two years, he complained in 1571 through a special messenger (does this imply that he was now himself in some part of his dominions again?), his infidel subjects had refused to pay the *kharadj* which was obligatory upon them; and the Vizier Pertev Pasha was instructed to take the matter in hand and see that the amounts in question were exacted. But this was not enough. In the following year, he once more alleged (again, by special envoy) that he had been unable to obtain his personal dues from his subjects for that year and the previous one, owing to the intrigues against him which were going on there and the attempt to overthrow his rule. This time the Captain Pasha was instructed to take the opportunity of visiting the Cyclades, where he was to summon the malcontents before him, to see that all debts to the Duke were punctually paid and to send any dangerous elements to forced labor.[19]

In the end, superficial order at least was restored. But the external menace continued, and in 1572 Giacomo Crispi was again soliciting the Venetian Republic for aid to recover his lost duchy, which he undertook to rule henceforth as their vassal. His labors were in vain, for in the peace concluded between Venice and Turkey in the following year no mention whatsoever was made of his former dominions, much less of his title to them. Still undaunted, in 1575, after Sultan Selim died, he set

out for Constantinople to press his claims upon the new
ruler, Murad III, whose mother, as it happens, had belonged to the ancient Venetian (or rather Corfiote) family
of Baffo. But he was again disappointed. Don Joseph's
position, though weaker, was still secure; he remained in
possession of his dignities as before, without any diminu-
tion; and in the following year the dispossessed Christian
ruler died (it was said, of a broken heart) after waiting
about miserably in the Turkish capital for many weary
months. Don Joseph continued to enjoy the title of Duke
of Naxos until his last day.

Even though he may have visited his island duchy
relatively little, he forewent nothing of the state and
pomp implicit in his rank. His residence overlooking the
Bosphorus now became a palace. His coreligionists referred to him, with unbounded pride, with the Hebrew
formula "May his might increase!" normally reserved
for reigning sovereigns. Official documents were drawn
up with all the pompous traditional formalities. The text
of one of them, part in Latin and part in Italian, conferring certain demesnes on the faithful lieutenant governor, has been preserved.[20] It is worth while to quote
the preamble and close at length:

Joseph Nasi, by the Grace of God Duke of the Archipelago,
Lord of Andros, etc. To all and single of our officers and servants who shall see these presents.

Be it known that having regard to the good, diligent and
faithful service of Fr. Coronello, Doctor of Either Law and Our
Lieutenant in the administration of all our Islands, both in the
matter of justice and in other things connected with Our service, and wishing to reward him in part. And considering that
Our aforesaid Lieutenant has humbly supplicated Us to gra-

ciously concede him the below-mentioned lands and pastures belonging to the Lordship which are to be found in the island of Naxos . . . . . &c. &c.

Given in the Ducal Palace of Belvedere near Pera at Constantinople, this 15th day of July, 1577.

Joseph Nasi.

At the Duke's Mandate.

Joseph Cohen, Secretary and Amanuensis.

Was the grant of the duchy of Naxos, too, connected with Don Joseph's far-reaching plans for the relief of Jewish suffering? This may be so. It is indeed most unlikely that he imagined that, as a sovereign ruler, he would be able to intervene on behalf of his much-oppressed coreligionists in Europe, anticipating thus one of the aspects of the modern Jewish national movement — the Turkish hold was too close and too jealous for this to be possible, though he could indeed count on the sultan's sympathy and assistance in emergency. It is not on the other hand impossible that he had the intention at the outset of developing his duchy, or part of it (perhaps one of the lesser islands), as a Jewish center, into which the persecuted might be admitted. But, if this were so, his plan was diverted by other dazzling prospects that were open before him. To set up an island of refuge in the Aegean could be at the best nothing more than a temporary expedient. The Jewish spirit would be stirred only by the prospect of a revival of Jewish life in Palestine.

CHAPTER V

Lord of Tiberias

DOÑA Gracia Nasi had desired to end her days in the Holy Land, and to be buried at the last by the side of her husband, whose body she had managed to transport, in accordance with his last wish, to the Valley of Jehoshaphat.[1] Such an ambition was by no means unusual among the Marranos on their return to Judaism. If they were forced to leave the place of their birth, there could be no more fitting refuge for them than the land bound up with their people's prayers and hopes for so many weary generations; moreover, here alone they could hope (some of them thought) to obtain forgiveness for the sin they had committed for so long in dissimulating God's holy faith. Accordingly, it was hither that their thoughts, and in many cases their steps, were turned.

Palestine was of course pre-eminent among the lands that had enjoyed Doña Gracia's lavish charities. She maintained there scholars and academies of rabbinic learning. Towards the end of her days, her plans became more ambitious and her work more practical. Like so much else, this was done in conjunction with her nephew and son-in-law, Joseph Nasi, who developed her ideas on a grandiose scale; and of all his many-sided activities, this was perhaps in many ways the most memorable.

The original Jewish settlement in Palestine had survived
the national disaster of the year 70, when Jerusalem was
raped by the Roman legions. With unbelievable tenacity,
it managed to maintain itself thereafter, though in ever-
dwindling strength and number, through a long succession
of catastrophes, until late in the Middle Ages. The
Crusades, followed by the Tartar invasions in the thirteenth century, proved to be the fatal blow. From this
time onwards, it may be said that the original *Yishuv*
was extinct over a great part of the area of the ancient
homeland; though there was a handful of agricultural
settlements in Upper Galilee (among them Pekiin, which
has survived to our own day) which according to report
continued even now to perpetuate the association of the
Jews with that beloved soil.

On the other hand, as early as the second half of the
thirteenth century, a new nucleus began to be formed.
No disaster and no hardship can ever discourage eager
Jews from attempting to implement their constant prayers, and the dreams of their prophets, and the paeans of
their singers, who never ceased to insist upon the indis-
soluble connection between the People and the Land;
and at intervals pilgrims would come to visit the sacred
sites and, perhaps, to fall under their spell and remain.
Greedy rulers in Europe looked askance at the emigration
of these useful sources of revenue; the journey was never
easy, sometimes perilous to a degree; life in the Holy
Land was hard when it was not hazardous. But still
they came — saints, mystics, rabbis, scholars and, above
all, ordinary, simple Jews and Jewesses — convinced that
merely to be in Palestine was in itself a meritorious deed.

In 1492, the highways of the entire Mediterranean

area became choked with homeless wanderers, victims of the heartless expulsion from the Spanish dominions. It was natural that some of the exiles, as they wandered from place to place without a home, without an objective, without a hope, turned their eyes to the Land which had been so long and so closely associated with their desires and dreams. Starvation there could not be more relentless than in any other spot on the world's surface, and its pangs would be alleviated by the thought that they were near, as they believed, to God's very footstool, and to that pathetic fragment left from His holy Temple, bathed for a dozen centuries and more by the tears of their people, whence prayer was assured of most speedy access to the Divine Throne. Moreover, if the recent tribulations were indeed the prelude to the comfort of Messianic days (and few doubted it in that time of woe), those settled in Palestine would be the first to enjoy the raptures of the great Deliverance.

In the circumstances, the Jewish population of the Holy Land grew beyond recognition.[2] A fresh impetus was added after the Turkish conquest of 1516, as a result of the war between Sultan Selim the Grim and the Mameluke rulers of Egypt, which brought the country under the rule of the great power which was at that time most consistently friendly to the Jews. Where a few years before there had been no more than a miserable handful, there was soon a virile settlement, flourishing spiritually if not materially. Scholars and rabbis, who had once been reckoned among the greatest luminaries of Jewish life in Spain, Portugal and Sicily, established themselves there in relative profusion, accompanied by many members of their flocks. Jerusalem, where a few decades before it had been difficult to muster a quorum of ten persons for prayer, soon harbored a community which was numbered by many hundreds, including a galaxy of eminent sages. Hither Isaac Solal, the last *Nagid*, or Prince, of Egyptian Jewry, dazzled by the luster shed upon the Holy City by the new arrivals, transferred himself and the seat of his lavish benevolence. Additional settlements sprang up in the other major centers of population. In the middle of the sixteenth century the Portuguese traveller, Fra Pantaleão d'Aveiro, who was exceptionally interested in the lot of his compatriots, found Jews — many of them ex-Marranos — more widely settled than they had been perhaps at any other time since the First Crusade.

The newcomers brought with them the technical skills that they had developed in their former homes. They established some petty industries, developed trade, fostered imports and did much else to revitalize the land, which had almost become a desert since the Arab and crusading armies had marched and counter-marched through its once-fertile valleys. Above all, they raised the cultural standard of the Jewish community. For the first time in centuries, Palestine was now a truly great center of rabbinic learning — a land to which the wisdom-loving Jew looked with veneration as well as affection. So great was the influx of scholars that in 1538 the very erudite Rabbi Jacob Berab (a Spanish exile, who had added to his reputation during a long residence in Fez, but had been driven thence also by the Spanish invasion) considered that the time was propitious for re-establishing the Holy Land as the center of Jewish spiritual life in a

PILGRIMS ON THE WAY TO JERUSALEM
(from an engraving of 1581)

PILGRIMS DISEMBARKING IN PALESTINE
(from a woodcut of about 1500)

formal sense. As a first step towards this, he proposed to
renew the venerable institution of rabbinic ordination, in
abeyance for over a thousand years. After this, it would
be possible, he opined, to restore the ancient Sanhedrin
as the spiritual ganglion of Jewry at large and the visible
expression of the supremacy of the Land of Israel in
Jewish life. Though some outstanding scholars associated
themselves with the scheme, there was a bigoted, unimagi-
native opposition, led by Levi ben Habib, rabbi in
Jerusalem, who in the end prevailed. His unquestionable
sincerity (not perhaps untinged with jealousy) was responsible for what was without doubt in the long run an
unmitigated misfortune to Judaism as a whole.

But Jerusalem was not at this time the only, nor
perhaps the principal, center of learning in the country.
Recent events had given a great impetus to esoteric studies
among the Jews. From the crushing vicissitudes of this
world, it was natural to seek refuge in the contemplation
of the mysteries of the next. Assuredly, these catastrophes
had been the veritable "pangs of the Messiah" spoken
of by the Rabbis of old — the darkest hour that proved
the dawn to be near. It was inevitable that more and
more attention should now be paid to the great mystical
classic, the *Zohar*, in the hope that in its rhapsodies
there might be discovered some indication of when the
Redeemer could be expected. Scholars of a mystical turn
of mind naturally directed their steps, therefore, to Upper
Galilee, where the action of the *Book of Splendor* was
staged, where its reputed author, Rabbi Simeon ben Johai,
had lived and where his grave was still to be visited; and
a remarkable settlement grew up in the principal city of

this area, lovely Safed, set within its diadem of hills. Here, there now came into being the strangest, strictest, maddest, most amazing community in Jewish history: a veritable Congregation of the Saints, recruited by eager mystics from all over Europe as well as Asia and Africa, passing twenty-four hours of every day in the study of the Holy Cabala, and maintaining in perpetuity the spirit of a revivalist camp.² The city, which, although it was the administrative center of northern Palestine, held at the beginning of the sixteenth century only the merest handful of Jews, whose rabbi had to keep shop in order to eke out his living, numbered within a couple of generations a Jewish population of thousands, who gave the entire area its specific background. The traditional life was lived with an intensity rarely equalled, coupled with a mystical fervor that was all its own. The multitudinous precepts of the Law were carried out meticulously, but with especial regard to their esoteric significance. Studies centered about the *Zohar* rather than the Talmud; and the anniversary of the death of Rabbi Simeon ben Johai was celebrated (as it still is) by a pilgrimage to his grave and the singing of mystical hymns throughout the night.

Safed was now the home of a group of remarkable personalities, headed by Isaac Luria, "The Lion of the Cabala,' who died in 1572 at the age of thirty-eight, the idolized exponent of the new school. It was here that Joseph Caro, the most eminent scholar of the age, alternated the composition of his famous ritual codex, the *Shulhan Arukh*, with strange esoteric visions during which he received, as he believed, direct communications from heaven; and here that Solomon Alkabetz composed the most famous modern Hebrew hymn, *Lekha Dodi*, for

recital by his associates as they went out into the fields
each Friday afternoon to greet the Sabbath Queen:-

> Belovèd, come to meet the Bride,
> Bid welcome to the Sabbath-tide.

These circumstances explain the reason for the exceptional position of the Jewish settlement in Galilee at this
time. But there was one historic site in this part of
Palestine which was barely affected by the revival. This
was Tiberias, at one time the most flourishing and most
important of the stately cities which studded the lovely
shores of the Sea of Galilee. After the ravaging of Judea
by the Romans, it had been for a long time the seat of
the Jewish Patriarchate and the main center of rabbinic
learning. It was the last city in which the Great Sanhedrin
had sat. It was associated with many of the outstanding
figures in Jewish spiritual and intellectual life in the early
centuries, from Rabbi Judah the Prince downwards. No
city figures more prominently in the Palestinian Talmud
and the literature of the Byzantine age, much of which
was compiled there. Even its sack in the fourth century,
after a local revolt, did not entail final disaster. Benjamin
of Tiberias, who had collaborated with the Persians against
the Byzantines in 614, was the last military figure in
Palestinian Jewry of antiquity; and it was in Tiberias that
the scientific text of the Hebrew Bible was formulated
and the current system of Hebrew vocalization and
punctuation was devised and perfected, in the early centuries of Moslem rule.

But now, in the middle of the sixteenth century, the
city, with its great memories, was all but desolate. The
only building intact was apparently the ancient church

built in the fourth century by the Empress Helena, which was opened once a year by the Franciscans for the celebration of the Mass. A typical wayfarer of the early sixteenth century (it was that same Rabbi Moses Basola who later on opposed and ruined Doña Gracia's scheme for the punitive boycott of Ancona) mentions the city in his account of his travels only for the sake of the graves of the departed which diversified the site:

In Tiberias, there rests a mighty congregation of the pious and the righteous and of godly proselytes.

The picture presented by a somewhat more practical observer of 1522 is no more seductive:

Tiberias was formerly a great city, the sea being its fortification, as our rabbis tell; but now it is desolate and waste, heaps of black [basalt] stones, as though it had been burned by fire. No man can go there from fear of the Arabs, except at the time of the caravan, when many travel thither under guard arranged by the governor of Safed, each person paying four drachmas for safe conduct . . . . Many date palms grow in the environs. There is still a village here, with ten or twelve Arab houses.

Another writer of the period tells us that the site was exceptionally dangerous because of the snakes which lurked amongst the ruins.

Towards the middle of the century, there seems to have been something of a revival in the region, partly due to the constant arrival of refugees from Portugal, and Tiberias could not fail to be affected to some extent. A French visitor of 1547, Pierre Belon, tells us that in the lovely country around the sea of Galilee there were in his day numerous newly-formed Jewish settlements engaged in fishing, such as Bethsaida and Chorazin, thanks to which that which was formerly desert had been repopulated. (How history repeats itself!) Some of the new arrivals settled in Tiberias, where another traveller, who passed that way two years later (1549), found a handful of Jews living uncomfortably among the ruins, the extent of which showed how important the city had once been. The settlers were, it seems, mainly ex-Marranos, for a New Christian renegade who returned to Portugal in 1557 informed the Holy Office of certain of his compatriots whom he had encountered there, known by Jewish names and practising Judaism. But the result of these attempts to revive the city and its Jewish community was negligible. Tiberias remained desolate, its former streets encumbered with reptile-haunted ruins and its old walls entirely destroyed.[4]

When Doña Gracia Nasi determined to settle in Palestine, this was the place that attracted her attention. (For a valetudinarian, the medicinal baths of Tiberias, famous since Roman times, were probably an added attraction.) Ordinary mortals went to the Holy Land, and then fixed on their accommodation. The *Señora* made her preparations first. Tiberias was in ruins? Then it should be rebuilt. There was no residence there fit for her luxurious style of living? Then let one be prepared. The Jewish population was sparse, and there was no established community? Then let Jews be attracted, and scholars subsidized. The political circumstances were unfavorable? Then it would be advisable to make a special arrangement with the Grand Signior. In everything, she worked in close association with her nephew, Joseph Nasi, who always acted as her agent and representative. The idea fascinated him, as it seems, and he began to develop it on his own more flamboyant lines. She had thought in terms of a Jewish community, of scholars, of a home where she could pass her last days. He, it appears, thought in terms of a quasi-autonomous settlement, of a city of refuge for the persecuted, of grandiose economic developments, perhaps of political action. She worked in the tradition of pious eleemosiny; he was in the direct line of ancestry of later Zionism.

It seems that his mind had long been running on the idea of a semi-political solution to the "Jewish Problem" of his time. Then, as in our own day, the fundamental difficulty had been that of finding a place of settlement for refugees — then, pre-eminently the victims of religious persecution in Spain and Portugal, corresponding to the fugitives from racial persecution in Central Europe in the middle of the twentieth century. Then, as in our own day, there was the complication that a sudden influx elsewhere might breed antisemitism and invite further persecution. Then, as in our own day, it was for this reason imperative to find not a temporary haven of refuge, but a permanent one, where there was no danger of reaction. Then, as in our own day, kingdom after kingdom and harbor after harbor were closed to these victims of man's inhumanity to man. (Turkey, indeed, alone in the world, opened its gates; but was it not possible that there was a limit to Turkish patience and generosity?) Then, as in our own day, logic made a "territorial" solution inevitable. It thus became a matter of primary importance at this stage to find some area where Jews could enter "as of right, and not on sufferance" — where, above all, in the sixteenth century, the unhappy fugitives from the fires of the Inquisition might safely come, confident that they would obtain admission. This ineluctably implied an autonomous or quasi-autonomous Jewish territory.

When he had been in Venice, years before, at the time of his aunt's tumultuous sojourn there, it is reported that João Miguez (not yet Don Joseph Nasi) had submitted a scheme of the sort for the consideration of the *Serenissima Dominante*. That government ruled over many islands, studded down the Dalmatian coast and across the Ionian sea as far as the Aegean and the coast of Asia Minor. He proposed, with a statesmanship so far in advance of its time that it was characterized as "effrontery," that one of those near Venice (which is not specified) should be assigned as a place of refuge for persecuted Jews, whither all who cared to come would be admitted without demur.[5] The settlement was obviously to be self-governing, though it is to be imagined that there would be some sort of Venetian overlordship, and that the advantages which would be brought to Venetian commerce were emphasized. (Not long after, another Marrano, Daniel Rodrigues, was able to make use of this argument when he created a Free Port at Spalato, thereby giving a much-needed impetus to the Republic's flagging economic life.) That the privilege was to be paid for, in hard cash, is self-evident. But the proposals were rejected. The Republic, at this time, was not in desperate need of funds. On the other hand, it was unwilling to sully its ostensible orthodoxy; and it was so far under the influence of Charles V (the expulsion of the Marranos at his request had taken place not long before) that such a gesture of sympathy on its part was unimaginable, as would have been the case, too, anywhere else in Christian Europe at this time.

But Don Joseph retained his vision. In fact, messianic dreams and cold logic pointed then as now to the same conclusion. There is only one safe place of refuge for persecuted Jewry, which will provide a solution to the problem of the Jewish spirit as well as a resting-place for wrecked Jewish bodies — the land that had been associated with Jewish hopes and dreams throughout the ages: Palestine.

Earlier historians gave the impression that the credit for the idea belongs to Don Joseph alone. But this was not the case. As we have seen, his good genius, Doña Gracia, stood behind him here as she always did, and contemporaries, in Palestine at least, associated the idea at the beginning with her as much as they did with him. Her practical interest, on a more modest scale indeed than his was afterwards to be, went back perhaps as far as 1558, or at any rate very shortly after this date. The precise nature of the concession that she received is uncertain, but it is reported that she paid the sultan in return for it the sum of 1,000 ducats yearly. It was not long before the results could be seen, on a modest scale. A visitor to Tiberias in 1561 found the nucleus of a settled Jewish population, with its synagogue and its scholars, who looked upon Doña Gracia as their patron. But there were already rumors that something on a more grandiose plan was intended, with which the name of Don Joseph was specifically associated.

He had the intention, it was said in Christian circles at this time, to make Tiberias into a Jewish center, filling it with "vipers" more deadly than those which already

haunted the ruins, and of course converting into a synagogue the ancient church which remained there from
former times. The apostolic delegate in Palestine, Fra
Bonifazio di Ragusa,[5a] was seriously perturbed by the
report, and when he was next in Constantinople voiced
his protest to the grand vizier, Rustam Pasha. He under-
stood the latter to inform him that he was opposed personally to the idea, and that nothing of the sort would
happen so long as the old Emperor Suleiman lived. But
Rustam Pasha was Don Joseph's closest associate (their
enemies said, his accomplice). It is highly unlikely that he
would have done anything against the latter's interests;
and, as a matter of fact, his success exceeded the friar's
worst forbodings.

In 1561, the year of Rustem's death, or not long afterwards, Don Joseph procured from the sultan a grant of
Tiberias and seven villages in the neighborhood, apparently as a semi-feudal dependency — "making him the
prince and ruler over them," in the words of a contemporary Jewish chronicle. The grant, issued in the name of
the aged Suleiman, is said to have been countersigned
by his son, Selim, the heir-apparent, and by the latter's
firstborn and successor, Murad, as a token that it was to
be valid for all time. The area in question was apparently to be set aside for Jews, who were ultimately to
predominate in it; but this development was still in the
future. The exact terms of the grant are unfortunately
not preserved, and to some extent it is necessary to rely
on conjecture. It is self-evident that a yearly tribute was
to be paid in consideration of the concession — certainly
not less then the sum of 1,000 ducats annually that had
been agreed to by Doña Gracia — and perhaps a heavy

outright payment as well. Probably, there was included in the grant the right of taxation and of exacting the *corvée*, or compulsory labor-service. From the Turkish viewpoint, the scheme was tempting not only on financial grounds, but also because it offered the possibility of attracting a loyal and industrious population to a desolate part of the empire, and strengthening its defences without expense by the addition of a new fortified city in a strategic area. (It may be, indeed, that this was one of the specific conditions of the concession.)

It is certain that a considerable stir was caused in the diplomatic world by the scheme. The French ambassador in Constantinople, for example, reported to the king in his despatch of September 13, 1563:

This Migues has received permission from the Grand Signior, confirmed by Sultan Selim and his son Sultan Murad, to build a city on the shore of the Lake of Tiberias, beneath Safed, wherein Jews only are to live. In fact, he proposes to begin his achievement here by this renewal, having the intention so far as one can judge of proclaiming himself King of the Jews. This is why he is demanding money from France so insistently.

Though this report was obviously, and grossly, exaggerated, it shows, nevertheless, that Don Joseph's plan was considered at the time to be basically political rather than charitable. The little plot of land on the shore of Lake Tiberias was to be, not merely a city of refuge, but the kernel of a Jewish state, dependent on the great, tolerant, benevolent but (if the obvious parallel to present-day conditions is to be pursued) somewhat unpredictable Turkish Empire.[6]

What was it that made Don Joseph chose Tiberias as the seat of his experiment, out of all the historic sites of

Palestine? In part, doubtless, it was simply that he continued and developed his aunt's less ambitious concession in the same area. To have fixed upon Jerusalem — the ancient capital of the independent Jewish state in the heroic days of the past — would have been more dramatic, and more obvious. But for that very reason it was safer to avoid it; for Turkish opinion was sensitive on this point, and the Jewish population of the Holy City was severely restricted for centuries thereafter, so as to prevent it from acquiring an Hebraic complexion. Safed, in Upper Galilee, with its large, ecstatic population of cabalists, might have seemed another possibility, and here Don Joseph would have had a considerable Jewish nucleus ready to hand. But Safed was the seat of the administration of the province, and a rival authority would certainly not have been welcome here. Moreover, Safed Jewry was entirely immersed in mystical exercises. It conceived that the redemption of Israel could be hastened only by prayer and study and the meticulous performance of the multitudinous commandments of the Law, with proper concentration on their esoteric implications. Men of this type were uninterested in practical work for the upbuilding of the Holy Land, such as was at the basis of Don Joseph's ideas; nor were they likely to favor the political supremacy in Palestine of any person less than the Messiah. If neither Jerusalem nor Safed was possible, desolate Tiberias, with its splendid site, its fertile surroundings, its great memories of the past, was certainly indicated for Don Joseph's purpose at least as much as any other place. And it was possible that the rabbinic advisers and mentors who came in and out of his palace in Constantinople had told him of the ancient rabbinic adage, quoted with approval by Moses Maimonides himself in his great Code,[7] that the city where the last flame of Jewish independence had flickered out on the extinction of the Patriarchate, thirteen centuries before, was to see the beginning of the reversal of the tide of fortune: "From Tiberias, the redemption will begin."

Don Joseph could not go to Palestine himself immediately to look after the interests of his embryonic state.[8] It was only by constant presence near the sultan and his entourage that he was able to maintain his position in the tortuous politics of the Sublime Porte; once he absented himself for more than a short while, his enemies would redouble their intrigues and he might go the same way as so many former favorites. He could not therefore afford to leave Constantinople; and he delegated his confidential agent, Joseph ben Ardut, or Joseph Pomar (presumably identical with the Joseph Cohen who acted as his secretary about this period),[9] to take his place. Before leaving for Palestine, probably in the summer of 1563, the latter had an audience with the sultan, who received him favorably and made him an allowance of sixty *aspri* daily, equivalent to some 450 piasters a year. He thus enjoyed the authority of an imperial officer, as well as that of Don Joseph's personal representative; and he bore with him both a copy of the imperial firman and letters patent to the governor of Safed and his superior at Damascus, ordering them to give him all possible assistance. Some stalwarts who were to be the pioneers of the new settlement accompanied him — the *halutzim*, as it were, of the sixteenth century. These included four of Don Joseph's personal retainers — former prisoners of war, who had been presented to him by the Prince Selim. He had with him, moreover, eight of the sultan's own servants, who had been assigned to him perhaps as bodyguard.

Ibn Ardut's principal task in Palestine was to superintend the restoration of the ruined fortifications of Tiberias, which, as has been suggested above, must have been one of the principal attractions of the scheme in the sultan's eyes, and was no doubt responsible for the official character of his mission. (The walls of Safed had been rebuilt, not indeed very elaborately, in 1549.) In any case, it was obvious that the first requirement of the new settlement was physical security, without which the settlers would have been (as in our own day) at the mercy of the inevitable Bedouin raids and the attack of any predatory forces which marched through Syria. Provision had already been made for this. The raw material was available in abundance, for the ruins of the city provided an ample supply of hewn stone, and there was an unlimited quantity of sand on the shores of the lake. The supply of labor was a more difficult problem, and it was for this reason that Ibn Ardut's mission had been commended to the authorities in Damascus and Safed. Skilled masons and workmen were compelled to come from these cities (for forced labor was the usual expedient then in such emergencies), while the mortar was made on the spot by the felaheen of the villages included in Don Joseph's domain. It may be imagined that the work was all the more unwelcome since it was on behalf of a Jewish master and under the direction of a Jewish agent. Nevertheless, it was pressed on.

Even now, the plan was not safe from intriguers and intrigue. Bonifazio di Ragusa renewed his protests to Ali the Fat, grand vizier since 1561 in succession to Rustam

Pasha, and was blandly assured of his personal sympathy and his profound opposition to the scheme. Though nothing effective could be done in the capital, underhand machinations were still possible in Palestine, and it was not long before the results were apparent. One of the local sheikhs, who had perhaps heard the Jewish legend that the deliverance would begin in that spot, came forward with the story that he had found in an old book that, when Tiberias was rebuilt, Islam would fall. This was sufficient to scatter the laborers to their homes, the work on the walls ceasing. Ibn Ardut was compelled to go to Damascus and demand the Pasha's assistance in having the sultan's orders obeyed. He came back with a military force, and two of the ringleaders were seized and savagely punished.

The work of restoration now recommenced. In the city (it is reported) there was unearthed the crypt of an ancient church, with its altars and images of the saints, which the pious discoverers destroyed; and three bronze church bells, hidden by the crusaders before they left three centuries before, which were melted down and made into heads for battering-rams. In the winter of 1564–5, in the month of Kislev in the Hebrew calendar (the same in which the festival of the Maccabees is observed), the walls of Tiberias were completed, though only a modest fifteen hundred yards in circuit. The nucleus of the new little principality was henceforth safe at least against a sudden onslaught. The success proved somewhat disconcerting to some contemporaries, such as a certain Safed Jew who had bound himself to make an inconvenient payment when the building of the fortifications was completed, and naively pleaded in self-defense that he had considered this to be equivalent to postponing settlement to the Days of the Messiah! We have a description of the new city, dating from the following century, which presumably describes faithfully enough how it looked when Don Joseph's restorations were complete:

> Tiberias is square-built, surrounded with walls and fortifications, three quarters of a mile in circumference. There is a city gate on the west side, artistically constructed of black and white marble, and a smaller one to the north. (I did not learn of any others.) The city is not very old, and much smaller than the former Tiberias![10]

The seventeenth-century French traveller, Thevenot, adds the detail (with reference to Doña Gracia's part in what had been achieved) that "the Walls . . . having been ruined, a Jewish widow afterwards built new ones in form of a Fort, with its Courtines."

Further building operations were, of course, needed inside the circuit of the city wall. Newcomers appropriated deserted houses, restored the roofs, cleared the ruins, opened up the blocked passages and on occasion quarelled over their respective rights. (We are informed of two scholars, who should have known better, who even came to fisticuffs and submitted a law-suit to the rabbinical authorities.) An ancient synagogue was reopened at the lake-side, abutting on the wall. Legendarily it was associated with Rabbi Simeon ben Johai, reputed author of the *Zohar*; and the mystic Isaac Luria, Lion of the Cabala, considered it exceptionally meritorious to worship there when he came down from Safed. (The Franciscans' forebodings as regards the fate of their ancient church were unjustified, at least so far as the Jews were concerned, though later on the Turks converted it into a mosque.)

Outside the city walls and not far from the famous hot baths, still frequented by visitors, as they had been since remote antiquity, Doña Gracia gave orders for the construction of a mansion for her private residence; and a visitor tells us how, at the beginning of 1565, the Jewish population of Palestine was all agog at the prospect that in the following summer the "Señora" would come to settle in their midst with her entire household and all who cared to follow. Great expectations were aroused among them by the news, for they imagined that this would greatly influence their status and prove the beginning of a new era in their history. Whether the transference actually took place is uncertain; possibly, it was forestalled by ill-health, though Doña Gracia's complete disappearance from the scene at Constantinople, for some time before her death, may perhaps be explained by the assumption that she had in fact carried her intention into effect.[11]

Meanwhile, Don Joseph had been exerting himself to establish his tiny domain on a sound economic basis. It is in this respect that his experiment is most strikingly modern in character. Like Baron Edmond de Rothschild, over three hundred years later, he realized that it would be impossible to build up a sound and healthy Jewish nucleus on the basis of the mystics of Safed and the petty traders of the other cities. It was necessary for some of them to be rooted in the soil; it was desirable that they should have manufactures and handicrafts; it would prove useful if they could build up an export trade. This could only be based, in the first instance, upon the textile industry with which, in spite of perpetual attempts to exclude them, the Jews of Europe had been associated

so long and so intimately. Domestic looms in every household could give employment to a large number of persons
and make possible a great increase of population. His
own interests in this branch of activity and his business-
connections all over Europe gave him special opportunities to be useful in this respect. He arranged accordingly for the importation of large quantities of wool from
Spain for the manufacture of cloth similar to that which
was made in Venice. (The prospect of damaging the
business interests of that proud city must have given
him particular satisfaction.)[12] It may well be that, as
historians have suggested, he tried to introduce from the
Peninsula merino sheep also, famous for their luxuriant
fleeces. But the branch of industry with which the Jews
of the Mediterranean world were most closely associated
was silk-weaving, which had at one time been almost a
Jewish monopoly in South Italy and Greece. (There was
an Italian Jew of this period, Meir Magino, who a few
years later was to receive from the Pope a patent for an
improved method of silk manufacture.) This industry
could provide a livelihood for a large number of persons
at every stage. The first step was to obtain the raw
material; and as a preliminary, plantations of mulberry
trees were planted for the silk-worms. Already there
were small Jewish fishing settlements round the shores of
the Sea of Galilee, which helped to solve the problem of
alimentation, and agriculture too was engaged in system-
atically.[13]

But this was clearly to be subsidiary. We almost see
working in Don Joseph's mind the same arguments and
reasonings which were advanced long afterwards by those
who, in a similar period of stress, were willing to accept

the proposals for the partition of Palestine and the establishment of a self-governing Jewish state in a fraction of the country. Industrialization would enormously increase the absorptive capacity of the restricted area and thus make it possible to open the doors widely to the homeless refugees who could find admittance nowhere else.*

The results soon became apparent. A traveller who visited Tiberias in 1564 gives a picture of the scene which is very different from the desolation described by the pious pilgrims of half a century before. The city of Tiberias, he writes, was visible from afar; it lay so near the Sea of Galilee that part of it looked as though it were actually sunk in the water; it was strong, being surrounded by solid walls. There was great abundance of date-palms, orange trees and pine trees. The natural luxuriance was so great that the scent of the plants was almost suffocating. Another visitor of the period informs us how of recent years "the habitations of the wilderness have been turned to a garden of Eden, and the parched soil like to the vineyard of the Lord." In the responsa of contemporary rabbis, we read of the perplexities of a pious Jew who had rented a piece of land for ten years from an Arab and wished to know whether, notwithstanding the fact that he employed Gentile labor on a crop-sharing basis, he had to let it lie fallow in the seventh year in accordance with the ancient biblical precept. From another record we learn that most of the householders had their gardens and vineyards outside the city, and a little later there is a record also of Jewish bee-keepers.

---

* In view of recent developments, it seems desirable to point out that this chapter was written in 1946.

The conjecture has been made[14] that one of Don
Joseph's principal agents at Tiberias was a member of a
very remarkable Marrano family, some at least of whom
settled there. Among the families who had been victims
of the forced conversion in Portugal in 1497 was that of
Gedaliah, or Guedalla (to use a spelling that has become
familiar in the English-speaking world). Some adopted as
Christians the name of Oliveira; and one of them, Mestre
Pedro, was one of the distinguished band of New Christian
practitioners who became body-physicians to the Court
of Portugal about this time. But their Jewish loyalties,
although suppressed, remained strong. Mestre Pedro,
indeed, and one of his brothers, Dom Manoel, of Villa
Nova, died before they could leave Portugal; but their
other two brothers, Joseph and Abraham, together with
a sister, fled to Turkey and there re-entered the Jewish
fold and re-adopted their ancestral name. Some time
later, one of Mestre Pedro's sons, David Oliveira, a man
of considerable wealth, also managed to escape and
apparently made his way to Palestine. It is he who, it is
said, acted as Don Joseph's agent for the imports of
Spanish wool to his little principality. There was a curious
sequel to the family history some little time later, when
he died without issue, and the members of the Gedaliah
family — particularly his cousin, Moses son of Joseph
Gedaliah, who had settled in Tiberias — attempted to
demonstrate their relationship to him in order to be able
to inherit his estate.

There were other immigrants too, with different interests. The mystics and scholars of Safed were overjoyed
at the prospect of the formation of a fresh center of

esoteric exercise, supported by the munificence of Doña Gracia Nasi, and several had already transferred themselves thither. Foremost among them was the scholar Eliezer ben Johai — one of those who had indulged in such a fierce dispute about his property rights in the house which he had retrieved from the ruins. He died in 1572, Abraham Kilai and then Samuel ben Saul succeeding to his position as rabbi. The lay head of the community was the erudite R. Zemah. A Yemenite traveller, who was in Tiberias about 1562, informs us quaintly of the awe he felt in the presence of the graybeards whom he found studying in the synagogue by the city wall, who made him appear a mere boy by comparison. Ultimately, nearly seventy scholars regularly frequented the academy supported by "the princess of all women in Constantinople the capital." For a short time, Tiberias must almost have rivalled Safed itself. The community was properly organized and possessed its official records, like any other; and we know that one volume contained at least thirty-three private agreements and public instruments signed, and in some cases drawn up, by Rabbi Eliezer ben Johai, a number of them being witnessed also by a certain Solomon Natiel.[15]

Doña Gracia's death in 1569 was a fatal blow to this scholarly element. It seems as though her nephew had little sympathy with it. He admired and supported scholarship in what he considered to be its proper place. But it had no role to fill in the tiny commonwealth he was hoping to establish, except as an occupation for leisure hours, and he withdrew the subsidy. The academy now dwindled, soliciting support from Turkey, Iraq, Egypt, Italy, even the Yemen. Its days were numbered nevertheless. Artificially created, it collapsed when support was withdrawn.

Don Joseph was more interested in the organization of immigration from abroad. Since the initiation of his scheme, the problem which so exercised him had become more pressing than ever. At an earlier stage, the plague-spot of Jewish life in Europe had been the Iberian Peninsula, where the fires of the Inquisition smoked continuously to heaven and it was suicidal for any person of Jewish stock to allow his allegiance to the religion of his fathers to be suspected. Little more could be done for the relief of these victims of misguided religious zeal. The "underground railway" for fugitive Marranos, with the organization of which Doña Gracia and her family were so closely associated, was still operating. It is self-evident that some of the fugitives were directed to Palestine; probably, indeed, this adventurous agency was responsible for the escape of the numerous Portuguese Jews who were found at this period all over the country (especially Galilee) by the inquisitive Fray Pantaleão d'Aveiro. Without doubt some of them were now diverted to Tiberias and the surrounding area by the Duke's agents (perhaps the Gedaliah family was among them). But there was now another class of sufferers whose requirements had to be taken into consideration, as life had become almost impossible for them as well in their former home.

Italian Jewry was the oldest in Europe and had hitherto been in many ways the happiest; for under the benevolent eyes of the Popes the ferocious expressions of Christian piety which had overwhelmed other lands were kept within moderate if not reasonable bounds. There were occa-

sional darker interludes, especially in those areas, such
as the kingdom of the Two Sicilies, where foreign influ-
ences dominated. But over a period of many generations,
Italy was the paradise of Jewry in Europe, and the
Italian communities took the lead in many aspects of
Hebraic intellectual life. Above all, during the Renaissance period, the Jewish magnates almost vied with the
Christian merchant-princes in their patronage of learning.
Jewish scholars associated on terms of the utmost intimacy
with Christian savants, almost every Italian ruler had his
Jewish physician, and the leaders of the Roman community enjoyed such a prestige that Gentiles solicited their
support at the Papal curia. In some ways, it was the
freest interlude in Jewish history, socially and economically, until the nineteenth century.

But recently there had been a catastrophic reaction.
The beginnings of the Reformation in Germany had
forced the Catholic Church to reconsider its own position,
the easy-going tolerance of the Renaissance period being
thus succeeded by the bigotry of the Catholic Reaction.
All the anti-Jewish restrictions of the Middle Ages, never
before regarded very seriously in Rome, were now put
into force with savage conscientiousness. Moreover, the
Jews were suspected, though quite unjustly, of having
fostered the Reformation, and it was considered necessary
to cut them off entirely from all intercourse with the
outside world. The reaction came to a head when in 1555,
shortly after he became Pope, the gloomy Paul IV issued
his notorious Bull *cum nimis absurdum*, in which he
stressed the "absurdity" of the ample toleration hitherto
enjoyed by the Jews and renewed, down to its last detail,
all the oppressive medieval legislation directed against

them. They were henceforth to be strictly segregated in
their own quarter (subsequently to be known as the
Ghetto). They were forbidden to practice medicine among
Christians, to employ Christian servants or workmen, or
to be called *signor*. They were debarred from owning
real estate, whether in town or country, having to dispose
at whatever sacrifice of what they already held. They
were forced to wear the distinctive badge, in the form of
a yellow hat. For the moment, this legislation applied
only to the Papal States. But these now comprised one
of the largest fractions of the peninsula, with nearly
half of the total Italian Jewish population, distributed
amongst nearly one hundred different centers, great and
small, throughout the Romagna, Campania, Umbria and
Marches of Ancona, where no township of any size lacked
its community and its synagogue. Throughout this area,
commissaries were appointed forthwith with instructions,
not only to enforce the new regulations, but also to
enquire into past misdemeanors; and as a preliminary
they sequestered the property of all whom they suspected.
As the months lengthened into years — and especially
after the accession to the papal throne in 1565 of the
former inquisitor general, Cardinal Ghislieri, under the
title of Pius V — conditions became worse and worse.

The result was wholesale, almost universal, ruin —
much similar to what happened in Germany when the
Nazis enforced their antisemitic legislation after 1933.
These who had formerly been considered the communal
magnates were beggared. Professional men were driven
out of business. The small manufactures had to be closed
down. Hardly any channel of livelihood was left open.
There was a wholesale wave of baptisms, which deprived

the stricken communities of many of their most capable members. Those left were least suited to face the battle of life independently.[16] There was only one avenue of escape — emigration. Yet emigration to other parts of Italy, where the Popes were pressing for their example to be imitated, was pointless. It was obviously necessary to find some haven of refuge abroad. The harbors were crowded with hopeless would-be emigrants, desperately anxious to find a new home; but where? As in the twentieth century, the problem of the refugee and of lands of refuge was uppermost in the mind of every sensitive and conscientious Jew.

This was the state of affairs in the Jewish world when Don Joseph Nasi was engaged in his Palestinian experiment; and the implications were obvious in the sixteenth century as they were to be in the twentieth — the people without a land should be directed to the land without a people. The tragedy of the Marranos of Ancona in 1555–6, when Doña Gracia and her nephew had striven in vain to organize reprisals, accentuated the need. The failure on that occasion made it obvious that, so long as the Jewish mentality remained unchanged, it was out of the question to attempt to relieve the pressure at its source by political and economic methods; all that remained possible was to bring relief to the sufferers. In 1566, indeed, Don Joseph was invested with the duchy of Naxos. But, though the possession of this island gave him political status, it could at the best make only a limited contribution to the radical solution of the problem that had suddenly become so pressing; for this, it seemed clear, only Palestine offered a solid basis. Nor was there then any need to use secret methods, or subterfuge. Manifestos were distributed

throughout Italy — or at least in those parts where the
clouds loomed most menacingly — inviting all who so
desired to come to assist in populating Don Joseph's little
principality. His summons was, however, not indis-
criminate; for (how modern, once again, this is!) he
specially invited craftsmen and artisans, who could assist
in establishing the settlement on a sound economic basis.
Transport fortunately presented no problem. The commercial interests of the House of Nasi extended, as we
have seen, to overseas trade and even ship-owning; and
he arranged for vessels to be sent at his expense to Venice,
Ancona and certain other Italian seaports, with instructions to take on board all refugees who wished to avail
themselves of his offer and to convey them, free of charge,
to the further Mediterranean shore.[17]

Among certain of the Italian communities at least, the
invitation from the Duke of Naxos was greeted enthusiastically — almost rhapsodically. We happen to be informed in detail of the reception in the little city of Cori
in the Campania, a little distance south of Rome. Here,
as elsewhere, the Bull of Paul IV had brought the community, numbering about two hundred souls, to the verge of
ruin, and some of the outstanding members had sought
refuge in apostasy. There was some slight alleviation on
Paul's death in 1559, but with the accession of Pope
Pius V, in 1565, the reaction was resumed in full measure,
reducing those who were left to utter despair. The summons to Tiberias provided a ray of hope in their darkness.
They joyfully assembled in the synagogue, with their
physician-rabbi, Malachi (Angelo) Gallico, at their head,
and there solemnly decided to emigrate to Palestine as
a body — men, women and children. An agreement to

this effect was formally drawn up and signed by all present; and four leading householders with influential connections in other parts were delegated to organize the glorious adventure.

One problem, however, remained: impoverished as they were, how could they scrape together the money to discharge their obligations and to defray the cost of the preliminary journey overland to Venice, where they proposed to embark on one of Don Joseph's vessels? Two of the four supervisors were accordingly instructed to go ahead to prepare the way and to collect money from their better situated coreligionists in those parts of Italy to which the reaction had not yet penetrated. We know of all this because of the eloquent credentials with which they were supplied, in the form of a letter to the Jewish communities far and near — a most interesting historical document, which it is worth while to quote at some length, in all its incongruous allusiveness and its pathetic biblical hyperbole:[18]

We the members of the exile in the Holy Congregation of Cori which is in the region of Campania, a day's journey distant from Rome, our eyes are always unto the Lord until He shall have mercy upon us . . . . . And it came to pass that when the days of woe and the tribulations and the imposts and the burdens encompassed us — while this was imminent, in the days of Pope Paul the Fourth, the cry of anguish came very near to the border of Israel; yea, he placed groaning and oppression in our loins by the hard labor which was imposed upon us by the Bull which he issued against us, until there was no possibility of livelihood left to us. These tribulations rose and clustered about our necks, for there went forth commissaries who took away our money and condemned us to the galleys or to death, so that those who did not have the strength to endure this and

to sanctify the Name of God abjured our holy faith. Thus, the
number of apostates increased at that time, and to those who
remained nothing was left but only their bodies and their
woe .... Above all was this the case in the region of Campania,
wherein our city is situated .... for they turned their gaze
upon us and we became as a heap of bones, and there is naught
left for us whereof to live, for we are brought very low.

At this stage, this bitter and hasty time came upon us, as is
notorious to all peoples, for the greatness of the groaning and
distress .... because of the stringency of the provisions of the
new Bull, so harsh and so cruel .... issued against us by Pope
Pius V (may his might increase!). It is not enough now to en-
close us strictly in every place wherein we dwell, but moreover
they have surrounded us in with walls which are entirely shut
in. Thus, no man can go forth to have any sort of intercourse
with our neighbors. Indeed, the regulations are so strict that
we cannot engage in any sort of commerce whatsoever, whether
in articles of food or in new garments, nor may we even occupy
ourselves with handicrafts. Moreover, the Gentiles are changed
against us from sweet to bitter, saying that it is forbidden for
them to give us any assistance or domesticity or to help us in
any way. From the time that all these woes came upon us, our
eyes have welled with weeping and the tears on our cheek have
given us no respite .....

When the woe encompassed us ... and our eyes were dark-
ened because of this .... we all strayed like cattle, and each
man turned his own way, to renounce the religion of the Holy
God; for every day there came entire families, great and small,
poor and rich, including even the wise and the learned, and
changed their faith. These were now numbered amongst those
who vexed us, and brought pressure on our fellow-Jews to go
over to their religion, besides oppressing us in other ways: and
every day we are slain because of the regulations of which we
have told. We are indeed placed like sheep for the slaughter,
pursued unceasingly, and there is none to deliver us from their
hands ..... As for us, we know not what to do ... and we
called to the Lord our God mightily, from the young to the old,

for the deliverance of our souls . . . from those who snare us to apostasy . . . . Oh, that we could go forth into the field, and lodge in the villages of our Holy Land and thus escape these impious apostates! Oh, that God would send us from on high a help and redeemer, so that Jacob might rejoice and Israel be glad!

Now, when the groaning and the prayer of the Holy Congregation of Cori and their tribulation became great, and their weeping became extremely heavy, behold, there came unto us the voice of the coming of the announcer and foreteller of peace . . . Yea, there came to these poor and miserable Jews who are eager to go out from this exile one who announced good tidings and grace and mercy to the holy congregations. We speak of the crown and glory and grace and honor of the Prince (*Nasi*), the Lord and Noble, head of those who are first and fortress among men, the pillar of the exile, in whose fair semblance and praise is the king's diadem and greatness; yea, the man exalted on high . . . . the exalted and aggrandized . . . . our Lord Don Joseph, to whom the Lord God caused to be given the land of Tiberias, wherein God chose to be the sign and symbol for our redemption and the salvation of our souls . . .

We have heard from the corner of the land the songs of glory addressed to the righteous one, the *Nasi*, the aforementioned lord, that he has lavished money from his purse and arranged in many places, such as Venice and Ancona, ships and help, in order to put an end to the groaning of the captive . . . to bring out the prisoner from duress and from the dungeon those who dwell in this dark and dreary exile: above all, those who have been brought low and who cannot by themselves go thither with their households . . . .

We have, indeed, learned that many have already set out and crossed the seas, with the assistance of the communities and of the aforementioned Prince. It has been told us, moreover, that he seeks especially Jews who are craftsmen, so that they may settle and establish the land on a proper basis; truly, "great is the good that he hath stored up . . . ."

On hearing all this, we became stirred with a single heart and

went as one man ... to the synagogue. There at our head was
Rabbi Malachi Gallico ... who is employed in our community
to teach our children and to cure the sick through his medical
knowledge ....[19] There we made agreement among ourselves ... about our proposed journey hence, to go to dwell
under the pinions of the Almighty, at the bidding of the honored
lord, the Prince, in Tiberias ... so as to give proper order to
this journey .... as is needful by reason of the poverty of the
Holy Congregation of Cori aforementioned. In the first place,
we picked four men, belonging to four different families, who
should be our leaders from one resting-place to another ....
From the above-mentioned four men we chose two who should
go as our emissaries to Venice before we set out, to see what
assistance will be forthcoming for us, and to go to the houses
of the generous ... in all parts of the Diaspora and ask them
to have pity on this congregation of ours. The names of the
two emissaries are R. Michael ben Aaron of blessed memory
and R. Joseph ben Menahem, residents in our community ...
whom we have chosen because they belong to worthy families,
well-connected in Israel .... In token whereof we have entrusted into their hands a register sealed with the seal of our
community and our dwelling-place, the city of Cori ...[20]
wherein they will be able to write down all the offerings ...
from each one who is generous of heart.

Wherefore, oh ye that are generous ... merciful sons of
merciful sires .... prepare ye provision ... to help the poor
ones to go in justice from the Exile to our Land, and to make
true the path of the righteous!

The outcome of this pathetic document cannot be
ascertained. We know that the two delegates reached
Ancona, where they were kindly received and had their
credentials endorsed in a further flowery letter commend-
ing their errand to the charitable. But the number of
the sufferers throughout the Papal States was so great
that it was out of the question to succor all, and it is to

be feared that the high hopes with which the emissaries set out were disappointed. Hence some part at least of the community remained in Cori, to face further tribulation later on.[21] On the other hand, it is probable that a considerable proportion left the country. The surname Cori, borne by their descendants, is still known in Turkey, and it may be that the cabalist Elisha Gallico, who flourished in Safed in the second half of the sixteenth century, belonged to the same family as the rabbi-physician, who had inspired the community's decision.

Even had they managed to embark *en masse*, as they had intended, their dangers would not have been over. When, in 1569, the papal onslaught on the Jews culminated with their expulsion from all the minor centers of the Papal States, large numbers assembled in the seaports of Pesaro and Senigallia, in the duchy of Urbino, in the hope of taking ship to the Levant. Now, Joseph Nasi's haven of refuge could have proved providential as never before. Many of the refugees had the definite intention to settle in Palestine. The Pesaro community, taking the lead, sent a circular letter to their coreligionists throughout Northern Italy, by the hand of the noble-hearted Solomon Mazliah Finzi da Recanati, begging for monetary assistance to enable the seven hundred refugees assembled there, who desired to go to the Holy Land "for the glory of our God," to continue their journey as far as Venice; hence, they would be able to take ship for their goal, where they would "rejoice and pass through, redeemed." But, until they came to port, there was continuous peril. A contemporary chronicler, speaking perhaps of this very convoy, tells us how

A Part of Old Tiberias

The Lake of Tiberias and its Surroundings in the 17th Century

Many Jews left Italy that year (1569) to travel to the East. On the journey, they were attacked by the Knights of Malta, who beset them. Many were lost at sea because of the attackers, and many others were enslaved at that sad time. Now, oh God, be Thou not remote! Speed Thou, oh our Strength, to save us!

We know of one group in particular, of over one hundred souls, who set out from Italy, their expectations roused to fever-point, with the object of establishing themselves in the Holy Land — presumably at Tiberias under the Duke's auspices. They were among those waylaid by the Knights of St. John on their journey and carried off to the island of Malta, to be kept as slaves or held for ransom.

This crowning outrage convinced the Pesaro Jews that it was imperative to take political action. It seems as though a conference of the local communities was held there, which decided to solicit the assistance of the Duke of Naxos. A few years earlier, the Sublime Porte had spontaneously attempted to stop these constant forays, which were carried on almost within sight of the Turkish coast. Could not the sultan again be approached — the sultan, the solitary hope of humanitarianism in international relations in those days — and asked to intervene once more, so as to stem this constant sequence of suffering? And would not Joseph Nasi, whose authority and influence at the Turkish Court were so great and so notorious, take the necessary steps, as he and he alone could do? "Except for you, Our Prince," the missive stated, "there is in the entire world no man who can reverse the wheel of fortune for these unhappy prisoners."[22] It is regrettable that the reply to this moving appeal has not been preserved.

Obviously, it was at this stage, and in the succeeding years, that the colonization experiment in Palestine could have been most useful. But, by this time, the question had apparently taken a secondary place in Don Joseph's fertile mind. It may be that with Doña Gracia's death in 1569 the idealistic force behind the experiment had waned, and that, notwithstanding the grandiose conceptions which he had momentarily elaborated, this now became a routine matter on the same plane as many others. He may possibly have decided in his superficial fashion that his island-feud in the Aegean gave him after all opportunities which were out of the question in the restricted area at his disposal on the shores of the Sea of Galilee, or that yet another area (which, we shall see) held the greatest potentialities of all. It is very likely, too, that his enemies had been at work, and warned the sultan of the danger of permitting anything in the nature of a Jewish state from developing in Palestine, and that he had decided that discretion was the better part of benevolence as well as of valor. There is evidence in rabbinic sources of an outbreak of violence, probably about 1575, when many of the wealthier inhabitants fled for safety from Tiberias to Sepphoris, leaving their property to be plundered, and for that reason refusing to pay a share in the taxation of their new home. In 1579, just before Don Joseph's death, there was a further Bedouin onslaught in the region, which is unlikely to have left Tiberias untouched. Arab acts of violence against the Jews became more common, so that it became positively dangerous for them to travel alone round the villages of the neighborhood as they had previously done.

Nor was the response among the Jewish masses such

as might have been hoped. Many had no objection to
receiving charity, but were not prepared to do anything
to help themselves, and we learn of one Egyptian woman
who refused to accompany her husband to Palestine because, forsooth, the country was ill-developed socially.
Little practical encouragement could be forthcoming
from rabbis, immersed in hair-splitting casuistry; or from
mystics, convinced that the Redemption could be hastened only by permutations and combinations of the
Divine Name; or even perhaps from fugitive Marranos,
only too happy if they had succeeded in saving their own
bodies. Conceivably, the Duke had been disappointed
at the relative feebleness of the response and the apathy
of those who were interested only in the establishment of
a new center of study, and considered his long-term economic planning to be almost a sacrilege. Whatever the
reason, the center of his interest changed. The Tiberias
experiment was not a failure, but it certainly did not live
up to the enthusiastic hopes that it had aroused.

Yet the idea did not die, and in its more moderate form,
without any of the original, almost Messianic, ardor, it
even survived Don Joseph's death in 1579. His position
at the Sublime Porte was inherited after a lapse of a few
years by another Marrano magnate, Alvaro Mendes, *alias*
Solomon Abenaish (ibn Yaish), who arrived in Turkey
in 1585, thereafter played a great part in Turkish foreign
policy and was enfeoffed with the duchy of Mytilene in
the Greek isles.[23] It seems that he secured for himself and
his son Jacob (formerly Francisco) a renewal of Don
Joseph Nasi's grant of Tiberias and the seven adjoining
townships. (What had happened there in the meanwhile
we do not know.) Not content with this distant sentimental

association, the younger man actually went and settled on his domain, as Doña Gracia had wished to do. Here he passed his time in study and prayer. We are informed by a contemporary that he built several houses in the city, as well as a fine "castle," and became very popular among the Arabs. His father, on the other hand, that shrewd man of affairs, considered him to be extravagant, not appreciating his idealism. As he wrote to his kinsman by marriage, Dr. Roderigo Lopez, the ill-fated body-physician to Queen Elizabeth of England:

Your Servitour, my son, is in his hol(l)y land(s) persisting in his folly. He hath spent me much money in his heate, without effecting anything, for not understanding well the people of the countrey. He is an honest man and of a good conscience; he spendeth all his time in *meldar*,[24] and procureth more for his soule than after the world. The Lord be with all.

This is unfortunately all we know. Don Solomon Abenaish died in 1603, and there is no possibility of ascertaining whether the grant of Tiberias and the seven townships continued to his death or survived it. We know however that in 1598 the local scholars were faced with starvation, the community of Safed having to issue an appeal on their behalf; and this makes it seem probable that outside interest had been withdrawn and the concession allowed to expire. In the second half of the seventeenth century, Tiberias again lapsed into a state of utter desolation and for many years no Jew lived there.[25] But the tradition of practical colonizing work remained alive, and in 1740 Rabbi Hayim Abulaffia of Smyrna settled there with a number of other Jews, at the invitation of the governor of Galilee. They threw themselves enthusiastically into the work of colonization, rebuilt the city, acquired rural holdings in the neighborhood, planted vineyards and olive-orchards and, notwithstanding the perils through which they passed, renewed in some measure the atmosphere of the autonomous Jewish settlement. Later on, they were reinforced by a number of pietists belonging to the new hasidic school from Eastern Europe, and Tiberias became one of the Four "Holy Cities" of Palestine (together with Jerusalem, Safed and Hebron), where the Law was studied continuously, and for which charitable oblations were sought from the faithful throughout the world.[26]

The ancient record was forgotten by now; and it was only in a much later day, when practical work began for the regeneration of Jewish life in Palestine on a sound economic and political basis, that attention has come to be devoted once again to the farsighted but ill-sustained experiments of Don Joseph Nasi, Duke of Naxos.

Additional Note to Chapter V

Up to a short while ago, the Tiberias episode was known to historians only from a brief account in the sixteenth-century Hebrew chronicle, Joseph ha-Cohen's *Emek ha-Bakha* or "Vale of Tears," which is still our primary source. It is desirable to cite the passage in full:

Then Don Joseph Nasi came to Ferrara, among those who escaped from the iron cauldron, Portugal, and lived there for some time. Thence he went to Turkey, where he found grace in the eyes of the King Suleiman, who loved him greatly. And the king gave him the ruins of Tiberias and of seven country townships round about it, and made him lord and prince over them at that time. And Don Joseph sent thither R. Joseph Adret [Ibn Ardut], his attendant, to rebuild the walls of the city, and he went and he too found favor in the king's eyes, and he gave him sixty *aspri* each day. And the king sent with him eight men born in his house, and gave him the order written and sealed with the imperial seal, and recommended him to the pasha of Damascus and the pasha of Safut, saying: "All that this man desires of you shall ye do."

The law was given in the king's name, saying: "All builders and porters who are in those cities shall go to build Tiberias; and he who does not go shall bear his sin." There was there much stone, for Tiberias had been a great city before the Lord, before the hewer went up against them, and there were twelve synagogues there in the days of R. Ammi and R. Asi [of the period of the Talmud]. And he commanded the inhabitants of these seven townships to make mortar to do the work, and more also; and there was there moreover much sand, for the Lake of Tiberias was near to them. But the Arabs were jealous of them; and a certain sherif who was advanced in years arose and called in the ears of the inhabitants of that land, saying: "Do not permit this city to be built, for it will be bitter for you in the end; for I have assuredly found it written in an ancient book, that when the city that is called Tiberias is built, our faith will be lost, and we will be found wanting." And they harkened unto his voice, and they were unwilling to go to rebuild the walls. "At that time, an end was made to the building of the walls" of Tiberias, and R. Joseph ben Adret was very sad, and he went to the pasha of Damascus and called before him: "Ho! my Lord! for the inhabitants of the country towns refuse to do the king's bidding." Then the pasha was afraid, and he hastened to send thither, and they took two of the heads of those peoples, and brought them down in blood to Sheol, so that those who remained might see and not act presumptuously furthermore. So they returned and hastened to make the walls of the city, and they found there a great stone, and under it was a ladder going down into the earth, and there was a great High Place filled with marble images and altars like unto the High Places of the uncircumcised; and the four servants of Don Joseph, which the king's son had given him, of those who had been captured in the Gelibite wars, broke them, and filled up that place with dust. They also found three bells at that time, which the uncircumcised had hidden away at the time of Guido, the last Christian king who reigned in that land, at the time when the hewer came up against them; and they made thereof battering-rams.

Now the city of Tiberias which they built was one thousand and five hundred cubits in compass. And the work ended in the month of Kislev, in the 5325th year. And Don Joseph greatly rejoiced, and gave thanks unto God.

And Don Joseph ordered and they planted many mulberry trees to feed the silk-worms; and he ordered wool to be brought from Spain to make cloth, like the cloth which they make in Venice; for the man Joseph was very great, and his report was in all the earth.

CHAPTER VI

King Aspirant of Cyprus

ON the night of September 13, 1569, Venice was shaken by a terrific explosion. It was obvious to the startled inhabitants, even before they thronged out from their houses, where the disaster had taken place. The famous Arsenal facing the Lagoon, the oldest and as yet indubitably the greatest in the world, was overhung by a pall of black smoke, and the sky was red with the flames of the conflagration that had broken out. Treachery was of course suspected. The gentry hastily took up arms, and great crowds gathered in the Piazza of S. Marco. When day broke, however, it became apparent that the first alarms had been exaggerated. The great powder-magazine at the Arsenal had been blown up — why and how was never discovered — and in consequence a great fire had broken out, which destroyed four galleys; but the damage was in fact limited. Nevertheless, highly-colored reports became current throughout Europe. It was generally believed that the entire fleet was annihilated, the disaster being on so vast a scale that Venice now lay powerless at the feet of her enemies.

In Constantinople, the news was received first of all by Don Joseph, the Duke of Naxos, from his faithful correspondents in Venice.[1] Later on, indeed, the rumor gathered force, and it was actually alleged that his agents

138

had been responsible for the catastrophe. That was, of course, ridiculous. Nevertheless, the information he received, which he immediately communicated to the sultan, made it possible for him to weigh down the scales decisively at a crucial turn in Venetian history.

We have seen that there were at this time two distinct tendencies in foreign affairs at the Sublime Porte. The Grand Vizier Sokolli Pasha had carried on Suleiman the Magnificent's European policy. For him, Turkey's ultimate enemy was the House of Habsburg, in Germany and in Spain; and it was for this reason that he championed the French alliance so fervently. He was supported by the generals who looked forward to the glory and booty which might accrue to them in further land campaigns. The recent revolt of the Moriscos in Spain, who appealed to their fellow believers throughout the Mediterranean for support, strengthened his position, for it seemed that this was a heaven-sent opportunity to strike. On the other side stood those who pinned their faith in sea power, who were somewhat dubious of the efficacy of the French alliance and who thought it more important to secure the flank before pitting the Turkish might against that of Spain. The Venetian empire was visibly past its prime, and the conquest of her possessions in the Aegean and Eastern Mediterranean — above all, the island of Cyprus, ingeniously acquired not long since by "inheritance" from the republic's adopted daughter — was essential in their opinion for the security and consolidation of the Turkish empire. Only after this was completed would it be wise in their opinion to make the decisive onslaught against a major opponent; and for this purpose a more reliable ally than France would be

needed. (These were the circumstances that prevailed,
as a matter of fact, a score of years later, Marrano statesmen in Western and Eastern Europe being partly instrumental.)²

This anti-Venetian policy, holding out the prospect of
facile expansion of territory, was highly congenial to the
sultan; it received the powerful support of Piale Pasha,
the admiral of the Turkish fleet; and of his brother, Lala
Mustafa, the general. The two parties were thus not
unevenly balanced, and the attitude of the Duke of
Naxos became extremely important. Knowing Spain as
he did, he counselled wariness as regards that power.
On the other hand, the recollection of the treatment he
and his family had received from the Venetians still
rankled; he was uncomfortably conscious that they resented his installation in the Cyclades; and he hated
their French allies too, who had attempted to defraud
him. Nor perhaps was there absent from his mind a
lingering reluctance to see the land of his residence, which
had treated him and his people so well, at war with that
of his birth, even though the latter had treated them so
ill; for patriotism is not a logical sentiment, to be modi-
fied or suspended in the light of pure reason.

Besides the reasons for Don Joseph's policy that have
already been indicated, there was another, more personal
and more ambitious. He had already been Duke of Naxos
now for the past four years, but the title lacked sub-
stance. If the war against Venice were successful, might
he not hope for a higher dignity still? Selim had as yet
refused him nothing; and he would then have a more
important fief in his power to bestow. The story went
that, on one occasion, on hearing that the excellent wine

he was drinking came from Cyprus, he threw his arms round the Jewish favorite who had provided it and vowed to make him ruler of the island if it ever lay in his power to do so. Thereafter, the tale continues, Don Joseph never forgot to ply him with similar vintages and to remind him of his promise. The monarch did not change his opinion. "If my desires are accomplished," he was once overheard to say, "you will be King of Cyprus."

This story, though so generally repeated by waspish historians, has all the appearance of a fable. Obviously, there were more serious arguments that Don Joseph might have used, and doubtless did — that the island was the key to the control of the Eastern Mediterranean, and important as a station for the Moslem pilgrims on their way to Mecca. Some of the chroniclers say that he had originally favored an attack on Spain in support of the Moriscos, but was converted by bribes to an anti-Venetian policy. Others add the embellishment that he was alienated by the fact that, when on Selim's accession the Signory had sent an embassy to confirm the peace-treaty, he was pointedly omitted from the number of those dignitaries to whom the conventional gifts were distributed. It was natural enough, for the Venetian government had declared him an outlaw not so long before. But, if this were indeed the cause for his change of policy, the Venetians were to pay heavily for their misplaced economy.

Already, in the previous October, before war broke out, the French ambassador, Grandchamp, was informed by his secret agent, the treacherous Jewish physician Daout (and in turn faithfully reported to Paris) that he had acted as interpreter in conversations between the sultan and the Duke over the question of the latter's elevation to the dignity of king, or at least perpetual governor, of the island, though (he added) the latter counted without his host. Henceforth the rumors became increasingly plausible and the amount of the yearly tribute that he had promised — 200,000 or 250,000 ducats — was specified. Some persons claimed that they had actually heard Selim, anticipating events, hail his Jewish companion as king.[3] It was said that he had made all possible preparations for assuming the royal dignity; that he had his crown manufactured in readiness for the great occasion; and that in his palace he kept a standard embroidered with the arms of the island and the legend in gold, "Joseph Nasi, King of Cyprus."

Was this mere ambition? Perhaps so; yet it half seems as though in his feverish, restless brain there was germinating a curious anticipation of the "territorial" idea as the solution to the Jewish problem; much the same solution as was evolved three centuries later by Theodor Herzl, before he centered his ideas on Palestine, though on an absolutist rather than a democratic basis. The ineffective Ancona boycott in 1556-7, under the auspices of the House of Nasi,[4] had made it clear that Jewish solidarity in the Diaspora was a chimera, and that it was impossible to rely on economic force to secure the amelioration of the Jewish position. A focal point was necessary, with a modicum of territorial independence. At one time the possibility vaguely offered itself that this might be attained in the environs of Tiberias. It had by now become manifest, it seems, that the Turks would not permit anything in the nature of Jewish independence in Palestine, of all places, and the movement became essentially one for relief and colonization. The duchy of

Naxos, too, may perhaps have been expected at one time
to provide a potential political fulcrum. Few Jews, however, were attracted thither; and the island's fervid
Christianity, its ineluctable political contacts, its constant need of military protection, its tradition of subservi-
ence, rendered any such development to the advantage
of Jews impossible, if indeed it was seriously considered.
Cyprus, on the other hand, might provide unique opportunities: political as well as geographical isolation, a more
absolute title, economic self-sufficiency, the possibility
of founding a new tradition, royal rank, and above all
such contiguity to Palestine that it might be regarded
almost as a stepping-stone on the way thither. There
should be no misunderstanding about what has been said
in the foregoing few lines. No inkling of this was stated
at the time. It is questionable whether anything of the
sort was ever formulated in Don Joseph's luxuriant
imagination. But it was the logical sequel to his reported
request to Venice years before for an island of refuge for
his brethren, as well as to his later somewhat nebulous
plans to constitute a self-sufficient Jewish center in Palestine. His mind seems to have been working subcon-
sciously in this direction, though he may not have realized
it.

That the name of a Jewish ruler should have been
associated with the island was indeed a curious irony
of history. It had probably been one of the oldest Jewish
settlements of the Diaspora, Jews being numerous there
long before the destruction of Jerusalem by Titus. In 116,
goaded by Roman maltreatment, they rose in revolt.
For a time, they seized complete control and (it was
alleged) perpetrated a great slaughter of their enemies,

But, after a strenuous resistance, the rising was put
down, with appalling bloodshed. The Jewish community was entirely extirpated and it was enacted that no
Jew was thereafter to be allowed to set foot on Cyprian
soil, even those driven ashore by adverse winds being put
to death. They began, indeed, to infiltrate again after an
interval, and more than one traveller has left an account
of the communities he found there during the period of
Byzantine, Latin and Venetian rule. After the fifteenth
century, we know little of them, and it seems that at this
period the island had only a scanty Jewish population.[5]
Was it now to receive a Jewish sovereign?

Reports of the sort had been circulating more and
more insistently of late. In 1568, Don Joseph was suspected of attempting to foment a rebellion in Cyprus
in favor of the Turks,[6] and the Venetian *bailo* in Constantinople reported at this time that he had all but
succeeded in procuring a declaration of war on Venice,
though Sokolli had momentarily triumphed. The Duke's
setback at the hands of the French representatives, in
the autumn of 1569, over the question of the embargo
at Alexandria, when his fall appeared imminent, seemed
to have averted the danger definitely. It was just at this
stage that the news of the disaster at the Arsenal reached
him. He did not fail to make full use of it. If (as was
generally believed) Venetian naval power was crippled
by what had taken place, this was obviously the moment
to strike. According to report, moreover, he emphasized
the point by bringing to the sultan for his inspection a
loaf of the coarse bread, made of millet-flour, to which
the Venetians were now reduced, of course sent to him
by his faithful coreligionists in Italy.[7]

His information clearly made a profound impression, and it was generally believed that this decided the day. The historians of the period — moderns as well as contemporaries — all concur, at all events, in ascribing the primary responsibility for the declaration of war on the Duke of Naxos, the sultan's Jewish favorite; one of the latter, Pietro Bizaro, even goes so far as to give the text of a long speech of his (obviously a rhetorical fiction, in the fashion of the time) which he says turned the tide in the imperial Divan. The Mufti Abu Saud gave his blessing to the project, on the plea that by the Turkish occupation of Egypt the sultan had become Suzerain of Cyprus, which had formerly paid an annual tribute to the ruler of that country, and that the island had been subject to Islam in the remote past, when it was occupied by the Saracens; and he intimated that he was prepared to issue an official pronouncement (*fetva*) approving of the enterprise and thus converting it in effect into a Holy War. Don Joseph was now confident of the outcome. "I am informed from various quarters," the Venetian *bailo* had reported to his government on November 23, 1569, "that Don Joseph Nasi is saying that this Signior is now going to carry out the enterprise of Cyprus, with such assurance as though it were already decided."

In the spring of 1570, the sultan presented an ultimatum to the Venetian government, demanding the surrender of the coveted dependency; and in May, a fleet under Piale Pasha's command, with 50,000 men on board, passed through the Dardanelles, bound southwards. The indignities that Doña Gracia Nasi and her daughter, now the Duchess of Naxos, had suffered at the hands of the Serenissima, nearly twenty years before, were it seemed to be avenged. The contemporary English dramatist, Christopher Marlowe, puts words which are very apt in the mouth of Barabas, his Jew of Malta, who has been imagined to be modelled on a distant caricature-impression of Joseph Nasi:

> I must confess we come not to be kings.
> That's not our fault; alas, our number's few!
> And crowns come either by succession,
> Or urged by force . . . .

Force was to be urged, for once, for the advantage and at the solicitation of a Jew.

As we have seen, on the outbreak of the war the duchy of Naxos was attacked by the Venetians. Notwithstanding a defense apparently directed in the early stages by Don Joseph himself, it was overrun without much difficulty, the authority of Duke Giacomo Crispi IV being temporarily restored. To compensate Nasi for this loss and for the material damage he suffered as a result of the military operations, another semi-independent fief was now considered for him. Wallachia, or Muntenia, a border province between Turkey and Poland, had like all this area been in the occupation of the Turks since the early part of the century, though it was valued by them mainly as a source of revenue and a transit route for their periodical expeditions against Transylvania and Hungary. It was ruled over (like Moldavia) by a voivode, nominally independent but in fact utterly subject to Constantinople, who generally acquired his dignity by payment — the incumbent of the office therefore changing with an indecent rapidity.

It was at this time ruled by Alexander, son of Mircea

"the Shepherd," a recent and insecurely-established nominee. Why should not Joseph, already a territorial ruler,
displace him, as he in turn had displaced his predecessor
so short a while before, transferring his rule thus from
the Islands to the *terra ferma*? He lost no opportunity of
pressing his suit on the sultan, informing him — certainly
without any minimization — of the extent of the losses
he had suffered in the Archipelago, and soliciting from
him the investiture of this less exposed fief. Selim proved
as amenable as usual and issued instructions to Mehemet
Pasha to this effect. Naturally, the grand vizier raised
objections: doubtless he had his own plans for the government of this lucrative appanage, quite apart from his
personal rivalry with Nasi. But he too was venal. Nasi
attempted to overcome his opposition with promises and
gifts — in the end, it may be, with success.

If so, his tenure of this office did not make any
impression. The voivodes, all interested only in self-
betterment, did not enjoy much standing in Constantinople; the province was itself still wild and lawless, the
state of the country primitive, the people mainly shep-
herds, and the houses (such as they were) built of clay
and wattle, without a single city worthy of the name
except the capital, Tîrgovistea. Nothing could have been
less like the delectable island-duchy of Naxos; and it
seems that Don Joseph was interested in this new appanage of his — as he was intended to be — only for the
sake of the financial compensation that could be derived
from it. He did not even visit the province, so far as is
known. To be sure, the negative character of his administration had its favorable side as well; for no abuses were
associated with his name as they were with that of his

immediate successors, who introduced the janissaries to the country and farmed out their possessions to the Turkish supporters who were necessary to maintain their rule. He, on the other hand, has left no trace whatsoever on local annals, and his connection was entirely forgotten until very recently.[8] But for the student of history it is an ironical consideration that the voivode of Wallachia was the lineal precursor of the later rulers of the kingdom of Roumania, which came into being in the nineteenth century by a union of the two so-called Danubian Provinces.

Yet on the other hand, the outbreak of hostilities could not fail to affect Don Joseph's standing in the Christian states, especially in those places where Spanish and Venetian influence was strong. So far was this true that in Ragusa, where he and Doña Gracia had formerly enjoyed such exceptional consideration, one of his relatives was actually arrested at this time on some charge (whether it was political or religious is not stated), put on trial and in the end executed. This threw the Duke, never likely to be passive under attack, into a towering passion, and he did his best to avenge himself. He roundly accused the Ragusans of working against Turkish interests, saying that they exported provisions from Alexandria in their ships and carried them to the island of Candia, the most important Venetian naval base, thus giving important help to the enemy: a charge which even Mehemet Pasha could not take lightly.[9] Already in the summer of 1570 one of Nasi's personal agents had been arrested, while he was on his way through Venice with correspondence from him, on suspicion of treason and stirring up disaffection.[10]

It was on July 1, 1570, that the Turkish troops under the command of Lala Mustafa began to disembark in

Cyprus. On August 8, Nicosia, the capital, was captured, after a siege of forty-five days, 20,000 of its inhabitants being put to the sword. In Famagusta, the Venetian governor, Marcantonio Bragadin, led a desperate resistance and the city did not capitulate until nearly a year later. The articles of surrender were shamefully violated by the victors, the governor being put to death with cruel torments and his skin, stuffed with straw, sent as a trophy to Constantinople. (It is hardly necessary to add that the Jews were alleged to have been instrumental in this; if the charge is true, the reason obviously is that in the Byzantine world they were compelled, among their other humiliations, to act as public executioners.) The whole of the island was before long under Turkish control.

But this act of aggression had brought about the conclusion of an alliance against Turkey between the Pope, Venice, and Spain, mutual jealousies being for the moment laid aside. Almost on the day of Bragadin's murder, Don John of Austria (Charles V's brilliant bastard) had received the admiral's flag from the papal legate at Naples, as commander of the united fleets of the League and the associated states. Two months later, they sighted the Turkish galleys under Ali Pasha lying at anchor in the Gulf of Lepanto. On October 7, the two fleets engaged. It was the greatest naval battle since Roman times. After a ferocious struggle — in which the reinstated Latin duke of Naxos took an honorable part — the allied powers gained a victory more complete and brilliant than had ever before fallen to the Christian forces in the centuries-long struggle against the Crescent. Nearly fifty of the Turkish ships were burned or sunk. The number of their dead amounted to 8,000, of the prisoners to nearly as many; and — outstanding glory! — upwards of 10,000 Christian galley-slaves were released. The victory would have been utterly overwhelming had not the Turkish corsair Ochiali (Uluj-Ali) Pasha, with whom the king of Spain was in private negotiation, been allowed to escape with his forty galleys. The Christian losses in dead and wounded were also heavy; among the latter was a certain Miguel de Cervantes, whose left arm was maimed and who in consequence was compelled in the end to embrace the career of letters.

The news of the great victory was greeted throughout Christendom with a delirium of delight. In Constantinople, there was utter consternation. The policy advocated in vain by Mehemet Sokolli, the grand vizier, appeared to be tragically vindicated. He had desired to measure forces with Spain before settling up with Venice. His advice had been neglected and Venice wantonly attacked — with the result that Spain had been drawn into the conflict and Turkey had received from the coalition, for whose creation she herself was responsible, the most serious defeat in her history. Notwithstanding the success of the Cyprus expedition itself, those who had advocated it were discredited by the sequel. The obvious course to follow was to attempt to break up the Triple Alliance, which in turn was possible only by restoring friendly relations with Venice. This Sokolli now set himself to do.

Fortunately, he was a man of sober, balanced character, and his profound personal antagonism to the most prominent Jew of the day did not make him indiscriminately anti-Jewish, as is so often the case in similar circumstances. Indeed, he was in extremely close relationship with one Jew in particular, whose star rose just as that of Don Joseph Nasi was obscured. The two men were poles apart in character: the one brilliant, volatile, dazzling; the other modest, solid, retiring, but perhaps in the long run the more influential. Solomon, the son of Nathan Ashkenazi (i. e., "the German": often called therefore in Italian accounts *Tedesco*) was born about 1520 at Udine in north Italy, almost on the Austrian frontier, being apparently a member of the same Basevi family from which Benjamin Disraeli was descended on his mother's side.[11] He adopted the career of medicine, probably graduating, like so many other Jews, at the famous medical school of Padua — virtually the only one in Europe to which they were admitted at this time. While still a young man, he went to Cracow, perhaps in the train of Bona of Savoy, wife of King Sigismund Augustus, whose body-physician he became. In 1564, he settled in Constantinople.

As a Venetian subject by birth, speaking Italian, and with relatives still living under Venetian rule, he was naturally in touch with the Venetian colony and was friendly with successive Venetian representatives. Marcantonio Barbaro, who was serving in this capacity at the time of the outbreak of the war, thought very highly of him professionally. When hostilities began and the *bailo* was placed under house-arrest, Mehemet Sokolli (who made no secret of his sentiments) permitted Ashkenazi to visit him. It happened that just at this time the bailo's dragoman died. Hence he began to use Ashkenazi as the medium of his communications with the vizier. The latter, who had not known him intimately before, came to entertain the highest opinion of his integrity, his good sense and his professional ability, and took him into his employment as medical attendant on his wife, the sultan's daughter, in whose train he went to Adrianople. Thus he became the secret go-between the *bailo* and the vizier, who was all along working privily against the foreign policy of which he was the official mouthpiece.

What was going on could not be kept secret. On one occasion, Ashkenazi was aroused from his sleep at dead of night and escorted to the imperial palace, trembling for his life. Here, in the ante-chamber of the Grand Signior (who was attentively listening from his own apartment) Cicala Bey roughly questioned him and asked what business brought him to the city. It is not recorded whether he had recourse to prevarication or mere diplomacy, but he escaped unscathed. Thus, while on the one hand Joseph Nasi was exerting his influence in favor of uncompromising hostility towards Venice and the vigorous prosecution of the war, the services of his coreligionist were being utilized to bring about a rapprochement with the Most Serene Republic.[12]

It did not in fact prove difficult to break up the Triple Alliance. The process was spontaneously assisted by the highhanded, not to say fraudulent, action of the Spaniards after Lepanto, when (it is said) the booty allotted to each Spanish man-at-arms exceeded that received by the Venetian admiral. The Turkish armed strength had made an amazing recovery after the recent disaster, and the fleet was once more cruising the Mediterranean. Meanwhile, a commercial crisis had set in at Venice, paralyzing trade and encouraging the peace party and Francophils there, who were convinced that the republic could expect no further aid from her nominal allies and, on the other hand, was quite incapable of continuing hostilities alone.

The Council of Ten now officially authorized Barbaro to enter into peace negotiations with the grand vizier, either directly or through the medium of the newly-arrived French ambassador to Turkey, the bishop of Acqs, a notorious Hispanophobe, who had acted as mediator for the original pourparlers. As it happened, Sokolli was absent from Constantinople when the *bailo* received his instructions, and in consequence the preliminary conversations were carried on through Hurrem Bey, the principal interpreter of the Sublime Porte, on the one hand, and the Jewish physician Solomon Ashkenazi on the other. Later on, they were taken up by the two principals. It was some time before agreement could be reached. When the question of raising the embargo on Venetian goods in Turkey was broached, Nasi urged Selim to refuse, saying that it was beneath the dignity of so great an emperor to take the first step. In spite of his opposition, all outstanding difficulties were settled and at last, on March 7, 1573, the treaty was signed.

It may be said that, while Turkey had lost the most important engagement of the war, she won the peace; for Venice, besides paying a large indemnity and making various miscellaneous concessions, ceded the island of Cyprus, which was henceforth a Turkish possession. Thus, the sultan attained the original object of the war and could go down to history, like his father, as one who had added fresh territories to the Ottoman state.

Indeed, in view of the process by which final triumph had been achieved, and of the grave danger that the

Turkish empire had run in the process, the original war
party was discredited. It could claim little glory in the
conquest or share in the spoils of victory. If it were true
that the sultan had promised Joseph Nasi the crown of
Cyprus when he had acquired it, the manner of its acqui-
sition put the project beyond the bounds of practical
politics. Sokolli certainly made it plain to his imperial
father-in-law — if indeed it were now necessary for him
to do so — that the fulfillment of his romantic promise to
his favorite would be unwelcome both to his Moslem
subjects and to the Christian world, who could not tolerate the idea of a Jewish sovereign. It was doubtless true;
yet he would not perhaps have insisted on it so warmly
but for his personal enmity — and for the fact that he was
himself granted the revenues of the new Ottoman possession.

This finally disposed of Joseph Nasi's naive hopes.
The sultan indeed invited five hundred Jews to settle in
Cyprus, to help in consolidating Turkish rule there.[13]
But if the Duke regarded this as a preliminary to putting
the island under his administration, he was disappointed.
Cyprus was never to be his; and, as a matter of fact, from
classical times down to the setting up there of deportation
camps in our own day for the refugees debarred from
Palestine, the name has never entered into Jewish history
except in a baneful sense.

As for Nasi, the day when the news of Lepanto arrived
in Constantinople marked the beginning of his decline.
Henceforth, his advocacy of self-sufficiency for Turkey,
which implied the abandonment of the French entangle-
ment and reliance rather on the northern powers, could
easily be misinterpreted as a pro-Spanish policy; and the

grand vizier took every possible advantage of this fact. In his conversations with the French ambassador, the latter spoke of the corrupt influence exercised at Constantinople by the king of Spain through the medium of certain persons prominent in political life, and stated roundly that the Duke of Naxos was acting as principal intermediary. He undertook that, if he were provided with convincing proof of this, he would be able to render his rival completely powerless and precipitate his ruin. The envoy in his despatches home did not fail to refer to this and asked for information which could help to bring to pass that consummation so devoutly hoped for by the French Court.[14] The details were not forthcoming, for the machinations were imaginary. Nevertheless, it is obvious that Nasi was now beset by a very powerful coalition and had to fight hard to maintain himself. The Venetian envoy, reporting home in 1573, spoke of the mortal enmity between the grand vizier and the Jewish favorite and told how the latter was able to maintain himself only as the result of the support of some of the principal courtiers whom he placated with gifts.

The conflict was not confined to the realm of politics. Though Nasi's financial concessions were unaffected by his setback, it was a question henceforth of preserving what he had rather than expanding into fresh fields. It was symptomatic that in this same year Sokolli succeeded in making his Greek rival, Michael Cantacuzenos, inspector general of taxes, in addition to the other lucrative appointments that he enjoyed. The latter showed no vestige of moderation in his activities, behaving almost like an independent potentate and arbitrarily making or removing ecclesiastical dignitaries, so that his fellow-

Greeks led the outcry against him. Nevertheless, from 1570 onwards he outdistanced Nasi completely in the financial sphere. The latter's economic as well as his political influence thus suffered a partial eclipse.

In fact, far from helping his coreligionists, his advocacy of the war of Cyprus nearly proved catastrophic to those who lived under Venetian rule. On the outbreak of hostilities, all Turkish subjects in Venice had been thrown into prison and stripped of all they possessed. (It is said that, on being advised to follow this example, the sultan replied that, however Christianly his enemies behaved, he would act in accordance with religion and justice.) It was the Levantine merchant-colony living in the Ghetto Vecchio who had especially suffered, Nasi's agent in Poland, Abraham Mosso, trying in vain to secure the liberation of some of them for whom he could personally vouch. Throughout the war, the local Jews had been suspected of favoring the enemy and had suffered accordingly — notwithstanding the fact that the fashionable physician and lexicographer, David de' Pomi, presented the doge with a memoir in which he ingeniously proved that the glorious victory of Lepanto was predicted in the Bible.

The news of that engagement had reached Venice in record time, after only ten days, on a swift galley laden with captured banners. The city was delirious with excitement. On December 14, the senate passed a solemn decree with reference to the recent happenings. It was desirable, they said, to make manifest the gratitude they felt towards the Almighty for the great victory He had accorded them; and they accordingly decreed that, on the expiration of the present agreement with them (*con-*

dotta) two years later, all Jews of whatever sex, condition or grade should leave the city, never to return. Such a measure had been contemplated ever since the outbreak of war, and there was no secret as to its reason. If the war was Joseph Nasi's revenge upon the republic, the expulsion of his coreligionists was the republic's revenge upon Joseph Nasi.

For a year and a half the Jews lay under sentence. But on July 7, 1573, when only a few months were left before the fatal day, the senate met and revoked the edict. It was stated that the reason for this was the difficulty in making other arrangements for loan-banks for the benefit of the poor, the Jews now undertaking, moreover, to reduce the rate of interest, already unremunerative, which they charged. But considerations of high policy also were involved. As the envoy who brought home the long-desired news of the conclusion of peace arrived in Venice (it is reported), his ship passed a convoy of dispirited Jewish exiles about to set sail for the Levant. When he saw the doge, he made it his business to expostulate with him; these new arrivals would assuredly strengthen the power of the Turkish empire, he pointed out, as those from Spain had done before them. Moreover, the Jews were still powerful at the Sublime Porte, and it would be folly to alienate this powerful section of the population of the Turkish empire precisely when an attempt was being made to re-establish good relations. It may well be that Solomon Ashkenazi and perhaps (even at this stage) Don Joseph himself had been active behind the scenes in Constantinople, and that Mehemet Sokolli had dropped a hint that what was proposed, involving Turkish subjects too, could hardly be regarded as a friendly act. Whatever the reason, the edict of expulsion was repealed; and in the course of the following generation Venetian Jewry was to attain the acme of its fame.

A year later, almost to the day, the wheel of fortune turned full circle. The grand vizier had promised the *bailo* Barbaro, in the course of the peace negotiations, that he would help the republic to obtain some compensation for the loss of Cyprus. Not long after, he instructed Solomon Ashkenazi to wait upon him together with the interpreter of the Sublime Porte and to propose a Turco-Venetian military alliance. If this were concluded, the sultan would aid the *Serenissima Dominante* to conquer the kingdom of Naples from Spain and add it to her own dominions, thus becoming the foremost power in Italy. Here was Jewish participation in something beyond even Joseph Nasi's dreams — the swaying of the Turkish power, not to wipe out personal grievance or to avenge a score of martyrs, but to inflict mortal injury on the great anti-Jewish power of the time and to plant a more tolerant rule in wide areas from which the Jews had ruthlessly been expelled a generation before. Such considerations must have added zest to Ashkenazi's errand, and perhaps eloquence to his tongue. But, for Venice, in her hour of decadence, the project was over-venturesome, and the Council of Ten declined to entertain the plan.

Still, the grand vizier did not abandon his project and sent Ashkenazi to Venice in the following year, 1574, to lay the proposal for an alliance before the Signory — a task for which his knowledge of Italian and of local circumstances gave him special qualifications.[15] He came with an authorization from the grand vizier only, for his mission was not altogether official, and a Jew was not perhaps the ideal ambassador at such a time and in such a place. Barbaro, in his despatches from Constantinople, had, nevertheless, recommended him in most cordial terms as "a man of high ability, and in my opinion well disposed towards you," and emphasizing how his coming would be useful to the Venetian republic, who could not easily acquire such valuable friends as this. Hence the Council of Ten proposed that he should be recognized and treated as though he were an ambassador from the sultan himself. Objections were raised, and long discussions ensued. But the path of tolerance and that of policy for once coincided, and it was decided to extend all the conventional honors to the envoy, notwithstanding his faith.

On July 7, 1574, Ashkenazi appeared officially before the doge and the dignitaries of state, with all the pomp that the diplomatic protocol required. The delight of the Jews knew no bounds. Prayers were offered up for him in the Levantine synagogue, almost as though he were a reigning prince. In the colophon to one of Rabbi Joseph Caro's new works published at Venice at the time, the episode is proudly mentioned as something of utterly exceptional moment:

I shall return thanks to the blessed God, Who has permitted me to complete this important book, *Yoreh Deah*, today, Tammuz 10, 5334, at the time that there was here the Lord and Prince, the expert physician, Solomon son of Nathan Ashkenazi of Udine, an envoy sent from Constantinople the capital by the great King Sultan Selim (may his might increase!) to the honorable government of Venice [and] to the Doge (may his might increase!). Our own eyes have seen what our fathers have known not since the day that Judah separated from Ephraim, the veritude of the glory and honor done to him by the princes here among us. Such has never been done to any Jew since the destruction of our Holy Temple.[16]

But the ambassador's eloquence was wasted. After four weeks of deliberation, the Signory decided to instruct him to thank the sultan for his friendly offer, but to inform him that they could not then undertake a new war and wished to remain at peace with Spain just as they intended to with the sultan. Ashkenazi took his leave, receiving every conventional token of esteem. During the following decade, there was hardly any figure in Turkish public life who was spoken of by successive Venetian representatives with more cordiality than "Rabbi Solomon," upon whom they relied at all times to use his influence on behalf of the Most Serene Republic.

Much was said, in the sixteenth century as in the twentieth, about Jewish solidarity and the manner in which prominent Jews attempted to forward one another's interests, regardless of any other consideration. Nothing can disprove this hoary fable more conspicuously than the fact that it was the Jewish physician, Solomon ben Nathan Ashkenazi, more than almost any other person besides the grand vizier, who was responsible for the loss to Joseph Nasi of the Crown of Cyprus.

CHAPTER VII

The Master of Belvedere

FROM the terraces of his villa of Belvedere, near Galata, one of the world's most memorable views opened itself daily before Don Joseph's eyes. Beneath him the Bosphorus, streaked with every variant shade of blue, carried the waters of the Mediterranean into the Sea of Marmora. The hills on either side were crowned with clusters of cypresses half concealing secluded villas, with walls painted white, pink or blue. Here and there, the minarets of mosques jutted skywards, from which the muezzin summoned the faithful to prayer thrice every day. The Asiatic side seemed sometimes incredibly near in that limpid air. Below him he could see passing a constant procession of white-sailed ships, bearing the commerce of Europe and Asia, while war-galleys manned by Christian slaves lay inshore. Thousands of screaming seagulls wheeled and turned above the masts.

It was from this residence, which he did not hesitate to term a palace, that Don Joseph exercised his influence. For an entire generation, he was without question the most prominent and most powerful Jew in the world. "He is the head of all his nation," reported the Venetian ambassador, Andrea Badoardo, in 1573; and there was nothing of exaggeration in this. Throughout the Ottoman empire, especially, he was regarded with obsequious deference. Rabbinic documents referred to him with the formula reserved normally for reigning monarchs — "May his glory increase!" In Christian Italy, as in Egypt and the other Moslem lands, his authority was little less, and he seemed to be the visible sign that the glory had not entirely departed from Judah and might soon return. There can be no doubt that among the Marranos of Spain and Portugal he, like Doña Gracia his aunt before him, became a legend even in his lifetime. A contemporary scholar, not of the sycophantic type, spoke of him not altogether exaggeratedly as being comparable in Jewish history only with Joseph the Patriarch, viceroy of Egypt, and Mordecai the Benjaminite, administrator of Persia.[1]

So long as Doña Gracia lived, he acted as her representative, and played a great role in the eyes of his coreligionists if only by virtue of this fact. But it was not a reflected glory alone. It is obvious that his position at Court, his intimacy with the Grand Vizier Rustam Pasha, and above all the favor he enjoyed with Selim, had been supremely useful when the intervention of the Sultan Suleiman was solicited on behalf of the Marranos at Ancona; and we have already seen how he represented his aunt during the organization of the boycott of the guilty port.[2] Later on, in her declining years and after her death, he worked in a similar sense independently. For his coreligionists living under Ottoman rule, he was a veritable providence. It is impossible to recover all the details; but after his death men spoke gratefully of the magnificent services rendered by him and his brother at all times of trouble and distress, and of the liberality they displayed whenever it was necessary.[3] Rabbis, scholars, collectors, mendicants, emissaries, came in and out of the mansion in an unending stream, deferentially standing aside from time to time as a *chaus* from the Seraglio arrived with a special message from the sultan or one of the ministers of state. We know, too, how non-Jewish notables, from the Greek patriarch and imperial ambassador downwards, came to visit him from time to time; and to the European colony in Constantinople, that remarkable household, with its memories of Lisbon, Brussels, Paris, Venice and Ferrara, must have seemed, notwithstanding its master's creed, a veritable oasis of occidental civilization.

His personal entourage was a remarkable one, recruited from all parts of the world and not confined to persons of Jewish stock. At this time of religious ferment, there were many persons throughout Europe, who, their interest in the Bible having been aroused by the process of the Reformation, carried it to the extreme conclusion and embraced Judaism, generally escaping for the purpose to some Moslem land. The tale was told, for example, of a certain Frenchman of noble family, named Roueries (?), who possessed considerable estates near Lyons, including no fewer than three châteaux. Deeply interested in religion, he proceeded by way of Calvinism to Judaism, becoming convinced of its superiority over other faiths. In conversation with the Marrano merchants of Lyons, he rated them soundly for continuing their life of subterfuge, and in the end went with his two sons to Venice, where they all adopted the Jewish faith. The whole of his fortune, to the amount of 30,000 ducats, he left in France, in the hands of New Christian acquaintances, to be sent after him. But he had chosen badly, for his agents swindled him out of the entire sum. Ultimately he arrived almost penniless at Constantinople, where the French trading colony jeered at him for abandoning all he possessed and throwing in his lot with a people who had defrauded him in this shameful fashion. "I did not come to seek the Hebrews, but the God of the Hebrews and the Hebrew way of life," he is reported to have answered. A man of this type clearly had spiritual affinities with the patrician ex-Marrano, who throughout his life had been engaged in assisting those who desired to come to shelter beneath the wings of the *Shechina*. In the end, Joseph Nasi came to his succor, receiving him in his house and supporting him "with the love and veneration deserved by such a person."[4]

It was natural that Nasi was appealed to by the various communities of the Ottoman empire to settle disputes which proved too thorny or too involved for the local authorities. Above all, he maintained his interest, as his aunt had done before him, in the great settlement of Salonica. A typical local problem which gave rise to a prolonged controversy was connected with the rabbinate of the Catalan synagogue here, to which a certain Moses Ovadia was elected in 1572 in succession to his brother Elijah, who had recently died of the plague. (Their father, Hayim, had formerly occupied the same post.) For some reason or the other, he estranged some of his flock, who engineered his dismissal. The aggrieved rabbi appealed for help to the wealthy Constantinople scholar and businessman, Meir ibn Sanche, an old friend of the Nasi family. The latter managed to enlist the sympathy not only of the rabbis of the capital, who obviously had some competence in the matter, but also of the Duke of Naxos, who supported them. (It was indeed a service of gratitude; had not Ovadia obliged him, some while before, by concurring in the excommunication of his enemy, the physician Daout?)[5] They wrote to the synagogue again and yet again, demanding the rabbi's reinstatement. It was not, however, until after the lapse of a long period, and with the utmost reluctance, that the governing body complied — and even so only ostensibly, for before long Ovadia was once more at loggerheads with his congregation, as he continued to be on and off indefinitely.[6] Such intervention (sometimes highhanded) to smooth over difficulties which arose in the various Turkish communities was doubtless a recurrent task which fell to the Duke's lot.

It was to him too that Jewish delegations which came to Constantinople from the provincial cities, for one purpose or the other, naturally had recourse for assistance if they needed it (and who did not?). Moses Almosino, rabbi of the synagogue founded by Doña Gracia in Salonica,[7] has left a very detailed account of one instance in which he took a leading part. When Suleiman the Magnificent had visited that city in 1537, he granted the Jewish community a valuable charter of privileges. Unfortunately, the original document was burned in the great fire of 1545, when a hundred persons lost their lives and almost all the synagogues were destroyed together with their libraries and records. Henceforth, the old abuses began to creep in again — for example, the imposition on the Jews (in addition to ordinary taxation) of the obligation to supply the imperial household every year with herds of goats, at crushing expense. The recurrent outbreaks of plague at this period weakened the community so much that such burdens became intolerable. Accordingly, in 1565, a mission was sent to Constantinople to procure the confirmation of the privileges and exemptions granted by the sultan, as well as to negotiate a final settlement regarding arrears of taxation. The members were the wealthy Jacob ibn Nahmias, whose house was a meeting-place of native and foreign scholars; Moses Baruch, also a distinguished savant; and, the youngest of the three, Moses Almosnino — no stranger to Constantinople, for he had been chosen to represent the community there on a similar occasion six years before, when he had been a frequent visitor at Belvedere and had made the acquaintance of the Grand Mufti, the cultured Abu Saud el Amadi, who, spectacles in hand, had propounded to him a problem in connection with the philosophical opinions of Aristotle and Galen.[8] The delegation left their native city at the close of February, we are informed, going by sea to Brusa, perhaps to discuss the question with the local community. Here Moses Baruch died, and the survivors then went by the dangerous road through Cara Hissar to Constantinople, Nahmias also succumbing on the journey. Moses Almosnino was thus alone when he reached the capital, dispirited and sick.

He received from the first moment the support and encouragement of Joseph Nasi, with whom he stayed throughout the period at his palace of Belvedere. With him, he met his brother Don Samuel, "sitting at his right hand" and participating in his work; and it seems that he came to entertain the highest opinion of this somewhat overshadowed member of the family. Unfortunately, the sultan had by now left for his last campaign in Hungary (May 1, 1566). Almosnino formed a committee of ten persons to press his petition, but the *Kaimakam* Iskander

Pasha, who was acting as regent, refused to do anything on his own responsibility. When the news of Suleiman's death in the camp before Szigétvár arrived, the work had to be begun all over again. Much was naturally expected at this stage from Don Joseph's influence at the new sultan's Court; but his position was not yet sufficiently certain, and he found himself opposed by a coterie of Greek renegades, headed by his deadly enemy Mehemet Sokolli, who advised the ruler not to renew his predecessor's concession.

Discouraged by the delay, even the members of the Jewish committee that had been formed began to show themselves lukewarm, if not antagonistic, fearing perhaps that a remission of taxes in one place would have to be made up for elsewhere. It was in vain that some of the leaders of the Constantinople community tried to help — Joseph Hamon, now the sultan's body-physician in succession to his father Moses; Judah Segura, another practitioner who enjoyed high favor at Court, especially with the imperial treasurer; and the wealthy, influential Meir ibn Sanche, who combined profound talmudic learning with considerable literary skill and was a member of the famous Poetical Academy of Salonica. Don Joseph, who knew the ins and outs of the seraglio as few other people did, was convinced that he would be able to settle the matter satisfactorily if he were authorized to spend 1,000 ducats on the inevitable baksheesh, but Almosnino's other associates thought the amount excessive. As a result, this favorable opportunity was missed. The community of Salonica became restive, pettily suspecting that their representative's delay was due to personal motives of a highly sordid nature. Six times in all he renewed his approach to the authorities; six times he failed. The utmost concession that he could obtain was a proposal to commute the extraordinary taxes for a fixed annual tribute of 50,000 *aspri* — far beyond the ability of the community to pay.

It was almost in despair that Almosnino followed the Court to Adrianople at the close of 1567, to recommence the apparently hopeless negotiations. Although seven notables of the local community escorted him on his first visit to Court, success seemed as remote as ever. At length (he recounts) he had one night a vivid dream, which impressed his somewhat superstitious mind and gave him new confidence. On the next day, he was received by the grand vizier for the seventh time. With him he took, to act as interpreter, Abraham Salama, who was assimilated to the prevailing culture to an extent unusual among the Jews of the Turkish empire and had managed to enlist the interest of the Grand Mufti, with whom he was on friendly terms. Through the medium of his friend, Almosnino once more explained the problems, difficulties and requirements of the Jews of Salonica. On this occasion (perhaps understanding the issue clearly for the first time) Sokolli proved more sympathetic, and agreed to recommend the sultan to confirm the Charter, with all the concessions contained in it, in return for an outright payment of 300,000 *aspri* in commutation of all extraordinary taxes (February 15, 1568). The Salonica community was thus erected into a *Musselemlik* — a self-governing political entity, independent of the city in which it was situated, as it was henceforth to remain for centuries.[9] The imperial firman approving this was signed almost immediately, and a few days later Almosnino returned in triumph to Salonica, bearing with him this new *Magna Carta* of his beloved community. He was received with jubilation, and a service of thanksgiving was held at the Talmud Torah, the hero of the occasion delivering an eloquent sermon in which he gave details of his achievement. He singled out for special mention twelve persons who had shown themselves especially sympathetic to him during the course of his mission and without whose support he could never have hoped for success. First and foremost among them was "the Prince, the Lord Don Joseph Nasi, the Duke (may his might increase!) who helped us from the time we went to him, while the sultan's father still lived, from the beginning to the end."

Of this mission of Almosino's there is a remarkable literary monument. While he was away from home, waiting for the success which never seemed any nearer, he used his leisure to compile a work describing the state of affairs in the capital at the time, together with a Chronicle (still much consulted by historians of Turkey) of Sultan Suleiman's reign, achievements and death, and of his son's accession. He devoted a good deal of attention to a description of Constantinople, emphasizing the paradoxical contrasts to be found there — the extremes of heat and cold, of wealth and poverty, and other matters, which had much impressed him and to which the book owes the title subsequently given to it. There are several sidelights, too, on Don Joseph Nasi, his career and his magnificence. The work, written in Ladino (i. e., Spanish in Hebrew characters), like most other of the vernacular literature produced by Jews in Turkey at this time, remained unpublished during the author's lifetime. But nearly three quarters of a century later a certain Jacob Cansino, "Vassal of his Catholic Majesty and Interpreter of Languages in the Places of Oran," who had lost his employment in the Spanish service in Africa, went to Madrid to secure reinstatement. He found interest in Turkish affairs considerable, but knowledge of them slender. Accordingly, he beguiled his leisure by transliterating Almosnino's book into Latin characters, re-arranging it, omitting various details of what he considered subsidiary importance, and publishing it, under the title *Extremos y Grandezas de Constantinopla* or "The Extremes and Greatnesses of Constantinople" (Madrid, 1638: it is dedicated to the Conde d'Olivarez, Philip IV's all-powerful minister of state) — one of the rarest works of Spanish Jewish literature. Thus, some details of Don Joseph Nasi and his magnificence became known, though in emasculated form, to the Spanish-reading public.[10]

Almosnino gives elsewhere a graphic picture of the palace of Belvedere in the days of its grandeur. Appended to his once-famous work of religious morals in Ladino, *El Regimiento de la Vida*, published in Salonica in 1564, there is a lengthy Treatise on Dreams, entitled *Tratado de los sueños,* "composed at the request of the most illustrious *señor*, the *señor* Don Joseph Nasi, whom may God preserve and augment his prosperous state: Amen!" In the prologue to this little work, which is addressed to Nasi himself, the author tells how, when he was in Constantinople, in the palace of Belvedere (clearly, on the occasion of an earlier visit, perhaps that of 1559), Don Joseph had told him one Sabbath, in the course of conversation, that he would very much like to read a capable treatise on the nature of dreams. (The topic suggests an aspect of the

Duke's interests which hardly accords with the keen politician and hard-headed businessman we know him to have been, but this was the sixteenth century!) At the time, Almosnino had given him a superficial answer. In the course of the annual cycle of the reading of the Bible in the synagogue, they had now arrived in mid-winter at the portion of Genesis which deals with the story of Joseph, and in consequence he had been reminded of the Duke's request. Moreover, he had himself recently had a dream, twice repeated, in which Don Joseph and his brother Don Samuel figured prominently; and this induced him to take the task in hand. His philosophy of dreams was somewhat unenlightened, and need not detain us here: but his description of Belvedere, as he saw it in his vision, deserves repetition. It was a feast-day, and Almosnino thought that he was in the *midrash*, or room of study, which Nasi had fitted up in his palace, where Divine service was being held. Rich carpets hung from the walls and were strewn about the floor; there were two seats of honor, one for Don Joseph and the other for his brother, Don Samuel, who (as has been mentioned) seems to have enjoyed especially great consideration in Almosnino's eyes; the sacred Ark was opened, and the Scrolls of the Law were taken out; a raised bench accommodated the scholars who attended the service; and in an adjoining room, separate from the men, sat their two wives, Doña Reyna and Doña Gracia *la chica*, together with their respective daughters, the rest of the female members of the household and others from outside. (It is a little remarkable that there is no mention at all of the redoubtable Doña Gracia Nasi, although this was written five years before her death; it may be that she was ailing, or

had by now left the capital.)[11] It was apparently the
Feast of Tabernacles, for the two brothers had in their
hands the traditional citron and palm-branch, and the
prescribed psalms of praise were being sung.... There
is no need to go further into the details of the vision, which
Almosnino diplomatically considered to presage, on the
one hand, victory and, on the other, certainty of male
offspring for the two brothers. His assurance perhaps
outran his judgment, as this last detail at least was not
destined to be fulfilled; but the picture of the Nasi
palace and its glories, even while Suleiman was still
sultan and before its master had been enfeoffed with the
duchy of Naxos, is both graphic and welcome.

That there was a luxuriously-fitted *midrash* in the
palace of Belvedere, as Almosino saw in his vision, was
only to be expected. It was traditionally part of the
function of the wealthy Jew to act as patron of scholarship,
thereby both acquiring fame in this world and at the
same time storing up merit in the next. Doña Gracia
had set a magnificent example in patronizing the circle
of Marrano litterateurs at Ferrara, building synagogues,
and maintaining academies for the study of Jewish lore
in Constantinople, Salonica, Tiberias and elsewhere. The
Duke of Naxos had been associated with her in this work
to some extent. He had acted as her intermediary, for
example, in the establishment of the new congregation,
Livyath Hen, and the annexed academy, for the Marranos
who arrived at Salonica, as was gratefully recorded by
Moses Almosnino in his inaugural sermon.[12] On her death,
he continued these benefactions, though not perhaps with
the same whole-heartedness. The academy of Tiberias,
indeed, speedily collapsed for want of adequate support.

That of Constantinople, on the other hand, had better fortune and apparently maintained its existence for many generations by the side of the synagogue of the *señora*. Don Joseph's own academy, too, had eminent scholars attached to it. We know, for example, of his dragoman-interpreter, Isaac Onkeneira, who is constantly spoken of as "trusted agent appointed to the sanctuary of the noble Duke"; and of Samuel the Levite (ibn) Hakin, formerly of Brusa, and Isaac Taitaçac, a member of one of the most learned of all Salonican families, to both of whom Saadiah Lungo refers as "belonging to the *yeshiva* of the exalted prince" in the elegies he composed in their memory.[13] Similarly, when in 1569 the aged scholar-bibliophile, Isaac Akrish, lost all he had owing to the great fire in Constantinople, he found a place in the household of the Duke of Naxos, where he continued to be supported for a number of years. It was he who preserved for posterity many medieval literary curiosities, such as the famous tenth-century correspondence between Hasdai ibn Shaprut of Cordova and the king of the Khazars, and various documents about the Lost Ten Tribes; and one may imagine that this constituted a bond of interest between the two men and a frequent topic of their conversation.

Hebrew printing in Constantinople had started at the end of the fifteenth century and was at present at its most active stage. Later on, the house of Nasi extended generous patronage to this branch of activity,[14] which enjoyed in the eyes of pious Jews a full measure of the sanctity attached to every sort of educational function; and there is reason to believe that Don Joseph set them the example, though with a degree of self-effacement which was unusual. In 1565, M. de Petremol, the French agent in Constantinople, wrote home to M. de Boistallé:

I have procured you a Bible in Hebrew, at least the Five Books of Moses and some of the Prophets, which have been published in this city. The said printing press was introduced by the Seigneur Joseph Nazi, otherwise known as Jean Miguez; but it has for some time been extinct, owing to the smallness of the profit, and has produced no other works than these few, which you will see on the very first occasion I have to send them to you . . . .

There are several inconsistencies in this report. Hebrew printing was introduced into Constantinople long before Joseph Nasi's arrival there, and even before his birth; the losses involved are unlikely to have been on such a scale as to have deterred him if he was really interested, and it is out of the question that he could have embarked on the enterprise for the sake of profit; anonymity in any such enterprise was hardly in accordance with his temperament; and it is nct easy to trace what precise Bible edition the informant can have had in mind. It is obvious nevertheless that Nasi's name was popularly associated in his day with this activity; and the story is certainly not wholly inconsistent with his character and interests. Most probably the editions referred to by the French envoy have been literally thumbed out of existence.

It seems that Don Joseph had a fine library, including numerous rarities, and gave the run of it to savants. He purchased many manuscripts, or had them copied at his expense, as several contemporary scholars gratefully acknowledged. The collection comprised, it seems, various rare works of religious controversy, as was to be expected

in view of his own interests; from one of them, Jacob
Catalani (who used the collection a great deal after his
death) subsequently copied for Isaac Akrish the polemic
against Christianity entitled *Eben Bohan* (The Touchstone) by Shemtob ibn Shaprut; while the same scholar
transcribed there a collection of medical recipes ascribed
to Maimonides, under the title *Arugath ha-Bosem* (Bodleian MS. Opp. Add. 4°, 161). More recent literature,
too, had its place — for example, the supercommentary on
Rashi's commentary on the Pentateuch by Moses Almosnino, a transcription of which, executed in 1582, is also
in the Bodleian Library, Oxford (MS. Mich. Add. 69).
Don Joseph was, moreover, liberal-minded enough to
admit sectarian compositions into his collection, and it
was from manuscripts owned by him that the *Gan Eden*
of the Karaite scholar Aaron ben Elijah was transcribed
in 1580 (this is now in the Library of the British Museum:
MS. Add. 22069) and the *Adereth Elijahu* by Elijah
Beschizi was republished two hundred and fifty years
after his death. In this respect, certainly, his good works
survived him.

There is a graphic picture of how, on one occasion,
while the scholars were discussing learned points around
the table in his academy, he produced for their inspection
an ancient manuscript which a gray-beard had given him
while he was "in the land of his enemies" — perhaps
following the Court on the Persian campaign. It turned
out to be the book *Reumah*, ascribed (no doubt, wrongly)
to the ninth-century Gaon Nahshon, on the laws of ritual
slaughter for food. He entrusted the editing of this
hitherto-unknown work to his learned retainer, Isaac
Onkeneira, who published it in 1565 with a double com-

mentary of his own; the printer lauding the Maecenas in an ingenious Hebrew poem at the close.[15]

Considering how late in life he was introduced to Judaism and had the opportunity of studying Hebrew, it is surprising to find that his interest in Jewish literature was so intimate.

His patronage is to be traced in several other works published in the sixteenth century. Amatus Lusitanus (the famous physician whose name has occurred so frequently in the foregoing pages),[16] at last able to practice Judaism in public, was now living in Salonica, where he died, during the great plague, on January 21, 1568 — the year before Doña Gracia and Samuel Nasi passed to their eternal rest. (An epitaph in Latin hexameters by his old friend, Pyrrho Lusitano, was inscribed on his grave.)[17] Here he built up in these years a flourishing medical practice, many details of which can be found in the seventh book of his *Centuriae*, which graphically illustrates the life of the local Jewish community — the notables of the place, the generosity of the Ibn Jachia family, the recurrent waves of disease, and the learned discussions (as, for example, one with the physician Aaron Afia and a colleague recently arrived from Portugal on the nature of laughter). Amatus' fifth *Centuria*, recovered so adventurously from Ancona[18] and completed at Salonica in 1559, had been dedicated to "Joseph Nasi, the Hebrew, a man no less illustrious than learned," in flattering terms:

Not only art thou learned thyself, but also a devotee, favorer and munificent patron of learning. So great is thy culture, that thou hast no rival in this eminence: to which is added a great liberality, such as always accompanies the other virtues. By reason of these qualities of mind, thou hast always been welcomed and honored by kings and princes wherever thou hast lived. This is shown by the favor thou hast enjoyed at the Court of the late Emperor, Charles V, as well as of his late sister Mary, Regent of the Netherlands, and of Francis, King of France. Now, moreover, all are aware of the influence thou enjoyest with Sultan Suleiman of Turkey and his sons, Selim and Bajazet . . . .

In editions printed in Venice it was found wiser to omit this dedication to a New Christian and to substitute for it an epistle from Giovanni Marinelli, the commentator of Hippocrates, to a certain Enrique Nuñes![19]

It was in Salonica that Lusitanus composed his famous Physician's Oath, which the censorship would not allow to be published in full in Christian Europe because it referred to an oath on the Ten Commandments and spoke of serving all persons impartially whatever their religious belief:

I swear by God the Almighty and Eternal [and by his most holy Ten Commandments given on Mount Sinai by the hand of Moses the lawgiver, after the People of Israel had been freed from the bondage of Egypt] that I have never in my medical practice departed from what has been handed down in good faith to us and posterity; that I have never practiced deception, I have never overstated or made changes for the sake of gain; that I have ever striven that benefit might accrue to mankind; that I have praised no one, nor censured anyone, to indulge private interests, but only when truth demanded it. If I speak falsehood, may God and His Angel Raphael punish me with Their eternal wrath and may no one henceforth place trust in me. I have not been desireful for the remuneration for my medical services and have treated many without accepting any fee, but with none the less care. I have often unselfishly and firmly refused remuneration that was offered, preferring through diligent care to restore the patient to health, rather than to be enriched by his generosity. [I have given my services in equal manner to all, to Hebrews, Christians and Moslems.] Loftiness of station has never influenced me and I have accorded the same care to the poor as to those of exalted rank. I have never produced disease. In stating my opinion, I have always told what I believed to be true. I have favored no druggist unless he excelled others in skill in his art and in character. In prescribing drugs I have exercised moderation, guided by the physical condition of the invalid. I have never revealed a secret entrusted to me. I have never given a fatal draught. No woman has ever brought about an abortion with my aid. Never have I been guilty of base conduct in a home which I entered for medical service. In short, I have done nothing which might be considered unbecoming an honorable and distinguished physician, having always held Hippocrates and Galen before me as examples worthy of imitation and not having scorned the precepts of many other excellent practitioners of our art. I have been diligent and have allowed nothing to divert me from the study of good authors. I have endured the loss of private fortune, and have suffered frequent and dangerous journeys and even exile with calmness and unflagging courage, as befits a philosopher. The many students who have come to me have all been regarded as though they were my sons; I have used my best efforts to instruct them and urge them to good conduct. I have published my medical works not to satisfy ambition, but that I might, in some measure, contribute to the furtherance of the health of mankind; I leave to others the judgement whether I have succeeded; such at least has always been my aim and ever had the foremost place in my prayers.

Given at Thessalonica in the year 5319 (1559).[20]

In his dedication, Amatus informed Don Joseph that he had inscribed to him also a translation of the Roman history of the Latin historian Eutropius; but this has unfortunately been lost. The choice of subject illustrates Don Joseph's own intellectual range. This was charac-

AMATI MEDICI
LVSITANI
PRÆSTANTISSIMI, CVRATIONVM
MEDICINALIVM.

CENTVRIA QVINTA.

D. IOSEPHO NASSINIO, HEBRÆO, VIRO
NON MINVS ILLVSTRISSIMI,
quam sapienti.

AMATVS MEDICVS
S. P. D.

IN Domini fub Paulo quarto, Antonio bubliti, vt intecti sorti noftri. Iofepho Nassino, omnium rerum mearum
factarum fecit, & ne à fuis commiſſariis etiam oppri-
meret, Piſarum primum, inde Regesſſum me ſubila-
xi. Vnde animo quietior, quam malum iactum me-
morie renoccerem, inter tot, tantaque mihi ſubrepta,
vt aurum, argentum, aulices pannos, precioſam veſtem, & ſupellectilem
non paucam, ac infructiſſimam Bibliotheam, à mente veruntam, Quinta
Centuria Curationum mearum, forte ad vmbilicum deducta, & Commen-
taria quædam, quæ in quartam Feu libri primi Auicennæ proximè anta
diebus parturiram: quæ ſimul atra quædam ſeruabantur. Pro quibus
ſcriptis recuperandis, rebus cæteris neglectis, quam multa machinor, Ex-
ce Abrahamus Cathalanus, cui ingenui ſus, & amicus non vulgariſsmi
tum Piſauri gebat, qui ſuadit, vt ad profeſtos commiſſarios litteras dicet,
incalceatque non eſſe difficile paucas libertas ab eis inter tantas, & tam
precioſa parta impetrare. Ego vero amici conſilio vſus ad Nauum Bona-
nienſem Latinè ſcribo : Ille vero, interueniente Hodara Theſſalonicenſi
mercatore, ſcripſi in Auiennam commentariis, ad me Centurias 5, re-

MM 4

mittit, quâ peſtea Piſauri abſoluiq, & Regiis magneiortiuſq : vbi Sta-
tam quoque literis mandaui. Quæ nunc quam Typographi Vineti per
literas vexit à me petant, in lucem ederepropoſui, tálque ſtatus illi di-
mitter. Sed quoniam à Veneto Domino decretum eſt, nihil poſsin-
primis ſuæ religionis conſpiciô, neſio, an quicquam adiunctum, diminu-
tiſque ſit : arbitror equidem eos, qui pro religione ſunt, maximè dili-
genter meam deſunctionem in Matthæolum Senenſem factam : ſed ſunt ta-
men me breuiterſpe-ruſarum eius apologie. Nunc ad rem. Cum his miſ-
ſem Centuriasdeliberandum diis non fuit : cui illaspotiſsimum dedicari.
Tu etiam in primis occurriſti vir Generoſe, & Ornatiſſime, quia muta-
remeliuſq magnis de cauſis, dignſſimam videri. Es eum & dicta,
& Ætran hominû non tantum ſtudioſus, ſed fautor etiam & prœt-
Eltr mirficus. Humanitatr vero tanta vt nemini hac noſtri animi do-
te ſecundus habearis, quibus accedunt, liberalitas inſignis, quæ ſemper
comitari ſolet cæteras animi virtutes. Quibus animi dotibus factum q;
vt Regibus & Principibus, gratus, & honorediguus vbique ſempe
habearis : vt huius rei teſtis eſt vniuerſa Diui Caroli Quinti Impe-
ratoris, nectnon eius ſororis Diuæ Mariæ apud inferiores Germanos præ-
ctis, veluti Francici Gallorum Regis, cura. Sed & nunc q; vt etiam apud
Solimanum Turcarum Imperatorem, & eius filios Selimum, & Baiacet
tum, valeas, omnes norunt : vt qui te inter ſuos primates, non errga
propheta, atque mercedis, reponerent, vt iure phœnix, & rara auis dici
merearis. Deus igitur Optimus Maximus te nobis hac ſaluata inco-
mem, & ſanum diu ſeruet. Interea verò manuſuilam hoc noſtrum hilari
fronte ſuſcipe quod, ſi tibi gratum eſſe intellexero : maiorsda ruque in
des ægreditur, vimesiadicet. Vel, & ſecundum Tonium hira-
Curationes, indies expedit, voſsit cum voli ex Europo Hiſtorico Rome-
no, à me in linguam Hiſpanicam verſo, & rubicato, animum mean
quantum laboris ſis higiocaſſimam, & tuis illuſtriſſmaque Dice gratia,
ac venuelis geniti noſtra amantiſſimam. Vale igitur, & cum tua Ro-
gius felicter venum.

Theſſalonicæ, Calend. Decemb. anni à
creatione mundi 5320.

AMAT.

AMATUS LUSITANUS' DEDICATION OF HIS "FIFTH CENTURY"
TO JOSEPH NASI (1559)

PHOTOSTAT OF THE TITLE PAGE OF DON JOSEPH NASI'S
BOOK *Ben Porat Joseph*

teristic indeed of the wide interests of Turkish Jewry at this time, still maintaining amid somewhat incongruous surroundings the humanistic tradition of the Spanish communities of former days; an interest which is illustrated also in Aaron Afia's Spanish work, *Opinions* .... *on the Soul derived from ancient writers* (Venice, 1568), in Jacob Algabe's Hebrew version of Amadis de Gaule (Constantinople, c. 1540), in an anonymous Spanish translation of the Orlando Furioso, still in manuscript in the Bodleian Library, in Gedaliah ibn Jachia's Hebrew version of the writings of Albertus Magnus, produced at the time of the plague of 1548, in a contemporary Ladino edition of Luis de Carvajal's play on the life of Joseph, and in a number of similar productions of the age. It was, of course, a point of honor to be interested in Hebrew literature also, though it is unlikely that Don Joseph was greatly exercised, save in exceptional cases, by adventures in the field of purely talmudic lore. He accepted, however, the dedication of the book *Yoseph Lekah* (Cremona, 1576) — a commentary on the Book of Esther by Eliezer Ashkenazi, the great Levantine talmudist, which embodied his name in the title and spoke of him in terms of the most unmeasured praise. Possibly the author had made his acquaintance while passing through Constantinople; but he informs us in somewhat guarded terms how, some time previous, he had been in danger of his life while living in Cyprus, and it is possible that he had been one of the Duke's agents there.[21]

He also patronized Hebrew poetry and poets, as was at that time almost *de rigueur*; for Turkish Jewry was experiencing a continuation, or even a revival, of the poetical passion which had formerly distinguished their ancestors in Spain. It is certain that he patronized generously Saadiah Lungo, of Salonica, the most gifted of the school, to judge from the effusive fashion in which the latter speaks of him and his house. But there is no need to rely on such indirect and sordid evidence. His palace of Belvedere is described by a contemporary as being open to versifiers who vied among themselves in friendly competition, the Duke rewarding them and defraying their sustenance with a lavish hand. One of this circle was Isaac ben Samuel Onkeneira, a member of an erudite Salonican family, who is described as his *meturgeman*, or translator, and was entrusted with the supervision of his "Temple" — the same who edited the *Sepher Reumah*. There is extant a graphic account of how, on one occasion in 1575, he met in the street his cousin and namesake, a second Isaac Onkeneira, author of the poetical collection *Ayumah ka-Nidgaloth* (Constantinople, 1577), newly arrived from Salonica, whom he accompanied round the town, introducing him without doubt to his patron and his patron's household; and how the two went together on country walks, with a lad accompanying them and chanting for their delectation Hebrew poems by the older writers, which they gaily tried to imitate or to surpass.[22]

Onkeneira's name is linked up with Don Joseph's only recorded literary production. One day, at the palace of Belvedere, the latter had a long discussion over various metaphysical problems with certain Christian scholars who had paid him a visit. Their talk drifted to astrology, to which the Duke declared himself to be utterly opposed. The rabbis had said that Israel is not guided by stars; and if astrology was part of the belief of other peoples, he was profoundly thankful that God had enabled him to return to his own. He accused his visitors, who differed with him on this point, of not troubling to think the matter out for themselves, but of relying wholly on what they found written by others. It was in vain that they adduced proofs from Arabic and Greek literature, as well as various folk tales which supported their view. "One must not bring evidence from the feeble-minded, or from exaggeration-loving men and women, who thereby strengthen their imagination and their inclination towards superstition," he retorted. "If now and again something of the sort is justified by facts, it can only be pure coincidence." (From this, it would seem that he is unlikely to have appreciated Rabbi Moses Almosnino's naive treatise on the nature of dreams which had been written for his benefit.) Prophecy, he went on, was essentially moral warning, rather than precise forecast; indeed, the prophets of Israel never tired of pointing out that the disasters and tribulations they foretold could be averted by true penitence. He recounted with gusto the story of one of the high Turkish dignitaries who carefully consulted the astrologers before building a fortification and followed out their instructions to the last detail — only to find that it was captured at the first assault . . . .

The colloquy ended. The visitors kissed the Duke's hands and withdrew. The latter received the congratulations of his retinue, among them his interpreter, Rabbi Isaac Onkeneira, and bade the latter record the arguments in writing *ad perpetuam rei memoriam*. This was the origin of the little work, *Ben Porath Joseph* ("Joseph is a fruitful bough": Genesis 49.22), published in Constantinople by Joseph Jabez in 1577, with approbations from several of the most eminent rabbis of the time, who clearly saw nothing heretical in the author's liberal views.[23] There can be little doubt that the editor, determined to make his hero appear in as favorable a light as possible, added something of his own erudition to the composition, but there is no reason to imagine, as some belittlers of versatility have suggested (to be sure, without a particle of evidence) that he was exclusively responsible for it.[24]

As is easily to be imagined, the Duke's fame was spread universally throughout Europe, among Christians as well as among Jews, though inevitably in a different sense. Visitors who had seen him passing through the streets of Constantinople preceded by his janissaries; diplomatic representatives who knew only too well of his influence; fanatics who resented his attempts to help his coreligionists; churchmen who bewailed his apostasy; merchants who feared his competition; all assisted to spread his reputation. The Spanish government knew of him as a renegade New Christian; the French as the man who had procured an embargo on their shipping in Eastern waters; the Venetians as an outlaw, exiled from their state, who had nevertheless succeeded in installing himself in one of their whileom protectorates as its Duke. It may even be that the antisemitic legislation of Pope Pius V, culminating in the Bull *Hebraeorum Gens* which drove the Jews out of the smaller places of the States of the Church in 1569,[25] may have been caused or at least exacerbated by exaggerated reports from the Levant of the magnificence and the activities of this all-powerful Jewish magnate. Venomous references to his activities and his career appear in theological and historical works written in several lands and tongues at this time.

There can be no doubt that his reputation reached England too, in however garbled a form. Of this, there is according to conjecture a remarkable literary record. In 1592, the brilliant young Christopher Marlowe produced in London his famous drama, *The Jew of Malta*, apparently begun a good while earlier. Its success was greater than that of almost any other contemporary play — perhaps because the leading part was taken by Edward Alleyn, the favorite actor of the day — and it is still considered by many to be the ill-fated author's masterpiece. Its theme is

> the story of a rich and famous Jew
> Who liv'd in Malta

at the time of the Turkish onslaught some time before. Maddened by persecution, he turns into a monster, attempts to wreak horrible revenge, conspires with the Turks and in the end falls victim to a plot he had prepared for his allies. (The close of the play degenerates into a sequence of impossible maleficence — very different from the relatively balanced psychological study with which it opens). It has long been imagined that the character of Barabas the Jew, with his overweening ambition, his machiavellian schemings, his anti-Christian bias, his great wealth, his trade in "the wines of Greece," his "argosy from Alexandria, Laden with spice and silks," the Spanish tags in his conversation, his rise to the rank of governor of the island of Malta (*scilicet* Naxos) under the Turks, his intimacy with "Selim Calymath, son to the Grand

Seignior," is based on dim reports that had reached
England of the fabulously rich Joseph Nasi, Duke of
Naxos. His commercial relations were similarly wide-
spread:

> In Florence, Venice, Antwerp, London, Sevill,
> Frankeford, Lubecke, Mosco and where not
> Have I debts lying; and in most of these
> Great summes of money lying in the bancho.

There are some passages even which reflect his personality faithfully enough. He, like Barabas, was

> Born to better chance
> And fram'd of finer mould than other men.

Most memorable are the great lines which show that
Marlowe, like Shakespeare after him, was not blind to the
facts of Jewish persecution and the reason for Jewish
failings. Here, if anywhere in the play, we have the
authentic Joseph Nasi:

> Who hateth me but for my happiness?
> Or who is honour'd now but for his wealth?
> Rather had I, a Jew, be hated thus,
> Than pitied in a Christian poverty . . . .
> The man that dealeth righteously shall live;
> And which of you can charge me otherwise?

ADDITIONAL NOTE TO CHAPTER VII

According to a conjecture put forward recently by H. Sinsheimer (*Shylock: the History of a Character*, London, 1947), Marlowe's *Jew of Malta* is not the only echo of Joseph Nasi, and his remarkable career, in sixteenth-century drama. The English strolling players (*Englische Komoedianten*), who gave performances all over Germany etc., at this time, had in their repertory one very popular item, composed by a Silesian student named Christoph Bluemel, which was variously entitled *Komoedia genanndt Der Jud von Venezien* (Comedy called, The Jew of Venice), or *Von einem Koenig von Cypern und einem Herzog von Venedig* (About a King of Cyprus and a Doge of Venice), or *Teutsche Komoedie der Jud von Venedig* (German Comedy, the Jew of Venice) etc. This opens on the island of Cyprus, where a Jew named Barabas is seen working to prevent the expulsion and spoliation of his coreligionists. Being unsuccessful, he goes to Venice disguised as a soldier, and changes his name to Joseph; and here he tries to secure his revenge, the tale of the Three Caskets and of the Pound of Flesh being brought into the story. This presents the story of the Duke of Naxos, as it were, in reverse, but follows it so closely that coincidence is out of the question. It opens in Cyprus, with which Nasi was so closely connected in the popular mind; it deals with a Jew of this place who later (instead of earlier) dissimulates his faith and appears as a Christian; it thus brings in a disguised Jew named Joseph; and it closes at Venice, where Nasi resided at an early stage in his career, and with which place he always had intimate relations. According to Sinsheimer, this play, or rather the earlier composition on which it is based, was known to and used by both Marlowe and Shakespeare: for we clearly have in it the original both of the former's Barabas (not only the name, but also the temperament) and of the latter's Shylock (the same stories and action). The intermediary between the German original and the extant English counterparts might be Thomas Dekker's lost *Josef, the Jew of Venice*, produced in London by the Admiral's Company between 1592 and 1594, but now no longer extant. This hypothesis is based on the material assembled by Albert Cohn, *Shakespeare in Germany in the Sixteenth and Seventeenth Centuries* (London, 1865) and Johannes Meissner, *Die englischen Comoedianten zur Zeit Shakespeares in Oesterreich* (Vienna, 1884), who, however, did not question that the influences were all in the reverse direction, there being no trace of the German play on this theme until 1611.

CHAPTER VIII

Afterglow

SO long as Selim the Sot lived, Don Joseph could perhaps have hoped to regain his influence at the Sublime
Porte. But, content with having qualified himself through
the annexation of Cyprus for the title, "Extender of the
Realm," borne by his ancestors, the sultan now confined
himself to the more pleasurable exertions of the Seraglio.
It was in vain that he was plied with the choicest wines
and the most unusual delicacies. He had no further desire to assert himself in the political sphere and surren-
dered the cares of state without a struggle into the
capable hands of Mehemet Sokolli, still grand vizier. In
December, 1574, less than two years after the conclusion
of peace with Venice, he died, prematurely exhausted if
not prematurely aged, before he had completed his fifti-
eth year.

His eldest son, Murad III (1574–1595) — known to
his European contemporaries, and celebrated by the
playwrights, as Amurath — succeeded him peacefully,
after butchering five of his younger brothers, in what was
now the conventional Turkish fashion, in order to remove
the possibility of dynastic competition. Though he owed
his throne to Mehemet Sokolli and retained him in office,
little love was lost between the two. This personal antagonism did not, on the other hand, imply a renewal of

Nasi's influence in the state. For the new sultan was not
to be won over by the old methods. Not that he was in
any sense a finer character. On the contrary, he was
sunk in debauchery unrelieved by any spark of genius
and made sordid by an inordinate rapacity. His bed was
placed, it is said, over a pit filled with his gold and treasure; the sale of offices became during his reign a fundamental feature of governmental policy; he fathered over
a hundred children; he maintained a retinue of freaks;
and he spent much of his leisure in witnessing buffoonish
comedies which the Jews — famous at this time as play-
actors — were compelled to present for his delectation.
But his weaknesses were different from those of his
slothful, gourmandizing father, which Nasi had known
how to turn to such advantage. On the first Friday of
the new reign, it is recounted, the usual hampers of wines
and delicacies, such as the former sultan had received
from him every week, arrived at the Seraglio. The gift
was refused, and the donor given to understand that
it was superfluous for him to trouble himself in this manner any more.[1] It was the old story, repeated so many
times in royal history. The new ruler belonged to another generation. His father's friends were not necessarily his friends; and he had no bond of sympathy with
the graying, elderly Jew whom Selim had found so amusing and so useful.

On the other hand — whether it was for Selim's sake,
or through the all-powerful harem influence, or merely
to annoy Mehemet Sokolli — Nasi was allowed to remain in possession of all his revenues and dignities . It
is said that, at the beginning of the new reign, the treasurer desired to revoke the wine-tax that Nasi adminis-

tered so lucratively. The sultan refused to consent,
saying that in his will his father had recommended that
his Jewish favorite should be left in enjoyment of it so
long as he lived, as in fact he did.[2] But this was all. At
the imperial Divan, his voice no longer carried weight.
He was a forgotten man.

With Murad's accession, indeed, a new chapter had
commenced in the history of the Jews of Turkey generally. Hitherto — at least since the capture of Constantinople in 1453 — the sultans had on the whole
followed a markedly pro-Jewish policy, that of Selim II
only accentuating the example of his immediate prede-
cessors. With his son, there was a different atmosphere.
He was the first Turkish ruler in whom there may be
discerned a definite and consistent anti-Jewish bias.
Contemptuous restrictions on the Jews' costume, activities and life now began to be enforced as well as enacted; and he is even said to have issued at one time an
order for the extermination of the Jews of the empire,
speedily indeed withdrawn.[3] Notwithstanding the influence still indirectly exercised by favored individuals, the
authentic Golden Age of Turkish Jewry was now ended,
and with it the atmosphere in which Joseph Nasi had
attained his eminence.

He did not yield his influence without a struggle.
Esther Kyra, the Jewish intimate of successive generations at the harem, was still active despite her great age,
having a particularly strong influence on the Sultana
Safieh, who in turn dominated the sultan. Through her
means, probably, Nasi made desperate efforts to reap-
pear on the political scene. At one time it seemed that
he might be successful; indeed, in a despatch of April 5,

1576, the French ambassador at Constantinople stated that, owing to his standing with the sultan's wife and mother, he now exercised more power, albeit indirectly, than he had ever done under Selim. He dabbled, too, in foreign politics, offering himself as mediator in this year in order to prevent a conflict between Hungary and Turkey over the succession to the throne of Poland. But the go-between he used was secretly attached to the French interest and played him false, deliberately suppressing the errand.[4] In any case, in the teeth of the opposition of the grand vizier and the indifference of the sultan, it would have been impossible for him to achieve anything solid, and he never returned effectively to the political stage. The Venetian ambassador, Antonio Tiepolo, in his report on Turkish affairs to the doge about this time, mentioned that the former "Giovanni Miches" still held the wine-customs, but did not think it worth while to say anything else about him, as he was out of favor and cut no figure at the Sublime Porte.[5]

There were, of course, compensations. His revenues were still very great. He was still enfeoffed with what had formerly been considered the premier duchy of Christendom, his authority in which had been restored as before after the short interruption during the course of the war; indeed, to this period belongs the only extant original record which we have of his rule, given in 1577 "at our palace of Belvedere near Pera," in Constantinople.[6] (It was in vain that the dispossessed Giacomo Crispi had journeyed to Constantinople two years before, on hearing the news of Selim's death, cheerfully hoping to be restored.) There is no reason to believe that the Tiberias concession, to which Murad's name had been subscribed at the very outset with those of his father and grandfather, was now allowed to lapse. Nor did Don Joseph lack domestic outlets for his restless activity. He sought solace in his library and in intellectual exercises, and the same year witnessed the publication of the colloquy with Christian scholars which was committed to writing by Isaac Onkeneira.[7] They were distractions, perhaps; but in view of his restless, ambitious nature they could be only minor ones, which could not compensate him for the fact that, for the first time, he was not a welcome visitor at Court and that he was no more, as he had been for so long, a force in European politics.

He did not, in fact, live for long in this gilded obscurity. He suffered from calculus, or gall-stones — that distressing complaint which, before the days of anaesthetics and skilled operative treatment, afforded little hope of relief or cure. On the Ninth of Ab each year, Jewish tradition prescribes a fast-day commemorating the capture of Jerusalem in the sieges by Nebuchadnezzar and by Titus, as well as manifold other disasters in the history of their people, down to the expulsion from Spain in 1492, which fell on or about the same date. This melancholy celebration, being postponed from the Sabbath, fell in 1579 on Sunday, August 2. That day, as the Jews of Constantinople were sitting barefoot in their dimly-lighted synagogues, a sad piece of news, in fullest accord with the disastrous associations of the fast, spread rapidly from mouth to mouth. Don Joseph Nasi, Duke of Naxos, had died in his palace of Belvedere overlooking the Bosphorus — the head of Turkish Jewry, the pride of his coreligionists throughout the world.

Services were of course held, and memorial addresses

delivered, in all the synagogues, as had happened when Doña Gracia had been gathered to her people; though Moses Almosnino, who had been the official orator at Salonica and elsewhere on that occasion, had himself recently been called likewise to the Academy on High (while in Constantinople on yet another official mission after the accession of the new sultan). The Duke was laid to rest probably (like his aunt) in the great cemetery at Cassim Pasha, which had served Constantinople Jewry since Byzantine times; but his tombstone has not been traced, nor is there any record of the inscription which marked it. The poets of the community — now at the height of their productivity — doubtless vied with one another in composing elegies to commemorate this great blow to their people; but only one has come down to us — that written by Saadiah Lungo, of Salonica, beginning:

> I voice my mourning in a bitter cry,
> And every ear shall hear my mournful strain.

Hardly was the Duke dead, when the carrion-crows began to gather round the body, hoping to derive some benefit from his fabulous, if exaggerated, wealth. Immediately the news was known, the sultan gave orders for an inventory to be made of his property, including his jewels and his treasure, which was to be kept under seal pending a final decision about its disposal. The wine-monopoly that he had long enjoyed of course lapsed, the plutocrats and financiers of the capital competing among themselves for the succession. In European diplomatic circles the news was heard with lively interest, not unmingled with malevolent pleasure. The new French ambassador, M. Jacques de Germigny, arrived in Constantinople not long after Nasi's death (which had been reported by the secretary of the embassy in the following week with ill-concealed exultation). It seemed that the time had now come for securing compensation at last for the loss France had sustained, a few years before, by the embargo laid upon her shipping at Alexandria. Application was immediately made (and was repeated shortly after) for reimbursement from the estate of the amounts then seized; and, in view of the cordial relations which now prevailed between the Courts of Constantinople and St. Germain, there seemed to be good hope of success.

But there was general disappointment. Don Joseph's wealth had been overestimated. He had lived magnificently, but not economically; and his expenditure far exceeded his income. In happier days, it had been possible for him to make loans to crowned heads of amounts of as much as 150,000 ducats. Now, among all his property and accumulated treasure, there was barely found sufficient (so at least the ambassador was assured) to repay the 90,000 ducats that the Duchess Reyna had brought with her as her dowry on her marriage.[8] The rest of that vast fortune had gone in magnificent living, in diplomatic intrigue, in support of the artificial ducal state, in outlay upon the sultanic pleasures. The vizier did not, of course, mention the sultan's own claims on the estate, which are unlikely to have been small. But they brought in little profit to the treasury, as the three *defterdars*, or paymasters, who had been entrusted with the administration could not resist the temptation, and before long were convicted of embezzlement.[9]

As for Don Joseph's former duchy, he had no son to inherit it, even had the enfeoffment been hereditary. In consequence, immediately the news of his death was known, the colony from Naxos, which had established itself in Constantinople in spite of his objections, petitioned for the restoration of the former Christian dynasty, now living in exile at Venice. The grand vizier is said to have favored the idea, but in vain. Instead, the islands were annexed outright to the Turkish empire, a *sandjakbey* assisted by a religious administrator, or *cadi*, being sent to rule them, and extremely favorable capitulations being granted by the sultan to a deputation from the islanders which appeared at the Porte. Gianfrancesco Sommaripa was, indeed, reinstated immediately after the Duke's death as Lord of Andros; but he found himself outbidden by the *chaus* Suleiman, who offered 40,000 *scudi* more for the privilege of enjoying the revenues for three years.[10] Some twenty years after Nasi's day, the ex-Genoese renegade Sinan (Cicala) Pasha endeavored to have his brother invested with the duchy.[11] But nothing came of this either, and Joseph Nasi was in fact the last Duke of Naxos and the Cyclades.[12] Francisco Coronello, his lieutenant, remained on the island, very popular among some sections of the inhabitants, who intervened in his favor when an attempt was made to compromise him in 1587.[13] In due course, his descendants intermarried with the proudest of the local nobility.[14] Almost to the present day, the family could be traced in the Cyclades — the only relic there, perhaps, of the rule of the Jewish Duke in the sixteenth century.

Cyprus remained under direct Turkish rule for some three centuries — an integral part of the empire and the most enduring memorial of Don Joseph's brief spell of influence at the Sublime Porte. During the period of international tension in 1878, at the time of the Congress of Berlin, the administration was taken over by Great Britain by amicable arrangement with the sultan, who nevertheless remained nominal sovereign until the island was formally annexed to British rule in 1914. It is a curious coincidence that the change of government in the nineteenth century was the work of Benjamin Disraeli, Earl of Beaconsfield. A Jew of Christian birth had been responsible for the union of the island with the Turkish empire; just three hundred years later, a Christian of Jewish birth ended the association.

In October, 1579 (it was a couple of months after Joseph Nasi's death), the Grand Vizier Mehemet Sokolli, who had so long opposed his policy and was ultimately responsible for the failure of his ambitions, fell victim at last to the intrigues of his enemies. His plan to build an observatory in Istanbul had aroused fanatical religious opinion, and his murder shortly afterwards by a discontented soldier is said to have been instigated by the sultan himself, jealous of his influence. (His creature, Michael Cantacuzenos, "the son of the Devil," who had represented the rivalry with Nasi in the financial field, had been disgraced and hanged not long before.) With him, said the Venetian ambassador, Turkish *vertù* sank into the grave. It was long before any outstanding Turkish statesman again emerged. There was now a succession of brief, precarious tenures of office, the harem exercising more and more power, and various coteries influencing policy now in this direction, now in that. Jews continued to

figure prominently in public life notwithstanding the
change in the general atmosphere; but instead of the one
or two sage, experienced, advisers who exercised their
influence consistently over a long period of years, henceforth there was a confusing succession of them, playing
a great role for a short period, owing to their acceptability
to one minister or another, and then suddenly disap-
pearing — sometimes, like their masters, tragically. To
complete our picture of the time, it is necessary to devote
some space to them and to their work.

An exception to the foregoing generalization was the
physician, Solomon Nathan Ashkenazi ("Allaman Oglou,"
as Turkish chroniclers call him), who continued to figure
prominently in public life for an entire generation, surviving two sultans and several grand viziers, who all
showed him unbounded confidence.[15] Since the time that
he had first been concerned in bringing about a rapprochement between Turkey and Venice, eight years before, he
had come to be universally recognized as one of the most
influential persons in diplomatic circles in Constantinople.
and "the favourite of all the Pashas."[16] Sokolli guided
public policy; Ashkenazi advised Sokolli; and it was he,
the Jewish physician, rather than Joseph Nasi, the Jewish
Duke, whom foreign powers now tried to conciliate. The
Signoria of Venice trusted him as they did few other
persons. In 1574, we find them instructing their *bailo*
at Constantinople to discover through his means who it
was that revealed their secrets to the Sublime Porte.[17]
Four years later, an attempt was made to persuade him
to use his influence to have an embargo placed on trade
between Turkey and the rival port of Ancona, which
still lay largely in the hands of Jews, though it was empha-

sized that great caution had to be observed lest the *Serenissima* should get into bad odor on this account.[18]

His part in the discussions in connection with the Polish succession, at this time, was especially noteworthy. In 1572 his former employer and patient, King Sigismund Augustus, died childless, and a national convention assembled in Warsaw in the following April for the purpose of electing a new king. Five candidates were in the field, one of them being Henri de Valois, Duke of Anjou, son of Catherine de Médicis and brother of the King of France. All were powerfully supported, and outside backing became a matter of primary significance to the candidates. That of Turkey, with its long common frontier with Poland, was all-important; but a French prince installed here might disturb the balance of power in Europe, which would automatically imperil the Franco-Turkish alliance. Solomon Ashkenazi was now asked for his help and persuaded Sokolli to throw the weight of Turkish influence, in spite of everything, on the side of the French claimant, who was duly elected. The Jewish physician did not minimize his services, notwithstanding the fashion in which the Bishop of Acqus tried to obtain the credit for the achievement; as the former wrote to Henri some years after, when he had become King of France: "In the election, when your Majesty was chosen to be King of Poland, it was I who was responsible for all [that was done here]."

Again, when, in 1578, the grand duke of Tuscany wished to resume diplomatic and commercial relations with Turkey, broken off at the time of the War of Cyrpus, Ashkenazi did his best to smooth over the difficulties created by the Tuscan envoy's exceptional tactlessness.

There may still be read a personal letter (sealed with the traditional Shield of David, surrounded by a garland) which he sent the grand duke advising him on procedure; and he was included in the list of state dignitaries whom it was thought desirable to placate by a gift.[19] In a communication of this period, the imperial dragoman, Hurrem, in close contact with whom he always worked, wrote that "Rabbi Salamone, because of his good conduct, takes part at present in most of the negotiations of this Porte." It may be added that he owed his influence no less to his reputation for personal probity than to his knowledge of affairs and his diplomatic skill, all of which are so amply attested in the records of the period.

His devotion to his coreligionists was profound. As we have seen, it was to his intervention, in all probability, that the community of Venice owed the withdrawal of the edict of expulsion against them in 1572. He used his influence, too, on behalf of those of the Danubian provinces. On one occasion at least, moreover, he was, it seems, compelled to intervene nearer home. Murad III, fanatical and somewhat unbalanced, needed little incitement to turn into a persecutor and in 1579 found his opportunity. His attention was attracted by the ostentatious and extravagant clothing of the Jewish women of Constantinople, one of whom wore personal jewelry around her neck worth (it was said) 40,000 golden ducats. It was reported at the time that the sultan so far resented the spectacle that, in a fit of childish rage, he issued orders for the extermination of all the Jews living under his rule. The imperial physician, however (it is thought, with good reason, that Ashkenazi was the person in question), secured the intervention of the sultana mother, who had great influence over her son; a large sum of money was raised among his wealthy coreligionists as baksheesh; and the fickle monarch was induced to change his mind.[20] But he would not be altogether deterred and issued stringent sumptuary legislation, against Jews and Christians alike, forbidding them henceforth to dress in silken garments and enjoining them to wear caps instead of the turban, which was to be reserved for true believers.

After Sokolli's assassination, in 1579, another Jew shared Ashkenazi's prominence. This was a certain "Rabbi" Isaac.[21] So intimate was he at Court, and so valued were his services, that the great officers of state considered him almost as one of their number. He was very highly esteemed, too, by all the foreign diplomatic representatives. The Venetians thought it important to gain his sympathy, in the hope that he would help them with Mustapha Pasha, the new vizier; the French ambassador used him as intermediary in communicating with the same official and promised him a regular allowance of 100 ducats. When, in 1580, the secretary of the embassy left for home on a secret mission, he was instructed to inform the king of Rabbi Isaac's outstanding importance and of the advisability of recognizing his services formally, thus making certain of his goodwill. It was reported as something noteworthy that he refused a bribe from the Spanish agent to use his influence for an extension of the armistice between the two powers. He had good reason. The Spanish sovereign, he said, only wanted to gain time; thus it might be possible for him to conquer Portugal, after which he would be able to turn with full strength against Turkey. If that happened, there would be no hope for himself, or for any other Jew living there![22]

Another very influential Jewish physician who begins to emerge into prominence at this time was Moses
Benveniste, known to the Turks as Hodja Moussahibi,
who was in attendance on the Grand Vizier Siavouch
Pasha and worked in frequent collaboration with Ashkenazi. He was closely associated with Turkish policy,
domestic as well as foreign, for many years, as we shall
see. It was his advocacy for example which was responsible for the reinstatement of Peter the Lame as Gospodar
of Moldavia in 1582. In the following year, he advised
on the currency reform which had such serious repercus-
sions later on, when the "Jews' Money" (as it was termed)
led to a revolt of the janissaries.[23] (The director of the
mint this time was, as it happens, another Jew, the *chaus*
Hodja Nessimi, or Nissim.)[24] Yet another influential
medical practitioner of the period was Dr. Mocato
(Mocatta), whose opinion was asked in matters of state
and who is recorded to have advised against the despatch of a fleet to Marseilles in 1596 to aid the French
king, as he was confident that, if this were done, not a
single vessel would survive.[25]

These years marked, too, the culmination of the influence of Esther Kyra, who even before Gracia Nasi's
arrival in Constantinople had acted as the intermediary
between the harem and the outside world and, though
now an octogenarian at least, was still active.[26] When,
during the reign of Murad, as a result of his excessive
uxoriousness coupled with sheer incapacity, the women
of the Seraglio began to direct the affairs of the empire,
it was she who manipulated the women. The sultan's
favorite wife, Safieh, belonged to the Corfiote family of

Baffo, and strongly inclined therefore to a pro-Venetian policy. Esther Kyra, having free entry to the palace, became the intermediary for all her negotiations and intrigues with the foreign ambassadors at Galata. It was alleged that she was informed of the most intimate state secrets through the medium of the diplomatic corps, while the ministers — sometimes even the grand vizier himself — were still ignorant of them. When once a tense international atmosphere was brought about through the capture by the Venetians of a Turkish ship coming from Algiers, with the governor's wife on board, it was she who was entrusted by Safieh with the delicate task of smoothing matters over in conjunction with the *bailo*. On another occasion, Catherine de Médicis, Queen of France, solicited the aid of the Turkish fleet against the Spaniards; it was Esther Kyra who informed the Venetian envoy of the episode and communicated copies of the correspondence to him. The diplomatic representatives of the *Serenissima* at Constantinople frequently alluded to her great influence at the palace; and their gifts to the sultanas were necessarily transmitted through her means. As a reward, she was permitted to organize a lottery in Venice — a right never given before to a foreigner.

The venerable intriguer seems to have dabbled in politics once too often. It is said that, on one occasion (it was probably in 1593), she succeeded in introducing her own nominee into some military employment, which had already been promised to someone else. The disappointed candidate vowed revenge. The result was a gruesome outrage, which attracted a great deal of attention at the

time. It is least embarrassing to use the words of an
English traveller of the period, John Sanderson, in his
Travels in the Levant:[27]

A Jewish woman of the greatest credit and wealth in Constantinople was brought out of her house and stabbed to death
in the Viceroy's yard, thence by a window in the seraglio wall
where the Grand Signior, Sultan Mahomet, stood to see, she
was drawn with ropes to the publickest place in the city, and
there laid for the dogs to eat; who did devour her all save the
bones, sinews of her legs, and soles of her feet. Her head had
been carried upon a pike through the city, and alike her shameful part; also many small pieces of her flesh, which the Turkish
Janizaries and other carried about tied in a little pack-thread,
showing to the Jews and others, and in derision said, Behold
the whore's flesh. One slice of her I did so see pass by our door
in Galata. Her eldest son the next day in like manner cruelly
stabbed and murdered in the said Viceroy's court; dragged
thence and laid by his mother, but was so fat and rank that
the dogs would not seize upon him, or else they were satiate
with the woman's flesh the day before, who was a short fat
trubkin.[28] So together with his mother's bones the next day
was the body burned in that place. Her second son became
Turk to save his life; so would his dead brother, if he could
have had the favor. The third son, a young youth, their wrath
being appeased, they permitted to live. This was an act of the
Spahi's in spite of the Great Turk's mother; for by the hands
of this Jew woman she took all her bribes, and her sons were
chief customers of Constantinople; who took all the gainful
business into their own hands, doing what they listed. The
mother and children were worth millions, which all went into
the Great Turk's coffers.

Meanwhile, although his original patron was dead,
Solomon Ashkenazi was not under eclipse. He was still
persona grata with all the diplomatic corps in Constantinople; and in 1583 his services were called upon as arbi-

trator to settle a squabble between the English and
Venetian representatives over a petty domestic matter —
a task which he was happy to perform. When an armistice
with Spain was concluded in 1586, it was he who, even
though privately he may have disapproved, signed the
preliminary articles on behalf of the sultan, his friend
the imperial dragoman, Hurrem Bey, being empowered
to act in a similar capacity for King Philip.[29]

He continued to enjoy the favor of successive ministers.
In 1591, we find him spoken of in a despatch of the imperial ambassador as "the famous Jew Solomon Tedeschi
[the German], at present factotum of the Grand Vizier."
The reference on this occasion is to Ferhad Pasha who,
indeed, needed all the assistance he could obtain; he was
a former pastry-cook, whose animadversions on the administration had been heard by Sultan Murad while he
prowled the capital incognito, had been appointed to
remedy what he ventured to criticize and, in the end,
had been elevated to the highest post of all. It was not
a peculiarly fortunate experiment. But Ashkenazi proved
faithful in adversity as well as in prosperity. When, in
1594, Ferhad was absent on an expedition to Moldavia,
his lieutenant, Ibrahim Pasha, and his rival, Sinan Pasha,
intrigued against him with such success that orders were
given for his arrest and execution on a charge of treason.
The disgraced minister tried desperately to secure the
intervention of the sultana mother, promising her all his
treasure if she would use her influence on his behalf. This
she did, and the order for execution was withdrawn
(though, indeed, a little afterwards Ferhad was infor-
mally but no less effectively strangled). It was "Allaman
Oglou," or Solomon Nathan Ashkenazi, who had acted

as intermediary in the negotiations to save his master and obtained the withdrawal of the death sentence.[30]

Another prominent Jew who greatly influenced Turkish policy at this period — one of the most prominent, indeed, though his name was long forgotten — was a certain David Passi, who for a long time enjoyed great fame in diplomatic circles throughout Europe. His antecedents are obscure. He was nephew, it was said, of one of the sultan's physicians — perhaps Moses Hamon, though this is dubious (it might equally well have been Joseph de Segura, the latter's successor). Like Joseph Nasi, he was by birth a Portuguese, but had lived for a time in Venice. Together with Moses Benveniste, he had some hand in the sultanic finances, and when, in 1589, the incensed janissaries invaded the Divan clamoring for the heads of those who were responsible for debasing the coinage, he was wounded so severely that he was reported dead. But he recovered completely. Already from as early as 1585, his name had begun to appear in the reports of the occidental diplomatic representatives as one who played a prominent role in all diplomatic intrigues in Constantinople, and was "always ready to take a part in such matters." A memorandum of his on the political situation was considered so important that it was read aloud to the French ambassador; he conferred at length with a visiting Englishman, apparently in the hope of bringing about a closer Anglo-Turkish understanding to oppose the mutual menace from Spain; and when the Englishman left, two members of Passi's household accompanied him. The Venetian ambassador, exceptionally well primed though he was, found his information valuable and trustworthy; the Spanish did their best to

gain his sympathy; and the viceroy of Naples suggested
that he should be given a regular allowance. The sultan
valued him very highly: he had slaves like the grand
vizier in abundance, he said, but none like David.[31] Such
services as his deserved a rich reward, and it was rumored
at one time that this new Jewish favorite had been elevated to the exalted rank of Duke of Naxos and the
Archipelago, vacant since Joseph Nasi's death six years
before. A news letter from Venice, dated August 17, 1585,
reported this as a matter of general interest:

By the last letters from Constantinople we learn that the
Grand Signior has invested David Passo (sic), a rich Hebrew
and nephew of his physician, with the Duchy of Nixia in the
Archipelago, in the jurisdiction of the Duke who is here, which
Jew has been in this city a long time.[32]

At about this period, there arrived in Turkey another
Marrano, whose career was to be bound up closely with
Passi's. This was Alvaro Mendes, a member of a New
Christian family of Tavira in Portugal.[33] (There is no
real indication that, as has been suggested, he was in any
way related to the founders of the great Mendes banking-
house with which Doña Gracia and Joseph Nasi were
associated.) In a ten years' residence in India, he had
made an enormous fortune by farming the diamond mines
of the kingdom of Narsinga. He then returned to Europe,
living in succession in Madrid, Florence, Paris and
London, becoming an intimate of the king of Portugal,
achieving the dignity of Knight of Santiago, being consulted by Catherine de Médicis, Queen-Mother of France,
and by Queen Elizabeth of England, and everywhere
playing a role in international politics. When the Spaniards seized Portugal in 1580, he embraced the cause of

the Portuguese pretender, Dom Antonio, Prior of Crato —
whose mother as it happens belonged to a New Christian
family — and became his trusted agent. The English
ambassador in Paris reported, in September, 1581, how
the king, Henri III, had dined with him recently together
with the dukes of Lorraine and Guise and the royal
mignons, or favorites. After being resident in France for
some years he went on to Turkey, presumably to see
whether concerted action could be arranged against Spain
and on behalf of the Portuguese pretender. Such importance was attached to his arrival that a safe-conduct
embodying various concessions was despatched for him,
as well as a special *chaus* to escort him on the last stages
of the journey. But his intentions were not only political.
On his arrival in Salonica, in April, 1585, he embraced
Judaism, together with all his family, and assumed the
ancestral appellation of Solomon Abenaish (Abenjaex)
or Ibn Yaish, recalling the name of a family which had
been prominent in Spain, and was to be prominent henceforth in Turkey, for learning and public spirit.

His future career seems to have been consciously
modelled on that of Joseph Nasi, whose recollection was
so fresh. He visited the embassies. He was in constant
touch with the imperial Divan. He was appointed high
commissioner (presumably, that is, purveyor) to the imperial Court. He was in close relations with diplomatic
and political circles. He maintained an elaborate information service all over Europe. He was created Duke of the
Mytilene (the ancient Lesbos), one of the largest and
most fertile of the Aegean islands, which had been under
Turkish rule since 1432. (It was calculated that this
brought him an income of between 16,000 and 18,000

ducats, though doubtless the greater part had to be made over to the sultanic treasury.)[34] He farmed the Ottoman customs-revenue, which was expected to secure 1,000 ducats daily and 40,000 nobles quarterly for the payment of the janissaries. (The administration of this was in the hands of one of his nephews, whom he brought to Constantinople.)[35] Like Nasi, though less ostentatiously, he managed to enforce payment of a debt owed to him by the king of France by obtaining the sequestration of the property of certain Florentine merchants who enjoyed French protection. He obtained (as has been told above) a renewal of Don Joseph's grant of the city of Tiberias and its environs, where his own son, formerly Francisco, but now known as Jacob Abenaish (who was not only deeply religious but, to his father's profound distress, also unpractical and other-worldly) went to settle, passing all his time in study. The French ambassador (to whom he had offered his services as soon as he arrived) treated him with contempt now it was known that he was a Jew, and gleefully reported every attempt made to ruin him.[36] But notwithstanding all intrigues, he maintained his position for nearly twenty years. The role that he played in the Turkish capital was almost as resplendent as Nasi's a quarter of a century before. One day, we are informed, when the Grand Signior was in his garden with the Captain Pasha, he sent for Don Solomon to come and join them in order to discuss important matters of foreign policy, bringing with him the *mapamundi*, or Atlas, which, to the envy of the savants of Constantinople (for only the French ambassador owned a similar treasure) he had brought with him when he arrived from overseas.[37]

Above all, he threw himself into the cause of an Anglo-

Turkish alliance against Spain, one of the corollaries of which was the support of the cause of the Portuguese pretender against Philip II. The association between Turks, Englishmen and Jews was not an unnatural one; had not Queen Elizabeth in a letter to the sultan appealed for him to make common action with her against the Spanish image-worshippers? Such was the consideration with which Don Solomon was regarded that when, in 1587, the Turkish admiral as a friendly gesture wished to set free nine English sailors whom he had captured off Tripoli, he handed them over, not to the English ambassador, William Harborne, but to the ex-Marrano, who in turn sent them to the embassy. On the other hand, Francis Drake was once instructed to release some Portuguese prisoners of war, captured at sea in a Spanish galleon, as a personal favor to him.

His activity was closely connected with that of the group of Marranos in London, headed by Dr. Hector Nuñes, who primed Queen Elizabeth's ministers with information from the Peninsula and contributed in some slight measure at least to the defeat of the Armada and, to a somewhat greater degree, to the frustration of Spanish plans for world dominion in the subsequent years. He boasted, with reason, that but for him peace between Spain and Turkey, leaving England isolated, would have been concluded in 1587,[38] in which case the whole course of European history might have been different.

A connection of his by marriage, named Roderigo Lopez, the queen's physician, was his principal channel for communicating with the English government. In the year of the Armada, Abenaish at last succeeded in per-

suading the sultan to sanction the despatch of a Turkish
fleet to help to put Dom Antonio on the throne of Portugal. This would have proved a solid help to England at
her moment of danger; but as the result of a bribe paid
by the Spanish ambassador to the grand vizier, Sinan
Pasha, the orders were cancelled, on the pretext that all
the available military strength of the Ottoman empire
was absorbed in the war in Persia. It was Abenaish, as a
matter of fact, who brought the Turkish government the
first intelligence of the defeat of the Armada — before
the English ambassador himself had learned the great
news and while the Ragusan representative was busily
engaged in putting about an opposite report.[39]

The question of obtaining support for the Portuguese
succession, which had originally been the reason for the
new Duke's interest in the Anglo-Turkish alliance in the
first instance, ultimately became secondary, so that he
favored the latter policy passionately on its own merits.
Dom Antonio had in fact revealed himself by now as weak,
vacillating and greedy; and as a result he and his former
champions became estranged. In the end, the pretender
broke entirely with Abenaish, whom he accused of building
up his fortune dishonestly at the expense of the Portuguese
Crown. (It may be mentioned that some time afterwards
the Spanish government investigated these charges, in the
hope of finding a pretext for the confiscation of his
property, but they could not unearth any evidence worth
taking into account.) He now transferred his favor to
David Passi, whom he appointed his representative in
February, 1591, notwithstanding persistent rumors that
he was a secret Spanish agent. The latter actually succeeded in persuading the grand vizier to promise his

master the armed support of Turkey — a spectacular triumph, but meaningless, as the undertaking was never carried out.

The English ambassador, Barton, had at first refused to have anything to do with David, but in due course was compelled to receive him at the embassy. This gave rise to a quarrel with Abenaish, and in May, 1591, the ambassador wrote to Lord Burleigh, Queen Elizabeth's minister, spitefully suggesting that the sultan should be told Dom Antonio's account of the source of the other's great wealth, which could then be confiscated and divided between the Turkish and Portuguese treasuries. The story leaked out. Towards the end of the same year, accordingly, the Duke sent to England as his personal representative a certain Solomon Cormano (Carmona?) who was to lay matters before the queen. (While he was in London, divine service was actually held in his lodging in accordance with Jewish rites — a welcome innovation for the little band of Marranos living in the city.) The mission was completely successful, and Cormano returned with a communication from Elizabeth to the sultan disavowing the action of her ambassador and testifying to Abenaish's high character. A covering-letter was sent to the latter from Lord Burleigh, which he was requested to transmit personally to the sultan; it would have been impossible to make a more unmistakable demonstration of confidence. There is still preserved in the English archives the Duke's original letter, written in Spanish but dated according to the Jewish year, thanking Her Majesty for her generous action.

Barton grumbled, naturally. Abenaish on the other hand, encouraged by his envoy's reception, was now emboldened to act even more independently. In the following year, at the sultan's suggestion, he sent a second mission to London headed by another of his retainers, Judah Sarfati or Serfatim, to make sure of the benevolent neutrality of England in the war with Hungary which was just beginning and was to continue for fourteen years. (The envoy went by way of Lemberg, which would seem to indicate that Abenaish inherited also Joseph Nasi's interest in Polish affairs.) He found English conditions changed for the worse in one important respect. Dr. Lopez, his master's relative by marriage and for a long time his London agent, had been indiscreet, if not far worse. He had received Spanish communications; he had conspired against Don Antonio; he was accused of treacherous intentions against the queen herself. Now, he was lying under arrest, in the Tower of London, on a charge of high treason. As was natural, Serfatim intervened on his behalf, pointing out how seriously his master's position might be affected if he were condemned. This was in vain, for popular passions were too greatly incensed; and though the secretary of state, Sir Robert Cecil, tried to save him, he was condemned and executed not long after.

Yet even this unhappy episode did not seriously affect Abenaish's position, which in fact was assisted by events that had been happening meanwhile in Constantinople. Barton had for some time been on amicable terms, not only with David Passi, but also with the physician Moses Benveniste and the Italian non-Jew Paolo Mariani, all three of whom were now suspected of being Spanish agents. But Passi's fall was imminent. In 1591, he had a violent quarrel with his former patron, the Grand

Vizier Sinan, conqueror of Tripoli and a great collector
of manuscripts: probably this break was the result of an
indiscreet letter Passi had written to the chancellor of
Poland, hinting that the minister's recent conciliatory
communication had been sent on his own authority, with
no object save to extract money.[40] The latter's fury
knew no bounds, and to save his life Passi took refuge in
the house of the Beylerbey (governor), only venturing
to stir from it on obtaining a safe-conduct from the sultan. Nevertheless, when the fiery old vizier caught sight
of him he was restrained from violence only with difficulty, and afterwards had him put in chains and deported
to Rhodes, where so many better men had been sent before him. He was not there indeed for long, for in August,
1591, Sinan Pasha was dismissed, but when he returned
to Constantinople in the following month, Passi was a
broken man and played no further part in public life.
The sultan's secretary informed the Venetian *bailo* that
the republic should consider Passi's removal worth
1,000,000 ducats!

The way was now clear for a rapprochement between
Don Solomon and the English ambassador. Other circumstances helped towards this. In 1591, a new voivode
had to be appointed in Moldavia in succession to Peter
the Lame. Solomon Ashkenazi, still active in public life,
exerted his influence to secure the appointment of a certain Pole of Jewish extraction, Emanuel Aron — perhaps
imagining (vainly, as it turned out) that this would
secure more humane treatment for the Jews of the province. More important than personal influence, however,
was the vast baksheesh which the latter promised the
grand vizier. At the prompting of the Italian intriguer

Paolo Mariani, with whom he was then hand-in-glove, Barton guaranteed the amount that was needed — some 300,000 crowns — hoping thus to extend English influence in eastern Europe. Aron got his appointment, but failed to honor his promises, with the result that Barton was besieged by his creditors. Abenaish ultimately undertook to advance the amount to the English government. Two years later, Ashkenazi went to Jassy to solicit compensation for his efforts, which had apparently entailed some expenditure. He was promptly handed over to the prince of Transylvania and thrown into gaol. The defeat of Sinan Pasha (now again in office, for the fourth and last time) when he invaded the province in 1596, seemed to seal Ashkenazi's fate. It was the English ambassador who now wrote to the prince requesting the release of "the Jew doctor of Sinan Pasha," as a personal favor. At last, accordingly, he was set free, though only (as was reported) after paying a ransom of 45,000 ducats.[41]

The influence of the Jewish statesmen, and amateurs of statecraft who considered themselves such, was intensified rather than otherwise, as was natural, after Sultan Murad's death in 1595. His son, Mohammed III, now ascended the throne: and Solomon Usque, the poet, formerly a dependent of the House of Nasi (of whom there has been occasion to speak more than once in the foregoing pages), presented the English ambassador an interesting report on conditions at the Turkish court, which was straightway sent to England and carefully studied by Lord Burleigh.[42] Solomon Abenaish's influence was undiminished in the new reign. In 1596, Judah Serfatim, his confidential agent, was sent to Spain on behalf of the Turkish government to negotiate an ex-

change of prisoners, his mission being followed with great
interest by diplomatic observers in the anticipation that
it might lead to something more vital. Another Jew now
attempted to enter the political sphere in opposition to
him — a certain David Ebrons, of Constantinople, who
claimed that he had performed great services to the
Spanish Crown, marauding and colonizing territories in
Asia, Africa and especially America. In 1597, this worthy
presented a scatter-brained petition to the king of Spain,
through the medium of the ambassador in Venice, requesting the withdrawal of the edict of expulsion, so that
well-wishers like himself might be able to serve the country more easily. His plans, he claimed, were more useful
than those suggested on behalf of Alvaro Mendes, from
whom he elaborately dissociated himself; for the other
was, he said, worth less than his gems, and his competence did not extend beyond jewelry![43] Notwithstanding
his self-advertisement, no attention was apparently paid
to him.

Hassan the Eunuch, who succeeded Ibrahim Pasha
as grand vizier in 1597, was said to be at the same time
avaricious, sagacious and friendly to the Jews, and his
relations with Solomon Abenaish were cordial. In the
following year (1598) the Spanish king decided to open
negotiations for a truce; and, though Spain was the most
intolerant of European countries, it was obvious that the
person best qualified to act as intermediary would be a
Jew who, besides having the necessary linguistic qualifications, would be acceptable to his powerful coreligionists in Constantinople. One was found who undertook
the task and was duly received, notwithstanding the
vigorous protests of the English ambassador. With him,

he brought a personal introduction to Abenaish, though the latter remained as much opposed to an understanding as ever before. Other Jews did not, however, share his views — so slight was the political solidarity among them. Indeed, it was generally held that the Turkish communities favored peace, if only because they were hoping to be permitted to establish themselves in Pisa in Tuscany for purposes of trade, which would have been difficult had a state of war continued with Spain and the associated powers. Among those who held these views was the physician Moses Benveniste, now confidential agent and adviser of the new grand vizier, Siavouch Pasha, who had always inclined to the Spanish party. He was, in fact, made one of the plenipotentiaries, together with two Turks, in the peace negotiations which were about to open. However, they exceeded their instructions and were banished; and though Benveniste tried to avoid the sentence by embracing Islam, his offer was refused and he ended his days as a political prisoner in Rhodes.[44] His end was more fortunate than that of another Jew who followed the same political tendency — Gabriel Buonaventura, who was sent as ambassador extraordinary to conclude an armistice with Spain, but was hanged with all his followers but one.[45]

The conclusion of peace, against his will, obviously implied the weakening of Abenaish's influence. He remained, however, in enjoyment of all his dignities throughout Mohammed III's reign and into that of his successor, Ahmed III, dying — an old man of over eighty — only in 1603. The details of his career have been recovered only recently, but there can be no doubt as to the importance of his position in the diplomacy of the day or of his utility to English foreign policy. The words of Lucien Wolf do not overstate the case:

He consistently supported Elizabeth's policy of an Anglo-Turkish alliance against Spain, and though he did not succeed in actually concluding an armed alliance he maintained cordial relations between England and Turkey, and thus defeated for many years all the Spanish schemes for securing the neutrality of the Sultan in the war between England and Spain. By his services in this latter respect he was instrumental in immobilizing in Italy and the Eastern Mediterranean large Spanish forces, which otherwise would have been turned against England.[46]

Not long before (probably about 1600), Solomon Ashkenazi, most influential of the Jewish statesmen of sixteenth-century Turkey, had died, full of years and honor. His reputation survived him. Ahmed I, who had recently ascended the throne at the age of fourteen, was suffering from smallpox or some allied illness, which his physicians could not cure. Rabbi Solomon's widow, Boula Eksati, who had retained some of her husband's medical proficiency and secrets, was now summoned to the palace and managed to effect a cure with her potions. As her reward, she was overloaded with presents. When, one or two years later, her son Nathan, who like his father combined ability as physician and as diplomat, visited Venice, he was received officially by the Doge Marin Grimani, to whom he brought letters of recommendation from the sultan; and the magnificence of his visit to the ghetto, and of his offerings to local charities, was long remembered.[47]

Meanwhile, the Duchess Reyna, Don Joseph's widow and Doña Gracia's daughter, had continued to live in the palace of Belvedere, still enjoying something of her

dead husband's glory. They had had one child only —
a daughter,[48] born not long after their wedding; but it
seems that she had predeceased her father, as nothing is
heard of her after 1564, and in 1576 Stephen Gerlach
referred to the marriage as childless. The Duke's estate
at the time of his death had (as we have seen) barely
sufficed to repay his widow her dowry-money of 90,000
ducats. But she had presumably inherited most of her
mother's vast fortune as well, and hence was not by any
means in reduced circumstances. She could perhaps have
continued to play a role in Turkish public life, as did
some of the other Jewesses of the time — all the more so
after Mehemet Sokolli's disappearance from the scene
a short while after her husband's death. She preferred,
however, to confine herself, as her mother had done, to
the more modest circle of Jewish communal life. It is
to be imagined that she continued the lavish charities
with which the family had been associated since their
first arrival in Constantinople. But she was interested
above all in intellectual activity — a phenomenon not
so outstanding among Jewish women as among men,
especially if, like her, they had obtained their first-hand
acquaintance with Judaism only in adult life.

She maintained, it seems, her husband's great library,
throwing it open to scholars who needed it for their re-
searches; and more than one copy was made in the subsequent few years from Hebrew manuscripts preserved
there, the colophons gratefully mentioning the late Duke's
name.[49] More active, however, was her patronage of
Hebrew printing, which for one reason or another had
never yet flourished in Constantinople as it did, for example, in Venice. Among the scholars whom she favored

was a certain Isaac Ascaloni, presumably a Palestinian
by birth. Depressed no doubt by the institution of
censorship in Italy, which prevented the untrammelled
publication of Hebrew books, and in many places made
it impossible, he prevailed on the Duchess to found a
printing press herself, as her husband was reported to
have done long before.[50] This she did in her own spacious
residence at Belvedere, its activities beginning in 1592.
The books blazoned the circumstances in magniloquent
phrases on the title pages or in the colophons —

Printed in the palace of the Honored woman Reyna Nasi,
widow of the Duke Don Joseph Nasi, at Belvedere, which is
near Constantinople, under the rule of Sultan Murad,

or

Printed in the house and with the type of the Crowned Lady,
crown of descent and excellency, Reyna (may she be blessed
of women in the tent!), widow of the Duke, Prince and Noble
in Israel, Don Joseph Nasi of Blessed Memory . . . near Constantinople, the great city which is under the rule of the great
and mighty King Sultan Mohammed (may his might increase!),

and the like.

The volumes chosen for publication, indeed, were
not memorable — Ascaloni had a penchant for trivialities,
and advised his patroness badly; and works such as the
Gan shel Egozim by Moses Egozi, comprising homilies on
the Pentateuch; *Torath Mosheh* of Moses Alsheikh; the
Kesher Nehosheth of Meir Angel; *Torath Hesed* or *Iaphek
Razon* — a commentary on the prophetical lessons by
Isaac Jabez — were hardly likely to usher in an intellectual revival on a major scale. (There was also one
work in Ladino, a guide book to the Holy Places of
Palestine; *libro intitolado Yichus ha-Zaddikim.*)

All these works appeared in 1592–4. Thereafter, the Duchess apparently had to give up the "palace" where she had lived with her husband. She now removed to a fresh residence, perhaps somewhat less magnificent, at Kuru Tschechmé, an adjoining suburb some little way further along the Bosphorus to the east, between Ortakewy and Arnaoutkewy (unless, as some authorities hold, it was only the printing press, and not the Duchess' private residence, that was transferred). In any case, in 1597 work was renewed here, under Ascaloni's uninspired direction as before. There were, indeed, certain manifest external changes, not all for the better. The first production was the fourth and concluding part of the responsa of Joseph ibn Leb, formerly Director of Doña Gracia's academy; other works included *Iggereth Shemuel* of Samuel di Uzeda; *Tapuhe Zahab* by Moses Alsheikh; *Minhath Kohen* by Joseph Cohen; a scholastic edition of the tractate Ketuboth from the Babylonian Talmud; and *Moshaoth El* by the Byzantine scholar Joseph ben Abraham Cohen — a production so poor that the author had to go to Venice to supervise the republication of a new edition in person. The press ceased to function in 1599. From that time on, we hear no more of Reyna Nasi. She had by now survived her husband by twenty years, her mother by thirty, and cannot have been much less than seventy years of age. There is little doubt that she died about this time.[51]

It was a lonely ending for the old woman in her great mansion overlooking the Bosphorus, even though the rabbis of the capital still waited upon her from time to time, dazzling her with displays of erudition calculated to stimulate her liberality. There she sat, dressed in the Spanish or Italian style of half a century before, waited on by her tirewomen. Thoughts crowded on her mind as she watched the shipping pass up and down the narrow stretch of water beneath her terraces. She dimly remembered perhaps the subterfuges of Marrano life in Lisbon, the glimpses of the Queen Regent's Court at Brussels, the elderly claimants to her hand, the headlong flight across the Alps, the pageants of Venice, the unpalatable discipline of the nunnery where she had been immured, the magnificence of the Este in Ferrara, the dangers and the escapes, the crossing of the Adriatic, the leisurely progress across the Balkans and the state entry into Constantinople. She could summon up still before her failing eyes the reunion with her cousin João Miguez, the festivities at their marriage, and the formal visit of the French ambassador himself to congratulate them. She recalled the banquets at the sultan's Court, the languid babel of the imperial harem, Sultan Suleiman's warlike demeanour and his sons' lascivious glances, her mother's open house to all who cared to come, the constant succor to fugitive Marranos, the indignation with which the news of Jewish persecution in Europe was received and the noble attempt to be avenged. Then there had come the glittering climax — her husband's enfeoffment with the premier duchy of Europe, their fleeting attempt to hold court in Naxos, the passing whim (if that was all it was) of establishing a Jewish territory in Palestine, and finally the brief period when the Crown of Cyprus almost seemed to be within their grasp.

The disaster of Lepanto had put an end to that dream. She was now an old and lonely woman, living on her memories. But still in her mind's eye she could see her

volatile husband, with his black beard and handsome
appearance, as he jousted in his palace garden with the
companions who had come with him from Portugal; or as
he left the sultanic presence on that memorable day at
Philippopolis, thirty years before, Duke of Naxos and
the Archipelago.

CHRONOLOGICAL TABLE

Expulsion from Spain *1492*
Forced Conversion in Portugal *1497*
Birth of Gracia Nasi .... c. 1510
Antwerp branch of Mendes firm opened 1512
Birth of Joseph Nasi .... c. 1520
Gracia Nasi married to Francisco Mendes 1528
Death of Francisco Mendes 1536
Inquisition established in Portugal *1536*
Doña Gracia Nasi settles in Antwerp 1536
Death of Diogo Mendes 1542-3
Doña Gracia settles in Venice 1544-5
Doña Gracia settles in Ferrara, and becomes a declared
    Jewess 1550
The Nasi family leaves Ferrara .... August 1552
The Nasi family reaches Constantinople 1553
Joseph Nasi arrives in Constantinople. He marries his
    cousin Reyna 1554
The boycott of Ancona, organized by the Nasi family to
    avenge the martyred Marranos 1556-7
Tiberias granted to Joseph Nasi .... c. 1561
Death of Sultan Suleiman the Magnificent and accession of
    Selim II .... *September 1566*
Joseph Nasi created Duke of Naxos 1566
Embargo on French shipping in Alexandria, at request of
    Joseph Nasi 1568
Death of Gracia Nasi 1569
Death of Samuel Nasi 1569
War of Cyprus *1570-1573*
Joseph Nasi nominated Voivode of Wallachia 1571
Death of Sultan Selim II and accession of Murad III *1574*
Death of Joseph Nasi, Duke of Naxos .... August 2, 1579
Death of Reyna Nasi, Duchess of Naxos .... c. 1599

BIBLIOGRAPHY

BIBLIOGRAPHY

I mention here generally only the works specifically dealing with the career of Don Joseph; they have sometimes been used in other chapters besides those in connection with which they figure. I have given exact references in the footnotes, to assist the student, only for statements which cannot be readily verified from these works.

GENERAL

BATO, YOM-TOB (LUDWIG), Don Joseph Nasi (a romanticized biography, in Hebrew). Tel-Aviv, 1942.

CARMOLY, E., Don Josef, Duc de Naxos. Brussels, 1855.

CHASSAZOGLU, N., Josef Nasi, der jüdische Prinz der griechischen Iseln.

GALANTE, ABRAHAM, Don Joseph Nassi, Duc de Naxos, d'après des nouveaux documents. Constantinople, 1913. (Cf. *Revue des Etudes Juives*, LXIV, 236–243.)

GRAETZ, H., Geschichte der Juden, vol. IX.

———, Don Joseph, Herzog von Naxos, Graf von Andros, und Donna Gracia Nassi, in *Jahrbuch für Israeliten*, ed. Wertheimer. Vienna 1856.

HALPHEN, ALICE FERNAND, Une grande dame Juive de la Renaissance: Gracia Mendesia-Nasi. Paris, 1929.

LEVY, M. A., Don Joseph Nasi, Herzog von Naxos, seine Familie, und zwei jüdische Diplomaten seiner Zeit. Breslau, 1859.

REZNIK, J., Le Duc Joseph de Naxos: contribution à l'histoire juive du XVIe siècle. Paris, 1936.

WILDENRAT, JOHANN VON, Joseph Nasi (a novel, translated into Hebrew by P. Kaplan). Warsaw, 1899.

CHAPTER I

DE VILLALÓN, CRISTÓBAL (*recte* Andrés Lagúna), *Viaje de Turquía*, ed. Antonio G. Solalinde. Buenos Aires, 1942. (Cf. also the works listed in the Bibliography to *Doña Gracia*).

CHAPTER II

HIRSCHBERG, H., "Udzial Józefa Nasi w pertraktacjach polsko-tureck-ich wr 1562" (The Participation of Joseph Nasi in the Turco-Polish Negotiations of 1562), in *Miesięcznik Zydowski*, IV (1934), pp. 426–439.

KAUFMANN, D., "Die Vertreibung der Marranen aus Venedig im Jahre 1550," in *Jewish Quarterly Review*, XIII (1901), pp. 520-32.

CHAPTER III

BERSOHN, M., "Einige Worte Don Joseph Nasi, Herzog von Naxos, betreffend," in *Monatschrift für die Geschichte und Wissenschaft des Judenthums*, XVIII, (1869), 422-4.

KOHN, S., "Oesterreichisch-ungarische Gesandsschaftsleichte uber Don Josef Nasi," in *Monatschrift für die Geschichte und Wissenschaft des Judenthums*, XXVIII, (1879), 114–121.

CHAPTER IV

CURTIUS, E., *Naxos*, Berlin, 1846.

HOPF, C., "Geschichte der Insel Andros," in *Sitzungsberichte der Kaiser-lichen Akademie der Wissenschaften*, XVI, (1855), Philosoph.-hist. Classe.

MILLER, W., *The Latins in the Levant*. London, 1908.

SANGER, R., *Histoire nouvelle des anciens Ducs de l'Archipel*. Paris, 1688.

CHAPTER V

BRASLAWSKY, J., "The Jewish Settlement in Tiberias from Don Joseph Nasi to Ibn Yaish" (Hebrew), in *Zion*, V, 45–72.

———, "Don Joseph Nasi's work in Palestine" in *Yerushalayim* (J.P.E.S.), dedicated to the memory of A. M. Luncz, 1928, pp. 67-77 (Hebrew).

KAUFMANN, DAVID, "Don Joseph Nasi and the Community of Cori in the Campagna," in *Jewish Quarterly Review*, O. S., II, 291-7. (See also *Algemeine Zeitung des Judenthums*, LIV, 255 ff.)

———, "A Letter from the Community of Pesaro to Don Joseph Nasi," in *Jewish Quarterly Review*, O. S., IV, 509-12.

———, "La quête pour les expulsés de Pesaro," in *Revue des Etudes Juives*, XX, 34 ff.

KLAUSNER, J., "Don Joseph Nasi" (Hebrew), in his *Historical Essays*, Tel-Aviv, 1936, etc. (French translation in his *Quand une nation lutte pour sa liberté*, Cairo, 1940.)

MOLHO, I. R., "The Falsification of the Picture of Don Joseph Nasi" (Hebrew), in *Behair haMizrah*, Jerusalem, 1944.

CHAPTER VI

DE LA GRAVIÈRE, JURIEN, *La Guerre de Chypre et la bataille de Lépante*. Paris, 1888.

HILL, G. F., *History of Cyprus*, vol. III. Cambridge, 1948.

ROMANIN, S. *Storia documentata di Venezia*, vol. VI, Venice, 1853.

CHAPTER VII

LATTES, *Notizie e documenti di letteratura e storia giudaica*. Padua, 1879.

MOLHO, I. R., "Moses Almosnino" (Hebrew) in *Sinai*, 1942.

CHAPTER VIII

Calendar of State Papers, Spanish.

Calendar of State Papers, Venetian.

DIENA, M., "Rabbi Scelomò Askenazy e la Repubblica di Venezia," in *Atti del R. Istituto Veneto*, VII, ix, 611–637.

GALANTE, A., *Don Salomon Aben Yaèche, duc de Mételin*. Istanbul, 1936.

WOLF, L., "Jews in Elizabethan England," in *Transactions of the Jewish Historical Society of England*, XI, pp. 1–91.

NOTES

NOTES

NOTES TO CHAPTER I

[1] The name is given in the account of Hans Dernschwam, quoted in full on pp. 8–9; but his evidence can be accepted only with reserve.

[2] *Al cual el Emperador había hecho caballero* (*Viaje de Turquía*, quoted below).

[3] It is hardly possible that (as has been stated) João Miguez is the same person as the Jehan Moniques accused of Judaizing at Antwerp in July, 1532 (Goris, *Les marchands méridionales . . . à Anvers*, pp. 65, 564, 588), for at that time he could hardly have been much more than twelve years of age, nor had his aunt Doña Gracia arrived in the Low Countries.

[4] See my life of Doña Gracia Nasi, chapter II, for full information. I shall not repeat in this volume details that can be found there. Romanin, *Storia documentata di Venezia*, VI, 271, quotes a despatch from Brussels of September 25, 1545, which confirms the picture given there. He adds the information that the exploitation of the family resulted from the advice given to the Queen Regent by her unpopular Florentine financial adviser, Gasparo Ducci.

[5] *Revue des Etudes Juives*, LXXXIII, 57. That he lived in Ferrara before going to Turkey is clearly stated by the contemporary chronicler, Joseph ha-Cohen, in the passage cited below, p. 136.

[6] A fanciful Dutch author has stated that he traded here under the extraordinary appellation of Don Tivisco de Nasao Zario y Colona. It hardly seems necessary to take this seriously.

[7] See *Doña Gracia*, p. 201. I am using the Buenos Aires edition of 1942 (ascribed, however, to Cristoval de Villalón) ed. A. G. Solalinde.

[8] As before, I am making use of J. R. Marcus' racy version, in his *The Jews in the Medieval World*.

[9] See below, p. 193.

[10] Some idea of the ceremonies may be had from Sir Richard Torkington's account of what he saw on a similar occasion at Corfu in 1517, as he gives it in his *Pilgrimage to Jerusalem*:

> The same Day ther was a Jewe maryed, and after Dyner I saw them Danse in a grett Chamber, bothe men and women, in Ryche apparell, Damaskee, Saten, velvett, weryng a bowte ther nekkeys

233

chenys of fine gold with many ryngges on ther fyngers with stonys of grett pryce, she that was maryed, she had upon her heade a crowne of gold. One of the Jewys be gan to syng, and then all the women Daunsed to gedyr by the space of an ower. And aftyr ther cam in young men, on of them sang: Thaune the men and women Dauncyd to geder. Aftyr that they callyd in ther mynstrellys, and so Dauncyd iii long howerys.

[11] J. Chesneau, *Voyage de M. d'Aramon* (Paris, 1887), pp. 48–9.

NOTES TO CHAPTER II

[1] It is possible that this was in fact the house where Doña Gracia had lived in the same area, not a new residence. The contemporary records generally give the name in the form *Belveder.*

[2] It is impossible to verify these three names, given by Laguna. But Don Samuel might be Samuel Usque (see *Doña Gracia,* p. 119) and Solomon could be Solomon Senior Coronel, who is spoken of just below.

[3] See below, pp. 87 ff.

[4] Below, p. 68.

[5] There is some vagueness about the name, but it may be imagined that the secretary, Joseph Cohen, who signed an official letter in 1577 (below, p. 96) is identical with the agent Joseph ibn Ardut (below, p. 112), who is again identified hypothetically with Joseph Pomar (Responsa of Moses di Trani, V, 8).

[6] See below, p. 180.

[7] See below, pp. 52–4.

[8] Cf. Amatus Lusitanus' dedication to the fifth book of his *Centuries,* dated Salonica, December 1559: "Your influence with the Sultan Suleiman and his sons, Selim and Bajazet, is common knowledge" (full text below, pp. 177–8). Don Joseph's intimacy with various European potentates is also referred to here.

[9] The historians say that Joseph earned Selim's good graces by bringing him a present from his father. In that case, it is difficult to see any reason for the former's extravagant gratitude. Possibly (but there is no indication that this was so) this episode took place at the turning point of the armed struggle between Selim and his brother, but it is curious that the sultan should have made use of the services of an infidel immigrant at this crucial moment. The version given in the text is borne out by Sereno, *Commentari della guerra di Cipro,* p. 7, and Gerlach, *Türkisches Tagebuch,* p. 426.

[10] Antonio Maria Gratiani, *De Bello Cyprio,* p. 15.

[11] The details are given by Almosnino, *Extremos y Grandezas de Constantinopla* (Madrid, 1638: see below, pp. 169–70) p. 77. Saadiah

NOTES 235

Lungo perhaps refers to this title of honor in the epithet "two well-born [or "illustrious"] brothers which he constantly applies to them in his Elegy. The word *muteferik* (Arabic) literally means "distinguished": it was a title given regularly to non-Moslem notables.

¹² See below, p. 68.
¹²ª Hill, *History of Cyprus*, III, 842–3.
¹³ See above, p. 10.
¹⁴ This passage shows that the Nasi family went from Antwerp to Venice *via* France, as already suggested.
¹⁵ This is improbable: all the indications suggest that Nasi was born in Portugal, though of Spanish parentage.
¹⁶ See *Doña Gracia*, pp. 55, 115.
¹⁷ *Doña Gracia*, pp. 70, 115.
¹⁸ Below, pp. 200–2, and *Doña Gracia*, pp. 105–7.
¹⁹ See ch. IV.
²⁰ H. Hirschberg, "Udzial Józefa w pertraktacjach polsko-tureckich wr 1562" (The Participation of Joseph Nasi in the Turco-Polish negotiations of 1562) in *Miesięcznik Zydowski*, IV (1934), pp. 426–439.
²¹ Hammer, VI, 118. The document was despatched by Sinan Pasha, Rustam's brother.
²² This clearly cannot refer, as David Kaufmann thought it did, to Nasi's hypothetical exclusion from Venice in 1550, but to an episode much more recent, at a time subsequent to Selim's accession to a position of authority, i.e., after (probably a good deal after) the year 1559. Possibly it was a result of the prominent part taken by him, in 1563–5, in the intrigue to induce the Duke of Savoy to put forward a dynastic claim on Cyprus (above, pp. 22–3).

NOTES TO CHAPTER III

¹ The correct details are in Almosnino, *Extremos y Grandezas de Constantinopla*, pp. 77–8 (See below, p. 169): the episode took place at Philippopolis, not Belgrade as is generally stated.
² These details are recounted by Almosnino in the original Ladino version of his *Extremos y Grandezas de Constantinopla*, extant only in manuscript, but were omitted in the published Spanish text: see M. Lattes, *Notizie e documenti di letteratura e storia giudaica* (Padua, 1879), pp. 18–19. This was not the only occasion when the Patriarch availed himself of the assistance of Jews: Gerlach, p. 240, tells of the manner in which he relied on the influence of the sultan's Jewish physicians.
³ Perhaps Hadef?
⁴ For the commercial relations between Joseph Nasi and Poland, see the article by Bersohn mentioned in the Bibliography, and Galante, *Joseph Nasi*, pp. 28–9.

[5] For an account of these, see Doña Gracia, pp. 105 ff.

[6] Galante, *Documents officiels Turcs concernant les Juifs* (Stamboul, 1931), pp. 112–3.

[7] Hammer, VI, 314–5. It is not correct to state, as has been done, that the gift to Nasi consisted of the sum of 2,000 ducats annually: it was only a part of that sum, allotted on one occasion. (As a matter of fact, there is no positive evidence that payment was actually made.)

[8] See above, pp. 13–4, for Verancsics' impressions of Nasi's personality.

[9] Schwarz in *Chajes Abhandlungen*, 1933, p. 225. One other Jew figures on the list — "Abraham Judt," who was to receive 100 thalers.

[10] I quote the full text from Halberstamm MS. 390 (now in Jews' College, London: Montefiore MS. 464) f. 57a.

[11] Above, pp. 34–5.

[12] It may be observed that this was not the only connection of a Jew with Polish diplomacy at this time: in 1567, the Khan of the Tartars had despatched a certain Meir Ashkenazi, from the ancient community of Kaffa in the Crimea, as his ambassador to Sigismund Augustus, though on his journey through the Mediterranean he was captured and killed by pirates.

[13] See Goris, *Les marchands méridionales à Anvers*, chapter VI, and *Doña Gracia*, pp. 27–8.

[14] Strada, *De Bello Belgico*, p. 135: cf. also Charrière, *Négotiations du Levant*, iii. 61.

[15] See chapter vii, *infra*: "King Aspirant of Cyprus."

[16] Charrière, iv, 747. The other information concerning this episode is almost all derived from documents in this very important work, except for the sultan's order to the Beylerbey of Egypt, which was published by Galante in his *Joseph Nasi*, pp. 31–2.

[17] So Almosnino, in more than one of his works (see below, pp. 166, 171–2). Saadiah Lungo, in his elegy on Don Joseph, speaks of Samuel's public work in generous terms.

[18] The sermon was delivered on Thursday, 28th Ab, 5329, corresponding to August 11, 1569.

I can think of no reasonable explanation of the duplication of name other than that given in the text: in all previous references, he is called Samuel. (It is out of the question that the biblical name of Moses would have been applied to him in his Marrano days.)

[19] I am at a loss to understand how the fact of the original redaction in Hebrew of a document so strongly antagonistic to Nasi's interests, and speaking of him in such a contemptuous fashion, should be ascribed to his influence — all the more so since he certainly knew French far better than he did the sacred tongue!

[20] The text is to be found in all the standard collections of diplomatic

documents bearing on Franco-Turkish relations — e. g., I. de Testa, *Receuil de Traités de la Porte Ottomane*, I (Paris, 1864), 91–6; St. Priest, *L'Ambassade de France en Turquie* (Paris, 1877), pp. 362–375.

[21] Du Bourg's despatch of 30th August 1569 *apud* Charrière, iii. 70; he adds that he will have this inserted in the Treaty, which he hopes will be ready in four or five days. The data are confirmed by the documents published in Reznik, appendix ii-iv. It is amazing that these facts have been overlooked by all previous historians, who have represented the Alexandria Embargo as wholly successful, and Nasi's greatest triumph, instead of nearly being (as it seems) the cause of his downfall.

[22] There does not seem to be any ground for Levy's identification of him as a member of the Hamon family: cf. Gross in *Revue des Etudes Juives*, LVI, 24–5.

[23] The text as promulgated at Salonica (and presumably elsewhere it was in similar terms) began as follows:

> *Per quanto se fallo en Constantina hombres tenidos por judios y procuraron de levantar cosa indiña contra el ilustrisimo Señor Don Josef Nasi, y era cosa de grandisimo peligro tanto al dicho señor, como y a todos judios ...*

[24] For the names of the signatories generally, cf. Rosanes, ii. 98, and for those of Salonica in particular, Emanuel, *Histoire des Juifs de Salonique* i. 219; the date is discussed in Graetz, ix. 393 note i; S. P. Rabinowitz, *Mozae Golah*, p. 332; and Rosanes, ii. 99n.

[25] Cf. Elijah Mizrahi's Responsa, *Mayyim Amukim*, §§ lv-lvi, etc.

[26] See especially for all this, besides the other sources cited above, St. Priest, *L'Ambassade de France en Turquie.*

NOTES TO CHAPTER IV

[1] The principal source for the succession of events, generally confused, is the statement of Moses Almosnino, Joseph Nasi's intimate, in his *Extremos y Grandezas de Constantinopla* (see for this work below, pp. 169–70), p. 77 f:

> *Luego que reinò, quando salio de Constantinopla para donde estava el campo (como avremos dicho) iba en su compania, y llegado à Phelipol le hizo merced del Estado de Nacasia ... Paris, y Ante Paris, Melo, Santorin, y otras Islas annexas à estas, que son pobladas, ademas de otras yermas, para hazer, y deshazer lelias a su voluntad, como cosa suya.*

From the phraseology, it seems probable that Almosnino had access to the original grant.

[2] For this and the general background later on, I am mainly dependent on William Miller's fascinating volume, *The Latins in the Levant* (London, 1908). Cf. also, for various details, Fotheringham, *Marin Sanudo*; E. Curtius, *Naxos*; M. H. Hauser, *Voyage au Levant de Philippe du Fresne-Canaye.*

[3] Cf. Almosnino *op. cit.* p. 78: *Despues le aumentò la isla de Andrea (que antiguamente se llamava Andros).* According to Miller, Antiparos formed part of the lordship of Andros at this time, but Almosnino specifically includes it among the islands comprised in the original grant. This passage also demonstrates that Miller was in error in stating (p. 592) that Andros never enjoyed personal union with the duchy of Naxos after the fourteenth century.

[4] Hopf, however, states categorically that these islands were dependent on and ruled from Tenos, a Venetian possession.

[5] So Immanuel Aboab in the important letter published by me in the *Jewish Quarterly Review*, n. s., XXIII, 153. In the only extant document of his administration (below, pp. 95-6), Nasi styled himself more modestly: "Duke of the Archipelago and Lord of Andros."

[6] Samuel de Medina, Responsa, *Yoreh Dea*, § liii.

[7] Almosnino, *loc. cit.*

Alli besò a su Alteza la mano, y le mandò (por medio de Hasan Baxà su Ayo) se bolviesse a poner en orden sus Estados, y escusasse el trabajo de ir mas adelante. I quote this passage verbatim, as it clears up many points about which confusion has reigned hitherto and proves definitely that Nasi was not a stranger to his duchy, as has always been said before now.

[8] The documents, unknown until recently, were published by Galante in his brochure, *Joseph Nasi,* and elsewhere.

[9] Historians, from Father R. Sauger in the seventeenth century onwards, have always said hitherto that Nasi never visited his duchy. This seems to be a deduction from the fact that his presence there is not recorded. On the other hand, Almosnino states clearly that he went there in 1566, immediately after his appointment, while it is almost certain that he was there in the spring of 1570, when it was rumored in Constantinople that he was captured during a Venetian raid. (See below, p. 93: this proves in any case that contemporaries who knew of his movements in detail did not regard him as a perpetual absentee.) Moreover, the official sultanic letter of March 23, 1568, to Piale Pasha (published by A. Galante, *Joseph Nasi,* p. 30), begins with the words: "Joseph, Duke of Naxos, and model of the princes of the Jewish nation, has despatched a messenger to bring to my notice" . . . . [certain facts regarding conditions in the Duchy]. This seems to suggest that he was there at the time; the document of November 24, 1567, on the other hand, speaks of information that he had brought in person

to the sultan, but that of June 13 of information contained in a letter from him. It may be taken for granted, nevertheless, that he was never long absent from the imperial Court if it could be avoided.

[10] The very interesting and informative contemporary memorials published by Lamansky, *Secrets d'Etat de Venise*, pp. 82–3, are quite definite on this point. Yet perhaps there is some confusion; for father and son to profess different religions, though both had left Spain, seems unlikely, and in my own mind I am not at all sure that the father enters into the picture. It may be noted that the family Senior Coronel was well known in Amsterdam in the following century.

[11] "The tithe was given by agreement with them to the Jew Joseph, without their suffering from any vexation." Capitulations of Murad III, 1580, quoted by Pègues, *Santorin* (Paris, 1882), p. 609.

[12] So Father R. Sauger, in his *Histoire nouvelle des anciens Ducs de l'Archipelago*, Paris, 1699. (Miller's attempt to explain this away is superfluous.)

[13] It may be mentioned that in the middle of the sixteenth century there was a famous North African corsair in the Turkish service who was of Jewish origin, "Sinan the Jew."

[14] The Turkish document published by Galante refers to "the traitor named Ducna, formerly Governor of Naxos." But his identity with the former duke is obvious, if only from the similarity of the pension given him by the Pope: presumably Ducna = Duke.

[15] See Chapter VI.

[16] For all this, see the letters from Tenos about Coronello in Lamanski, *Secrets d'Etat de Venise*, pp. 83–3, and Paolo Paruta, *Storia della Guerra di Cipro*, ed. 1827. Miller places this before the outbreak of the Turco-Venetian war; but Paruta, the contemporary, seems definite on the point.

[17] Charrière, *Négotiations du Levant*, IV, 767.

[18] The letter of the Teniote ambassador to Venice about Coronel, with many interesting details, together with the covering letter of the Council of Ten dated October 10, 1571, is published by Lamansky, *Secrets d'Etat de Venise*, pp. 80–83.

[19] These additional documents about Joseph Nasi are published by Galante in his *Appendice a l'ouvrage "Documents officiels turcs concernant les Juifs"* (Stamboul, 1941), p. 44 sqq.

[20] The document was found by the historian Curtius a hundred years ago, in the possession of one of the Coronel's descendants. For the subsequent history of the family, see below, p. 194. I am informed that Mr. J. Harosin (formerly Reznik), of Tel Aviv, now owns a further document signed by Joseph Nasi as Duke, about the settlement of a dispute in a church in Naxos: but I have been unable to obtain further details.

NOTES TO CHAPTER V

[1] The information is given by Hans Dernschwam, about whom see above, pp. 8–9; it is amplified in *Doña Gracia*, pp. 119-20.

[2] The origin of the present Arab inhabitants is an independent question. At the time of the Tartar invasions of the thirteenth century, Palestine had been depopulated to a great extent; and in just the same way as the Jewish population had to be built up again almost from nothing, so too the Moslems had to depend on immigration in order to reinforce their numbers. There were Bedouin from the desert, agriculturalists from the Yemen, military colonists from Turkey and Egypt and slaves from every part of the Moslem world. It is often forgotten today that a very great part of the population of the Holy Land, Moslem and Christian as well as Jewish, are equally newcomers.

[3] The phrase is that of Solomon Schechter, who devoted a vivid chapter to sixteenth-century Safed in his *Studies in Judaism*, vol. II, pp. 202-306.

[4] The general insecurity in the country at this time was, of course, partly responsible for this state of affairs. The Turkish conquest of 1516 had in fact barely affected the administration, save that the revenues were henceforth despatched to Constantinople instead of Cairo. The Palestinian annals of the period record little save the sanguinary quarrels of the local sheikhs and their relentless oppression of the long-suffering felaheen. Public security barely existed. The German botanist, Lenhard Rauwolf, has left a vivid picture of the conditions which he found in 1575, a little time after the period with which we are dealing, even in the immediate neighbourhood of Jerusalem, where conditions were better than in Galilee. Jaffa, where he landed, was in ruins, and a safe-conduct had to be obtained from the governor of Ramleh before the party could proceed inland. On the way, at Yazur, they were stopped by an official who extorted heavy blackmail, on the pretext that he had been given custody of the Holy Places and was forbidden to admit anyone to them without payment. Later on, they had a brush with some Bedouins. At last, after nearly completing the rough and stony road that led to the Holy City, they were kept waiting about outside the gate until the governor decided to permit them to enter. It was against a background such as this that Don Joseph made his historic attempt.

[5] The information is given by more than one contemporary — e. g., A. M. Gratiani, *De Bello Cyprio* (Rome, 1624), p. 21: Luigi Maria Benetelli, *I Dardi Rabbinici infranti* (Venice, 1705: dedicated to the Archangel Michael!), pp. 177–8; etc.

[5a] His official title was Father Custos of the Holy Land — i.e., Custodian of the Holy Places, a position reserved for the Franciscan order: his interest in the project was thus natural.

[6] The Tiberias experiment has been variously interpreted — as a philanthropic venture, a political experiment, an anticipation of Zionism, even an economic speculation. There is a certain degree of truth in all these hypotheses, but unfortunately our sources of information are too sparse to permit any definite conclusions, and Don Joseph himself was not probably altogether clear on this subject in his own mind.

[7] *Hilkhoth Sanhedrin*, XIV, 12.

[8] It is generally stated that he never went there at all. But it is impossible to be dogmatic upon this point: this same is said also as regards his duchy of Naxos, which as we have seen (above, p. 86), he visited repeatedly. From the language both of the chronicler Joseph ha-Cohen (below, p. 137) and of the letter of the community of Cori (p. 128), it seems as though he was on the spot for a short while at least at the time of the completion of the city wall.

[9] See above, pp. 12, 234.

[10] See p. 134.

[11] The point is discussed elsewhere: *Doña Gracia*, p. 182.

[12] The woollen industry was one of the mainstays of the community of Safed about this time, and there, too, wool was imported to manufacture cloth which competed with the Venetian product: see the very interesting anonymous account, based on the responsa of Rabbi Moses di Trani, in *Hemdath Israel*, ed. A. Elmaleh (Jerusalem, 1946), pp. 147–156, where there is, too, some further information on Tiberias at this time.

[13] The agricultural (not commercial) basis of the settlement is emphasized also in an overlooked reference by Antonio Maria Gratiani, *De Bello Cyprio* (Rome, 1624), p. 15: *urbem in veteribus Hebraeorum sedibus habitandam, ac frequentendam, agrumque colendum, impetraverunt.*

[14] Rosanes, *History of the Jews in Turkey* (Hebrew), II, 211.

[15] Responsa of Moses di Trani, III, § xxix, referring to a deed drawn up in Tiberias in 1558, which formed the subject of a lawsuit some fifteen years later, when the records were still extant. In most cases, the chronology of the responsa is not so exact, and conditions may not perhaps refer to the exact period with which were dealing here.

[16] For a full description, see my *History of the Jews in Italy*, chapter VII.

[17] I am inclined to believe that we can trace the terms of this letter of invitation, at least in part, in the account of the Tiberias episode inserted by the chronicler Joseph ha-Cohen (incidentally, no connection of Joseph ibn Ardut, with whom he has been confused by some writers) in the *Emek ha-Bakha*. The passage is quoted at length in the Additional Note at the end of this chapter.

[18] The date of this communication, discovered by that remarkable scholar and bibliophile David Kaufmann in a model letter-writer, is not given. However, it was clearly written some while after the accession of Pius V (1565) and his renewal of the onslaught on the Jews, but before the expulsion from the minor places in the Papal States by his bull, *Hebraeorum Gens*, of 6th February, 1569.

[19] It is interesting to note the rabbi including among his official duties the functions of physician as well as those of teacher.

[20] This seems to imply that the mission, in the name of the Jewish community, was endorsed by the City Council.

[21] The community was still in existence in 1582, when a bishop complained that they had managed to evade the edict of expulsion: *Revue des Etudes Juives*, IX, 85.

[22] Kaufmann originally believed that this letter, also found by him in a model letter-book, was written on behalf of the Marranos expelled from Pesaro in 1557 (see *Doña Gracia*, pp. 171-2), but subsequently changed his mind on the subject; there can be no doubt that it belongs to the period with which we are now dealing.

[23] There is a detailed account of his extraordinary career, hardly less remarkable than Don Joseph's, in chapter VIII, below.

[24] ="study": the word is still traditionally used among Spanish Jews.

[25] That there was a continuity of tradition is nevertheless not entirely out of the question. There is in Tiberias a Sephardi synagogue styled the Synagogue of the *Señor*. (The present building was erected by one Samuel Cohen, who died in 1873.) The name of the founder is unknown. But, since the places of worship supported by Doña Gracia were called *Kahal de la Señora*, it is possible (at least) that this institution was the solitary surviving record of the munificence of her son-in-law, Don Joseph Nasi (who may well have been styled similarly by his coreligionists "*The Señor*"), and his short-lived colonizing enthusiasm.

[26] There are extant a number of Hebrew hymns in praise specifically of Tiberias (not of the other "Holy Cities" in Palestine), obviously written for publicity purposes. It is, I think, conceivable that they represent a tradition which goes back to the period when Joseph Nasi was trying to arouse interest in his scheme.

NOTES TO CHAPTER VI

[1] Contemporary observers are unanimous on this point; see B. Sereno, *Commentari della Guerra di Cipro*, p. 16; A. Guarneri, *De Bello Cyprio*, p. 6; A. M. Gratiani, *De Bello Cyprio*, pp. 33-4; and, a little later, Luigi Maria Benetelli, *I Dardi Rabbinici Infranti*, pp.

177–8, etc. The details are repeated in Codice Gradenigo 49 in the Museo Correr, Venice (Grewemboch, *Habiti de' Veneziani*, vol. iii. p. 62). This accompanies the drawing of a Turkish merchant reproduced in *Doña Gracia* as illustration no. 13.

² See chapter VIII, below.

³ Gratiani, op. cit., p. 38.

⁴ See *Doña Gracia*, chapter VII.

⁵ Elijah of Pesaro, on his way to Palestine in 1563, found in Famagusta only 25 quarrelsome Jewish householders; they had a beautiful synagogue, however, and economic conditions were good.

⁶ Lamansky, *Secrets d'état de Venise*, p. 031 (sic). The document is interesting: the Captain of Famagusta was to seize various Christians and Jews, as well as a number of Cypriotes who had become Turks, "who go about the island and give treacherous accounts to Giovanni Miches." The captain was instructed, moreover, to report on the number and occupations of the Jews in Cyprus.

⁷ Gratiani, op. cit. But the story has a suspicious similarity to what was told about Coronello (above, p. 9).

⁸ This story is based upon a despatch of the Venetian *bailo* in Constantinople to the Doge of March 11, 1571, published by L. de Humazaki, *Documente privitóre la Istoria Românilor*, viii. 162 (n. 234):

> The aforesaid Giovanni Miches, moreover, with many suits and complaints, has greatly exaggerated the extent of the damage which he says he has suffered in his islands from the Venetian galleys. By availing himself of this opportunity, he has brought matters about so that the Grand Signior has given orders to the Magnificent Pasha to give him the state of Wallachia in exchange for these other possessions. Thus, Your Serenity would have been the occasion of this benefit to him, were it not for the fact that His Magnificence [the Grand Vizier] was opposed to the idea, and disturbed the matter so that, as is thought, it will have no effect . . . .

The Imperial envoy in Constantinople had reported to the emperor to much the same effect, three days earlier, saying that Don Joseph of Naxos, or the "Great Jew," had set his mind on the province in question, had managed to win over the Sultan, and was doing his best to overcome the grand vizier's opposition with promises and bribes (*ibid.*, II. i. 612–3). That Don Joseph actually obtained the investiture is stated by M. A. Halevy, *Comunitatile Evreilor din Iasi si Bucuresti*, p. 47 (Bucharest, 1931: Kindly consulted for me by Dr. Joshua Starr, whom I have to thank for other references also), and in *Encyclopaedia Judaica*, IX, 365–8. Without access to Roumanian sources quoted here, I am unable to determine whether the information is to be accepted implicitly. N. Jorga, "Contributiuni la Istoria Munteniei," in *Analele*

Acad. Romane, XVIII (1896) p. 9, states on the other hand that the grand vizier's opposition was successful.

[9] Unpublished despatch of M. A. Barbaro to the Doge of March 11, 1571, in Venetian State Archives (kindly copied for me by Prof. G. Luzzatto):

> *Li Ragusei sono qui al presente in qualche contumatia, perchè Gioan Miches sdegnato con loro per haverli quei signori fatto morire di giustitia in Ragusa un suo parente hebreo, fa con molte accuse contra di essi offitii assai dannosi, dicendo che con navi loro levano via vettovaglie di Alessandria et le conducono in Candia, del che il Bascià ne mostra grande alterazion.*

[10] Romanin, *Storia documentata di Venezia,* VI, 279.

[11] Cf. *Archivio Storico Italiano,* 1862, n. s. XVII, 81: "Privileges to the Basevi family (Jews) granted in 1574 by the Council of Ten in Venice at the request of a Turkish ambassador, a Jew, who was a relative of theirs" (C. Cavattori, *Informazione delle cose di Verona,* 1600).

[12] Most of this information is from the despatches of the Venetian ambassadors in Constantinople, published by Albéri, which contain a good deal more unused information; cf. also Paolo Paruta, *Storia della Guerra di Cipro,* ed. 1827, pp. 399, 412.

[13] Galante, *Histoire des Juifs d'Istanbul,* I, 11.

[14] Charrière, *Négotiations du Levant,* n. 280.

[15] It is interesting to note that the report of this episode reached even England. Sir Philip Sidney referred to it in a letter written to Languet in June, 1574: *Cras Judaeus quidam Selimi medicus aget cum Venetiis de pace certis conditionibus stabilienda (Notes and Queries,* cxix, 408).

[16] It may be noted that Nathan is not referred to as a rabbi in this Hebrew source, though this was almost always the case when the non-Jews mentioned him.

NOTES TO CHAPTER VII

[1] Eliezer Ashkenazi, preface to *Ioseph Lekah* (see below, p. 179).

[2] *Doña Gracia,* chapter VII, "The Ancona Boycott": there is cited here, p. 165, an extraordinarily graphic description of an audience with Don Joseph while he was on the point of leaving Constantinople, derived from the responsa of R. Joshua Soncino.

[3] See especially the memorial elegy of Saadiah Lungo, cited below, p. 192.

[4] The story is told by Immanuel Aboab in the letter published by me in the *Jewish Quarterly Review*, N. S., XXIII, 121–162.

[5] See above, pp. 68–73; and for Meir ibn Sanche, p. 167 in this book, and *Doña Gracia*, p. 165.

[6] Emanuel, *Histoire des Juifs de Salonique*, I, 217–8 (from Responsa of Solomon de Medina, etc., and Bodleian MS. Hebr. 1986, ff. 133–7).

[7] See *Doña Gracia*, p. 129. There are important monographs on Moses Almosnino by Carmoly in French, and I. R. Molho in Hebrew (in *Sinai*, vol. VI. 1942; cf. also ibid., VI, 133–9 and *Marx Commemoration Essays*, pp. 7–9). The latter states erroneously, that Nasi was his nephew: this is based on a confusion of the references on the title page.

[8] Lattes, *Notizie . . . di storia giudaica*, pp. 16–8.

[9] The details are from Almosnino's sermon, preached on his triumphant return home and included in his volume, *Meamez Koah*: they have been used by Emanuel in his *Histoire des Juifs de Salonique*, I, 210–6, and in the various monographs on the author cited already.

[10] The unpublished Ladino "original" of this work, embodying some interesting details on Joseph Nasi which are not in the published Spanish version, is described by M. Lattes in his *Notizie . . . di storia giudaica*.

[11] She was eagerly expected in Palestine in 1565, but that was a year after the date of the vision.

[12] *Doña Gracia*, pp. 128–9.

[13] It is of interest to note that Theodor Herzl was descended in the female line from the Taitaçac family.

[14] Below, pp. 217–9.

[15] The work is dated 1st Tevet 5326 = March 23, 1565.

[16] *Doña Gracia*, pp. 27, 53, 71, 138, 146, etc.

[17] It is included in Pyrrhus' published poems and reprinted by Emanuel in his collection of Salonica tombstones, n. 228. The Salonica cemetery was desecrated and most of its monuments destroyed in the course of 1941–6, the wilful devastation continuing even after the liberation of the city, and it is now improbable that the original monument — for which many had already sought in vain — will ever be traced.

[18] *Doña Gracia*, p. 146.

[19] It is a coincidence, but no more, that this was the name by which one of the progenitors of the Nasi family was known: see *Doña Gracia*, pp. 10, 95.

[20] I have made use of the translation by Dr. Harry Friedenwald: the bracketed passages were omitted in the editions printed in Catholic countries.

[21] There is an interesting characterization of him in the travel-letter of Elijah of Pesaro, who met him as a wealthy householder when he visited Cyprus on his way to Palestine in 1563.

[22] See *Ayumah kaNidgaloth*, preface. In the *Jewish Encyclopedia*, and other authoritative works, both earlier and later, the two Isaac Onkeneiras are fused into one. On the other hand, some writers suggest that there was yet a third, to whom they ascribe the editing of the book *Reumah*; but the constant recurrence of the same epithets and ascriptions make this assumption, in any case gratuitous, impossible. The two Isaacs were cousins, both being grandsons of R. Judah Onkeneira.

[23] This little work is not, as many eminent writers have stated it to be, an anti-Christian polemic. The pages are numbered 30–36 (the title-page is unnumbered), which makes it appear that it was intended to be part of a larger publication, in which case Don Joseph may have been far more prolific than has been imagined hitherto.

[24] There is a work of religious polemic, *Hoda'ath Ba'al Din*, by David Nasi of Candia (Crete), steward and intimate of the Venetian Cardinal Francesco Bentiviglio, who was a student of Hebrew. But the author had nothing to do with Don Joseph Nasi, and, indeed, lived long before him.

[25] See above, p. 130.

NOTES TO CHAPTER VIII

[1] S. Gerlach, ut supra.

[2] Ibid., p. 426: the reference is obviously to the accession of Murad—not of Selim, as might appear from the text.

[3] See below, pp. 198–9 for fuller details.

[4] Charrière, *Négotiations du Levant*, III, 648; cf. IV, 280.

[5] Albéri, *Relazioni*, III, ii, 166.

[6] See above, pp. 95–6.

[7] See above, pp. 180–2.

[8] Testa, *Receuil de Traités*, I, 126; Charrière, *Négotiations du Levant*, III, 808.

[9] Hammer, *Geschichte des osmanischen Reiches*, VI, 59–60.

[10] Hammer, VII, 59.

[11] Albéri, *Relazioni*, III, iii, 432.

[12] See, however, below, p. 205.

[13] The document was discovered and printed by Galante in his *Don Joseph Nasi*, pp. 32, 39.

[14] Thus, in the seventeenth century, Adriana Coronello, daughter of Crusino Coronello, married Crusino Sommaripa, great-grandson of the last Lord of Andros.

[15] For details, cf. A. Galante, *Médecins juifs au service de la Turquie*, Istanbul, 1938; Rosanes, *History of Jews in Turkey* (Hebrew), III, 268–274.

[16] Charrière, *Négotiations du Levant*, III, 883. In his case, too, the Turkish government once sent a *chaus* to Venice to secure payment of a debt owed by a local merchant who had failed, and he also had difficulty in obtaining the repayment of a sum lent to the French ambassador, Grandchamp (*ibid.*).

[17] Lamanski, *Secrets d'état de Venise*, p. 744.

[18] *Ibid.*, p. 882.

[19] *Rivista Israelitica*, VI, 145 ff.

[20] Albéri, *Relazioni*, III, ii, 299.

[21] "Rabbi" Isaac's surname is unrecorded. Rosanes (III, 274–5) suggests that he was one of the Hamon family; it has been conjectured, on the other hand, by Lucien Wolf and others, that "Isaac" is a slip for "Solomon," the reference being to Solomon Ashkenazi; but this is hypothetical, and not very likely. The information may be found in Testa, *Receuil de traités*, I, 129–30, 137.

[22] There is an echo of the fame of the Jewish physicians in the sultan's service at this time in Robert Greene's play, *The Tragicall raigne of Selimus, sometime Emperour of the Turkes* (first produced in London between 1588 and 1592). This has among its characters Abraham "a cunning Jew professing physicke," who is used by Selim for his nefarious purposes, but succumbs to them in the end.

[23] Rosanes, III, 279–80; Galante, *Turcs et Juifs* (Stamboul, 1932), p. 101.

[24] Galante, *Documents officiels turcs concernants les Juifs*, Stamboul, 1931, p. 137 ff.

[25] *State Papers, Venetian*, 1595, p. 159; 1596, p. 190.

[26] See *Doña Gracia*, pp. 105–7.

[27] *Purchas his Pilgrimes*, IX, 435 ff.; the data supplement those in Galante's monograph on Esther Kyra. Although Sanderson implies that her fall took place under Mehemet III (1595–1603), it was probably in 1593; but the chronology is very confused.

[28] i. e., dumpy.

[29] *State Papers, Venetian*, 1583, p. 572.

[30] Rosanes, III, 63; Galante, *Juifs d'Istanbul*, II, 48.

[31] The personality of David Passi (i. e., "of Fez") was first pieced together from various scattered sources, in connection with its possible bearing on the figure of the Jew in Elizabethan drama, in a letter by C. F. Tucker Brooke in the London *Times Literary Supplement* of July 6, 1922; my account has been supplemented from the data in the *Transactions of the Jewish Historical Society of England*, vol. XI, and various references in the British *State Papers* series (Venetian, Spanish etc.) covering the last decades of the sixteenth century.

[32] *State Papers, Foreign*, 1585, p. 663.

[33] Solomon Abenaish is a discovery of the late Lucien Wolf's, and most of the data given here are from his article on the "Jews in Elizabethan England," in the *Transactions of the Jewish Historical Society of England*, vol. XI. On the basis mainly of this, Abraham Galante published a separate monograph, *Don Solomon Aben-Avèche, duc de Métélin* (Istanbul, 1936). My data are from these two sources, supplemented from the *State Papers*; Charrière, IV, 488, 490, 517, 524; etc. See also my *History of the Jews in England*, Oxford, 1941, p. 141.

Wolf originally stated (and I repeated) that Abenaish was knighted by the Queen of England, but this is not correct: his knighthood was of the Spanish Order of Compostella.

[34] The principality of Mytilene had been conferred on a Genoese adventurer named Francisco Gattilusio by the Eastern Roman Emperor in 1355, his descendants continuing to reign there until the Turkish conquest. Descendants in the female line of the last ruler, then belonging to the English family of Wickham, continued to lay claim to the dignity as late as the beginning of the present century! Full data may be found by those interested in that curious compilation, *The Legitimist Kalendar*, of which the issue for 1899 lies on my desk.

The Duke's agent described his master's fief to the English government as being on *terra ferma*, 15 or 16 days from Constantinople. Either his geography or his nomenclature are obviously at fault.

[35] Wolf ingeniously suggested that this was not his nephew, but his connection by marriage, Jacob Anes, born in Crutched Friars, in London, in 1552, whom Thomas Coryat met as a professing Jew in Constantinople in 1612.

[36] *State Papers, Spanish*, 1587, p. 92; Charrière, *Négotiations du Levant*, IV, 517, 524–5.

[37] Abenaish also patronized Hebrew scholarship: an edition of the talmudical tractate Shabbath, published in Constantinople about this time, announces on the title page that "he who engaged himself and assisted in the good deed with his means and his money in the service of his Creator, to enmerit the public, behold he is the Lord Don Solomon Aben Aish ... May the God of Abraham be his help and favor the work of his hands and implant him and his sons in the midst of Israel ....." There is a similar panegyric prefixed to the tractate Yoma. These allusions (which help to date the editions in question, previously vague) are the only references to Abenaish in Hebrew sources.

[38] *State Papers, Spanish*, 1587, p. 92.

[39] Similarly, it was one of the Marrano group in England, Dr. Hector Nuñez, who one day rose from table to bring Walsingham the news that the Grand Armada had sailed from Lisbon.

[40] *State Papers, Venetian,* 1591, p. 533.

[41] Rosanes (III, 275–6) suggests that the physician here in question is a certain Eleazar Iscandri, who perhaps had been attached to Sinan Pasha in Egypt. But in view of the fact that Ashkenazi is known to have been one of Aron's supporters, it can hardly be doubted that the reference is to him, especially as he seems to have spent some time at Peter the Lame's court (Jorga in *Anelele Acad. Romane,* XX. 438). Aron's Jewish origin is hypothetical.

[42] Cf. my article in the *Jewish Quarterly Review,* N. S., vol. XXIV, pp. 65–85. I had not noticed at the time of writing this that Wolf, in *Transactions of the Jewish Historical Society of England,* XI, 32, note 65, ascribes Usque's letter to Abenaish and draws erroneous conclusions from this.

For Solomon Usque, see *Doña Gracia,* pp. 118–9.

[43] Duquesa de Berwick y de Alba, *Documentos escogidos del Archivo de la Casa de Alba,* Madrid, 1891, pp. 228–235.

[44] Rosanes, III, 55; Charrière, *Negotiations du Levant,* IV, 246–7; Galante, *Juifs de Rhodes,* pp. 109–110.

[45] *State Papers, Venetian,* 1600, p. 430; cf. also J. Paz y Espeso, *Archivo General de Simancas,* Cat. ii: "Informaciones sobre el judio Gabriel Buenaventura, in Cartas de Alemania, 1604–7."

[46] Attention may be called at his point to "a Jew of the black bonnet" named Saul Cohen who arrived in Constantinople in May, 1586, was concerned in the diplomatic relations between Venice and Spain, corresponded with the doge, became converted to Islam and claimed back from Abenaish, with the deliberate intention of ruining him, a diamond pledged with him for 80,000 ducats (Charrière, IV, 517; *State Papers, Venetian,* 1581–91 *passim*). Another interesting character was the Jew Angeli (Mordecai?), agent of the Swiss cantons, through whom they tried to open up diplomatic relations with Turkey during Sokolli's regime (Hammer, VII, 53).

[47] Rosanes, III, 68, 284–5.

This is not the place to deal with the Jewish statesmen and diplomats who took a part in public life in Constantinople in the seventeenth and eighteenth centuries, such as Israel Conegliano (1650–1720), physician and diplomatic adviser to the Venetian ambassador, who was prominent at the time of the conclusion of the Peace of Carlowitz in 1698; or the Marrano Daniel Fonseca (c. 1690–1750), formerly a Catholic priest, who was body-physician to the sultan, adviser to Charles XII of Sweden, and friend of Voltaire; or Moses Berberi and his son, successive Swedish ambassadors to the Sublime Porte (to mention only a few).

[48] She is referred to in Almosnino's vision of the palace of Belvedere in the *Tratado de los Sueños* appended to the original (Ladino) edition

of his *Regimiento de la Vida* (above, p. 171), together with a daughter of Don Samuel Nasi, who similarly is mentioned nowhere else. ("Nuesa beatísima señora y las señoras su hija y sobrina, que el Dios guardi.") But later on Almosnino again speaks of "your daughter and niece" — in the singular — in such a way as to suggest that the two are identical: i. e. that Don Joseph had no daughter of his own, and that the reference is to Don Samuel's child, who stood in filial relation to him.

[49] See above, p. 175.

[50] The latest and best account of this press is in Haberman's Hebrew brochure on *Jewish Women as Printers*; cf. also B. Friedberg's *Hebrew Typography in Italy . . . . Turkey and the Orient* (Antwerp, 1934), and *Hebraïsche Bibliographie*, I, 67–8; II, 33–4.

[51] With Reyna's death, the famous house of Nasi came to an end. Nothing is known to connect it with certain eminent persons of the name who figure in Jewish history later on, especially in the Marrano colonies of Europe and America. But it is worth while to call attention to the fact that several of them showed something of the same keen political interest that had distinguished the Duke of Naxos. In 1652–8, one David (Cohen) Nasi, alias Joseph Nuñez da Fonseca, one of the collaborators in Blaeu's great Geography, received a series of concessions from the Dutch West India Company for tracts of land in Curaçao and Guiana on which to settle agricultural colonies of his coreligionists. When, in 1689, Surinam was attacked by a French fleet, it was Captain Samuel Nasi who led the defense, and other soldiers bearing the name served in campaigns against the Bush negros. A hundred years later, Dr. David Nasi, the leading Jew of Pernambuco and author of a famous book on the colony, was the intermediary in opening up relations between the community of that place and the Portuguese government, which had begun to take an interest in them.